A COMPARATIVE ANALYSIS OF ECONOMIC REFORMS IN CENTRAL AND EAST EUROPE

A comparative analysis of economic reforms in Central and East Europe

Edited by
CARLO FRATESCHI
Department of Economics
University of Padua
and
GIANNI SALVINI
Department of Public Economics
University of Pavia

Dartmouth
Aldershot . Brookfield USA . Hong Kong . Singapore . Sydney

Published by
Dartmouth Publishing Company Limited
Gower House
Croft Road
Aldershot
Hants. GU11 3HR
England

Dartmouth Publishing Company
Old Post Road
Brookfield
Vermont 05036
USA

Printed and Bound in Great Britain by
Hartnolls Limited, Bodmin, Cornwall.

ISBN 1 85521 155 6

Contents

Introduction vii

List of contributors xiii

1 Resistance to change, large enterprises and soft budget constraint: a property rights perspective
Jan Winiecki 1

2 The ten commandments of economic reform
Ruud Knaack 25

3 Is there a role for macroeconomic planning in Eastern Europe ?
Bruno Dallago 53

4 Labour redeployment and cooperatives in the Soviet Union
Silvana Malle 83

5 Economic reforms in Poland: a post mortem
Andrzej Brzeski 115

6 Private sector and economic reforms in the Soviet Union and China
Gianni Salvini 127

7 The reform of industrial enterprises in East European economies and the incentives to export
Marie Lavigne 143

8 Manufactures export performance and perestroika
Giovanni Graziani 162
9 Economic reforms and foreign trade policies: reflections on the East European experience
Carlo Frateschi 179

Introduction

This book contains the papers prepared for the Conference on 'The Socialist Enterprise Between Autonomy and Constraints. A comparative Analysis of Economic Reforms in the USSR and East European Countries', held on September 11-12, 1989 at the University of Padua.

The conference was organized as part of an ongoing research endeavour, carried out by a network of Italian and foreign scholars, on the economic problems of East European countries and the USSR. The aim of the Conference was to explore and clarify, from different perspectives and with various methodological approaches, the issues raised by the wave of economic reforms which, under the impact of a severe deterioration in both internal and external economic conditions, had emerged in all these countries in the second half of the eighties. To reach this aim, economists from Eastern Europe, Western Europe, and the U.S.A. contributed papers dealing either with the experience of specific countries or with more general and/or comparative issues.

The contributions can be roughly divided in three groups (each consisting of three papers), dealing respectively with these main issues: 1) the conditions and possible outcomes of reforms in Soviet-type economies; 2) the experience with reforms of specific countries (Poland, China, and the USSR); 3) the foreign trade aspects of the reforms.

The first paper, by Jan WINIECKI, tackles a somewhat intriguing question: why the industrial sector, while possessing in Soviet-type economies the highest priority from the planners' point of view, has been so resistant to reforms? The answer in found in the theory of property rights, as applied by the 'new economic history' school. In particular, the author explains why the resistance to change in the property rights structure is the strongest with respect to industry, and within industry with respect to large enterprises that offer greatest opportunities for appropriating the rent by bureaucrats and apparatchiks. The property rights approach is shown, moreover, to be in accord with the widely accepted description of the mechanism of the Soviet-type economy, while supplying a more coherent rationale for its continuing existence.

In his contribution, Ruud KNAACK formulates a decalogue containing the conditions for a successful economic reform in Soviet-type economies, based on a thorough account of the relationship between reform processes and (mostly negative) economic outcomes in the Soviet Union. The author stresses that these outcomes are not a surprise: an economic reform must have a negative effect on the economy because it unbalances the economy as the logical outcome of the decentralization of decision-making. These unbalances might be fortified by over-ambitious central development programmes. In this respect bureaucratic resistance to the reform is not necessarily the cause of the reform failure, but more the logical behaviour of the bureaucrats to restore order. Another important aspect stressed by the author is that in reality no reform process could be free either of conflicts or of objective contradictions, because a reform is fundamentally a social process, one of learning by doing, trial and error; therefore by far the most relevant point of any reform is the preservation of its political dynamism.

Bruno DALLAGO's paper addresses an issue which is of extreme importance for the economies of Central and Eastern Europe that are now trying to find the best route for a transition 'from plan to market'. According to the author, in (former) Soviet-type economies macroeconomic planning - together with a true market - is still necessary, albeit in a radically changed form, to drive the direction of the transformation of the economic system. The paper is devoted to present and discuss a theoretical approach that appears to be particularly useful in order to analyse the role of macroeconomic planning, namely the heterogeneity hypothesis of the neoinstitutionalist school. From this point of view much of the misunderstanding, and with it the rejection of planning as such in many former socialist countries, arises from the identification of one particular type of planning (namely the directive or administrative planning), with macroeconomic planning tout court, while attributing to it a political value of an instrument of implementing communist or socialist policies.

The main purpose of Silvana MALLE's paper is to analyse economic reforms in the Soviet Union from the point of view of the methods and means capable of increasing the efficiency of labour. The author examines labour redeployment within the state sector and from the state sphere into other forms of economic enterprise: the question is raised of whether cooperative and individual activities, which may be considered the embryo of a developing private sector, are presently recipient of unemployed or redundant labour or compete for workers in a still taut labour market. The paper tries an assessment of the relative tautness of republican labour market, examines the results obtained so far in the field of labour redeployment and discusses some possible options in this field. Some aspects of the traditional employment policy are also outlined in order to put emphasis on present alternatives.

The issue addressed by Andrzej BRZESKI in his contribution are the failures of all past attempts at reforms in Poland, and in general the 'unreformability' of centrally planned socialist economies. The Polish 'reform process' of the last three decades is likened to a treadmill: a lot of movement, but no advance. The paper tries to identify some of the causes of this outcome, which has been characterized by a cyclical pattern, consisting of recurrent attempts to solve the same problems. The resistance to reforms, according to the author is grounded in four overlapping groups of motives: vested interest, distrust of benefits, Marxist ideology, and most importantly, political considerations. It is stressed in the paper, in fact, that a 'comprehensive' economic reform represents an immensely complicated task, entailing a high degree of uncertainty, which not surprisingly acts as a conservative influence against reform: for Party regimes, programmatically and historically inseparable from the economy, these uncertainties seem intolerable.

The contribution of Gianni SALVINI deals with a comparison of the role of the private sector in the Soviet Union and the People's Republic of China, and considers some implications of the related changes on the economic reforms under way in these two countries. The main conclusions drawn from his analysis are the following: a) In both countries reformers are trying to introduce market processes in order to improve the efficiency of their economies. In so doing they are finding that they must face the issue of ownership of land and capital assets: in other words property rights and the sequence of reform are closely linked; b) Great importance is attached to expanding the private sector in both the USSR and the People's Republic of China: nevertheless, the conditions under which private economic activity is required to take place differ greatly between the two countries; c) to have any hope of implementing their privatization programme the Soviet and the Chinese governments must not only liberate all forms of private economic activity, including those now denounced as speculation, but even guarantee by law the enforcement of private contracts, secure private property rights, create a credit system favouring the private sector rather than the government-owned monopolies, and finally command 'social respect' for private economic activity.

Marie LAVIGNE's paper covers various aspects of the changes which occurred since the early eighties in the traditional state trading system in Eastern Europe and the USSR. One interesting point underlined by the author is the specificity of the Soviet approach in the way it has integrated foreign trade and domestic economic reforms: in other terms, according to the author, the foreign trade reform in the USSR, unlike in the other countries, was not a by-product of the domestic reform but came first, under the pressure of the external constraint. A second important remark is that the desire to provide enterprises with incentives to export has led several countries to contemplate the full implications of internal convertibility, but that at the same time the balance of payments constraints act as a powerful brake to substantial moves towards convertibility. The general conclusion of the author is that the reforms which occurred in the field of foreign trade have been at large unable to spur exports or to induce a structural modernization of the export pattern. On the other hand, the foreign trade reforms played their part in the general trend toward marketization and monetization of the domestic economies, and in this systemic sense they appear as more significant than as instruments of structural changes in foreign trade.

Giovanni GRAZIANI's paper deals with the crisis of the Soviet export model based on raw materials and fuels, and with the difficulties in achieving the goal, stated by Soviet policy-makers, of modifying the commercial flows in the direction of increased sales of Soviet manufactured goods in the Western markets. The author develops a thorough statistical analysis in order to assess the structure of Soviet trade, evaluate the degree of resource dependence and factor intensity of the Soviet trade in manufactures, and estimate the evolution of market shares and international competitiveness of Soviet manufactures. The main conclusion of the paper is that the reforms undertaken up to now do not seem capable of inducing an export promotion of Soviet manufactures. Administrative decisions from above and decentralization are not sufficient by themselves to stimulate an expansion of manufactures exports to the extent that the systemic obstacles are not removed: irrational price structure, inadequate technological base, chronic shortages which frustrate any incentive system, and finally the residual role assigned to exports.

The first part of Carlo FRATESCHI's paper traces the evolution of the debate on the 'effectiveness' of foreign trade, which has been alive in East European economies for more than three decades: the main conclusion is that in a situation were the domestic economy of all these countries was still characterized by widespread shortages and excess demand, the use of financial, fiscal and other incentives to export was bound to yield very scarce results.

The second part of the paper addresses the issue of the desirability and feasibility of a switch, in East European economies, to a new strategy of development based on outward-oriented and export-promoting policies. A comparison of the development strategies and foreign economic policies of East European, Latin American and East Asian developing countries in the last decades yields the following main results: a) the three groups of countries appear distributed along a continuum going from extremely open to almost autarkic economies, but the Latin American countries seem to be much closer to the East European ones, with which they share quite a number of common features, policies and outcomes, than to their East Asian counterpart; b) on the other hand, while in the developing countries the selection of certain development strategies has arisen as a result of a policy choice, East European countries appear characterized by a 'built-in' and invariable inward-orientation stemming from their centrally planned economic system, which causes trade policies to be highly protectionist and makes the economy extremely inflexible in responding to external economic signals. The paper ends with an evaluation of some important lessons, derived from the experience of developing market economies in the last decades, that East European countries should not forget in their efforts to design new strategies of development in their transition.

The Conference took place exactly at the beginning of one of those swift accelerations of historical development which, rightly deserving the name of revolutions, can change the face of the earth in a few months: the result of this revolution was, as we know, nothing less than the termination of communist regimes in Europe.

The contributors to the Conference were therefore confronted with the challenging task of producing well conceived scientific analyses of an object, the 'socialist economies', whose main features and attributes were in a state of flux and whose very essence was undergoing a catastrophic transformation. Our judgement is that the contribution presented at the Conference and the ensuing debate, which touched many empirical, methodological, analytical and theoretical issues, were up to this challenge.

All the contributions have been revised and updated to October 1991. Still, some aspects of the analyses and some data presented in the papers have been obviously overcome and made obsolete by the rapidity of changes: the direction and qualitative nature of these changes, however, have been correctly understood and clearly shown.

The papers deal with economic systems and institutions and it must be stressed, in this regard, that in evaluating the present situation in Central and East European countries one should be careful not to think that an economic system can change with the same speed as the electoral and political processes, international politics, popular discontent, and above all in accordance with the superlatives and sensationalisms used by the press. From this point of view, therefore, our judgement is that the contributions retain all their validity, since the economic problems that were dealt with at the Conference, contrary to political institutions, are not going to change substantially or disappear in the short term.

The conference, organized by the Department of International Studies of the University of Padua, was financed with a grant from the Italian Ministry of Public Education. Our most sincere thanks, together with those of the contributors and participants in the conference, go to this institution for its substantial support of our research efforts.

Carlo Frateschi, Gianni Salvini

List of contributors

Andrzej Brzeski, University of California (Davis)

Bruno Dallago, Department of Economics, University of Trento

Carlo Frateschi, Department of Economics, University of Padua

Giovanni Graziani, Department of Economics, University of Brescia

Ruud Knaack, Department of Economics, University of Amsterdam

Marie Lavigne, University of Paris I

Silvana Malle, Institute of Economics, University of Verona

Gianni Salvini, Department of Public Economics, University of Pavia

Jan Winiecki, Catholic University, Lublin

1 Resistance to change, large enterprises and soft budget constraint: a property rights perspective

JAN WINIECKI

Introduction

So far only reforms of the agricultural sector in Soviet-type economies (STEs for short) brought about, in some cases, positive effects. No such cases exist with respect to the industrial sector (the more recent literature justifiably rejected some analysts' optimistic assessments of successes of post-1968 Hungarian 'regulated market economy').

This being the case, it can be assumed that industrial reforms in STEs did not go far enough toward the private ownership-based market-type economy (MTE for short). In this paper the present writer tries to answer the question why the industrial sector has been so resistant to change. The analysis is conducted from the property rights' perspective.

Large industrial enterprises: a case of aggregate political clout

This author noted earlier that although there have been (rather modest) improvements in the functioning of agriculture in some STEs, nowhere were similar effects achieved in industry [1]. The verdict in favour of agriculture is surprising at first glance. Throughout communist rule industry has been a pampered child that received most attention and resources, first at the expense of agriculture and later increasingly at the expense of services. The whole effort to cut short the developmental distance to the industrialized West centred almost exclusively on industry.

After decades of Soviet-style industrialization, however, the effort looks increasingly misguided. Not only demand continues to exceed supply on both producer and consumer goods markets but also the quality of STEs products falls increasingly behind that of other - not only Western! - countries. To give but one example STEs, that in 1965 obtained about 50 per cent of the average unit (kilogram) price got by everybody else for their engineering products on the EEC market, obtained only 28 per cent in 1985 [2]. And not only the prices they get are lower but also their shares in manufactured imports of the West fall, showing STEs' inability to sell even at markedly lower prices.

An answer to the intriguing question why the industrial sector has been so resistant to reforms is difficult without looking closely into the property rights structure in STEs. It is possible, of course, to obtain an indirect answer that just because industry is the core of centrally managed 'socialist development', ideological purity has prevented ruling groups from making even those modest concessions to decentralized market-type economy they made in 'less important' agriculture.

Ideological answers are usually unsatisfactory and this particular case is no exception. Communists generally turned out to be very adept at resolving conflicts between requirement of their continuing rule and ideology - in favour of the former. Thus, another question arises: if the core sector turns increasingly into a problem sector, why do the rulers resist solutions that would make industry to perform better and accordingly facilitate their continued rule?

The theory of property rights as applied by the 'new economic history' school posits that in societies with a pre-representative type of government a typical conflict arises between the efficient property rights structure designed to lower transactions costs, i.e. to facilitate an increase in wealth, and actual property rights structure designed to maximize rent to the ruling stratum [3]. In spite of the obvious discrepancy between the two, the rulers tend to maintain the inefficient property rights structure in order to avoid offending powerful segments of the ruling stratum who benefit most from the existing arrangements. The foregoing methodological guidance makes the author look more closely at those in the ruling stratum in the Soviet system who benefit most from the present, patently inefficient property rights structure in industry.

This author stressed elsewhere [4] that beside the traditional mode of extracting rent under the dictatorship there exists under the Soviet-type dictatorship yet another mode. It enables maximizing rent of, primarily, two segments of the ruling stratum: party apparatchiks and economic bureaucracy.

This system-specific mode of rent maximization occurs in two ways. The first is through *nomenklatura*, i.e. the right of the communist party apparatus to 'recommend' (read: appoint) candidates to all managerial positions in the economic and public administration. Since appointments are made primarily on the basis of loyalty to those who appoint managers rather than competence, apparatchiks and bureaucrats see no obstacles in appointing themselves and their card-carrying cronies to these well paid jobs.

The second rent-maximizing way is through the upward flow of goods and services from enterprises to those in the party apparatus upon whose continuing favours depends the position of nomenklatura-appointed enterprise managers. The flow of underpriced goods in short supply increases wealth of those who have access to it (either directly or through higher income if goods are resold later at higher free or black market prices). Underpriced services contribute directly to apparatchiks and bureaucrats' well-being through building or renovating apartment or country houses, designing, manufacturing and installing the one-off, custom-built furniture, etc. A myriad of goods and services may be profitably acquired in this way in a shortage-plagued economy.

The foregoing brief outline of the property rights structure in the Soviet-system sets forth the general framework within which this author explains the place of industrial sector as the most important rent-seeking area for apparatchiks and bureaucrats.

Let us begin with official salaries. It is a well known fact that wages and salaries in STEs are generally higher in industry (mining, manufacturing, electricity and construction) than elsewhere in the economy. It is less well known that managers in industrial enterprises earn more than their counterparts in enterprises and institutions in the remaining sectors of STEs. A look at Table 1.1 yields a differential of one third to one quarter (if managerial salaries in industry are made equal to 100) in the case of Poland. Thus, the industrial sector offers higher managerial salaries than other sectors.

Industry offers other advantages for those segments of the ruling stratum who benefit most from the present property rights structure in STEs. Extremely high levels of industrial concentration in STEs, much higher than elsewhere in the world (see Table 1.2), leave the industrial sector in STEs with many very large enterprises and many layers of management. With size determining to a considerable extent managerial salaries, very large enterprises offer well paid managerial jobs in large numbers. Thus, the industrial sector offers not only higher managerial salaries but also more of them.

Table 1.1
Salary differentials between comparable managers in Industry and managers elsewhere (outside Agriculture) in Poland in 1987
(monthly salaries in units of national currency)

	Managers	Range	Average (unweighted)
1.1	General managers in industrial enterprises	55647 -70035	63341
1.2	General managers in some other so-called productive sectors (railways, post, telecommunications, forestry)	39245 - 44212	41219
1.3	General managers in some so-called non-productive sectors (municipal administration, justice, public health, banking)	40164 - 46876	43248
2.1	Divisional managers in industrial enterprises	37521 - 42116	38953
2.2	Divisional managers in some other so-called productive sectors	25918 - 38936	30581
2.3	Divisional managers in some so-called non-productive sectors	27925 - 32915	29568

Source: Extracted from data on salaries of non-manual workers, Ministry of Labour and Social Affairs: March 1987 Survey.

Moreover, the complexity of industrial production (a number of manufacturing phases, a number of parts and components required, etc.) makes industry particularly prone to increase in the size of enterprises. As this author has shown elsewhere [5], uncertainty generated by the centrally planned economy is an important factor increasing the size of enterprises as each manager tries to produce as much as possible internally in order to reduce the dependence upon external suppliers. This, coupled with import substitution, results in the industry's hypertrophy. The share of the industrial sector on GDP and employment is between one fifth and one third higher than in MTEs at similar development levels. Thus, the industrial sector not only offers higher salaries for more managers at comparable managerial positions than other sectors but also offers to apparatchiks and bureaucrats an increased number of these well paid posts in industry due this sector's oversize.

Table 1.2
Structure of Employment in Industry [a], according to size of enterprise establishments in selected European STEs and MTEs, in percentages

<table>
<tr><th rowspan="2">Country, year of the census</th><th>Up to 50</th><th>51-200</th><th>201-500</th><th>500 and over</th></tr>
<tr><th colspan="4">persons employed</th></tr>
<tr><td>GDR (East Germany), 1970</td><td>5.6</td><td>10.9</td><td>10.2</td><td>73.3</td></tr>
<tr><td>Hungary, 1970</td><td>3.9</td><td colspan="2">27.3</td><td>68.8</td></tr>
<tr><td>Poland, 1970</td><td>7.4</td><td>14.8</td><td>13.2</td><td>63.6</td></tr>
<tr><td>F.R. of Germany, 1967</td><td>10.1</td><td>17.1</td><td>15.0</td><td>57.9</td></tr>
<tr><td>Sweden, 1973</td><td>19.7</td><td>16.6</td><td>11.5</td><td>52.2</td></tr>
<tr><td>Italy, 1951</td><td>27.6</td><td colspan="2">34.2</td><td>38.2</td></tr>
<tr><td>Belgium, 1961</td><td>31.7</td><td>18.6</td><td>12.8</td><td>36.9</td></tr>
</table>

[a] Mining, manufacturing and utilities (excl. construction).

Note: STEs passed in the 1970s through yet another concentration drive, while MTE in general moved at least both toward and later away from greater concentration. Thus, comparable data for the 1980s would show even greater differences in this respect.

Source: E. Ehrlich, G. Kramarics and L. Tuu, 'Enterprise Establishments Size in Industry in East and West', Wiener Institut für Internationale Wirtschaftsvergleiche, Forschungsbericht n. 61, 1980.

It follows from the above that it is large enterprises in industry that are regarded as the most important rent-seeking area for apparatchiks and bureaucrats. The special position of large enterprises (which so strongly affects their performance, see following section) is best explained by a diagram showing *nomenklatura* linkages between the traditional command-rationing hierarchy of central planning and various levels of party apparatus (see Figure 1.1). Thus, a general manager may be appointed through central committee *nomenklatura*, his deputies through regional *nomenklatura*, factory managers through district or town or county *nomenklatura* and divisional managers within factories through enterprise *nomenklatura*. Thus, rent-seeking becomes a unifying factor: every level of the communist party apparatus keeps its share of the pie.

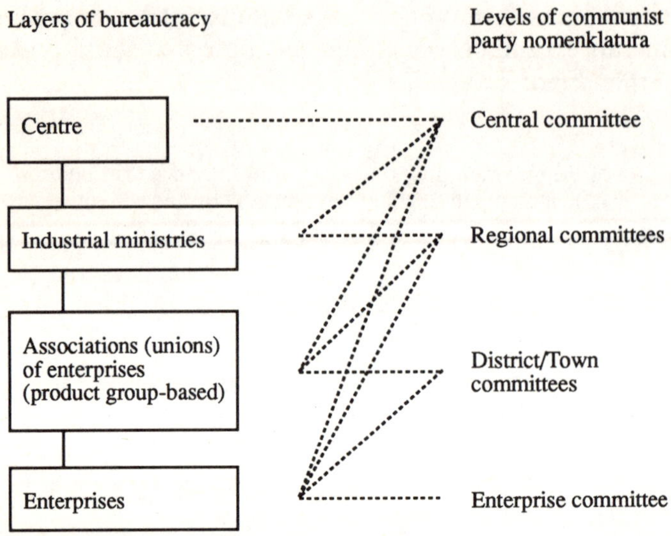

Figure 1.1 Linkages between bureaucratic and managerial positions and various levels of the communist party nomenklatura

However, higher salaries and associated 'perks' (chauffeured cars, etc.), that this author called authorized corruption, are by no means the only source of income and wealth for those segments of the ruling stratum that benefit most from the present inefficient property rights structure. The second way of rent extraction, as stressed above, is through the acquisition of underpriced goods and services on the basis of personal linkages between enterprise managers and those upon whose favours their position depends. As spoils are divided locally and without the authorization from the centre this way may be labelled unauthorized corruption (in contrast, e.g., with coupons to buy a car at much below the market price that are distributed from the top down).

Here, industry becomes an even more promising rent-seeking area relative to other sectors than in the case of authorized corruption. A plethora of durable and non-durable manufactured goods can be acquired at the source, i.e. from producers, in case of shortages. And, as a commonly heard remark in communist countries has it, temporary shortages are the most permanent feature of a Soviet-type economy.

Industry has an advantage as a source of consumer goods in short supply (except agricultural produce) but it also has an advantage with regard to highly valued services. For example delegating workers to renovate an apartment or build a dacha (and adding the necessary building materials to such a favour) is much easier in a large enterprise where costs of such favours can be more easily hidden among thousands of items hiding other transgressions and pure and simple waste. Moreover, beside the scale of operations that enables hiding the cost of such favours, construction divisions of manufacturing (or mining) enterprises or construction enterprises themselves are simply better supplied with labour and materials than resource-starved service sector enterprises.

Altogether, given the rent extracted from industry, it is not surprising that well paid managerial jobs in industrial enterprises are kept 'in the family', i.e. among the party apparatchiks and their card-carrying cronies. Exact data across countries and over time are of course hidden from view (just as the whole *nomenklatura* procedure) but a few glimpses can be made nonetheless.

According to reports on the four country study on managers in industry [6] prepared under the aegis of COMECON, a full 100 per cent of general managers in Czechoslovakia and Poland belonged to the communist party. The same figures for Bulgaria and Hungary were 87.5 and 83 per cent respectively. Altogether, with respect to both general managers and their deputies, party membership figures were 95.9 per cent for Poland, 94.4 per cent for Czechoslovakia, 79.1 per cent for Hungary and 77.4 per cent for Bulgaria [7].

This extremely high share does not seem to change much over time in spite of all 'liberalizations'. For example in Poland in the 1970s more than 90 per cent of managers had belonged to the communist party. The percentage fell, according to one study, to 75 per cent among managers who went through a competitive selection process in the 1981-1983 period [8], but this figure hides more than it reveals. It includes selection of managers in 1981 when 'Solidarity'-supported self-management committees were free to choose managers, regardless of nomenklatura. In the 1982-1983 period the rules of competitive selection were changed, and self-management committees found themselves under political pressure and secret police intimidation campaigns. The percentage of managers who are communist party members went up again. Accordingly, five years later it was reported that (again) 'about 90% of managers in state enterprises belongs to PUWP (communist party - J.W.)' [9].

They are, thus, part and parcel of the ruling stratum in the Soviet system, being recruited predominantly from its two segments: bureaucrats and party apparatchiks. Consequences of that state of affairs are very far-reaching. They belong to the world where rewards are distributed on the basis of loyalty: in fact, obedience, to those who decide about their actual position. As this author has argued elsewhere [10], they do not need to be exceedingly concerned about the balance sheet as long as their superiors are satisfied. They are not even expected to give the true picture of enterprise performance for their bosses are also interested in sending upwards optimistic reports on enterprises within their industry or region.

Managers that are obedient and moreover mindful of the needs of their superiors with respect to goods and services in short supply may be reasonably sure that premiums and bonuses, as well as 'perks' distributed from the centre, will always be forthcoming. Not every manager may expect generous rewards, of course. There are important differences in this respect and these differences result mostly from the political clout of managers in the sense of belonging to a strong *coterie*. Being well connected means being appointed to a high position in a large, important enterprise. And the larger the enterprise, the more numerous are such *nomenklatura* positions and, consequently, the greater is the managers' aggregate political clout.

Political clout and resource allocation

This author already mentioned large enterprises as the most important area of rent-seeking within the already privileged industrial sector. Salaries of *nomenklatura* managers are the highest there, 'perks' associated with their position (authorized corruption) are most numerous and profitable, benefits from the stream of underpriced goods and services (unauthorized corruption) are greater than elsewhere. Those are components of the appropriated rent that directly affect their income and wealth. But the fact of being a manager in a large 'priority' enterprise brings also other, less tangible benefits.

In the Soviet world the unlimited relativism extends also to resource allocation, which is not based upon efficiency criteria (not even those pseudo-criteria established by central planners). Consequently, political clout bears heavily upon resource allocation. And in shortage-plagued STEs it matters whether enterprise is given a preferred access to supplies of inputs, foreign exchange, investment grants, credits, and - if the need arises - subsidies. It makes all the difference between easier and more difficult implementation of planned output targets.

Following further the trail of aggregate political clout, it is worth noting that not only plan implementation can be made easier if political clout facilitates the inflow of resources to 'priority' enterprises but also planned output targets can be made less demanding as well. Bargaining with enterprise superiors is also the more successful, the stronger is the enterprise managers' aggregate political clout.

Thus, aggregate political clout is positively correlated with both easier output (and other) plan targets and easier access to resources needed to implement these targets. It enables managers in large enterprises to benefit indirectly, through leisure-on-the-job, from their privileged position within the loyalty-based system of *nomenklatura*. Given level of income and wealth is achieved with less effort.

The privileged position of large enterprises did not go completely unnoticed in STEs. Probably the best known is a critique by the Hungarian economist Andras Hegedus in the mid-1980s [11]. But without resorting to the Northian perspective of the inherent conflict between the actual, inefficient property rights structure (but the one that maximizes the rent of the ruling stratum) and the efficient property rights structure, convincing explanations are hard to find. Only when it is pointed out that both the centre and managers of large enterprises belong to the ruling stratum and that the aggregate political clout of the latter is considerable, reasons for the centre's unwillingness to press for radical reforms can be explained in terms of its unwillingness to offend powerful segments of the ruling stratum. Pieces of the puzzle fall into their proper places.

It is also worth remembering that often it is not managers of large enterprises themselves that are so powerful but first of all people who appoint them or support their managerial position and who subsequently draw various benefits from these appointments (mainly through what this author calls unauthorized corruption). Analysing the relative clout of a manager in a STE, a commentator in a Polish management journal says that the 'manager's stand is as solid as is the influence of those who stand behind him' [12].

Although everybody knows in STEs about various preferences for large enterprises whose managers enjoy strong political clout, the scale of the phenomenon remains unknown. To the best knowledge of the author only one little known study by Maria Csanadi ever attempted to measure it in quantitative terms. Published in Hungarian in an obscure mimeographed bulletin [13] that study deserves more attention than it received. The next few pages present its main results (as seen from the vantage point of property rights).

The authoress decided to answer the question which enterprises have a 'priority' or - more precisely - which enjoy preferential access to scarce resources. As an object of study she took engineering industry, the most important manufacturing industry in Hungary (let it be noted that she also selected an industry which itself enjoys a 'priority' at the branch level). Although she obviously recognized the close link between large size and political clout, Maria Csanadi nonetheless decided to study both variables separately, as well as jointly.

Consequently, the authoress divided engineering enterprises into three categories with respect to size: large, middle-size and small, according to the size of their fixed assets. She used a dichotomous classification with respect to political clout. As a measure she used the participation of enterprise managers and/or other employees in executive and plenary bodies of the Hungarian communist party (HRWP) at central committee, regional committee and Budapest district committee level.

Membership in these bodies is a reasonably good proxy for the aggregate political clout as defined earlier by this author. Informally, *nomenklatura*-covered managerial positions link their holders with different executive party committees: the larger the enterprise, the more links are established at more *nomenklatura* levels and the greater is the aggregate political clout as a result.

But large enterprises are also formally linked with the communist party through the participation of party members from important enterprises in its executive and plenary bodies. Managers themselves are sometimes 'elected' to these bodies if they belong to an important *coterie*. More often, however, it is some decorative miners, steelmakers, lathe operators and others that are 'elected' there. The latter, even if 'elected' to the central committee, are inconsequential in terms of their own political clout but their presence is a good measure of the enterprise's political importance. Even if Csanadi's dichotomous classification rules out measuring the aggregate political clout by degree, it is nonetheless useful in this respect.

Armed with the knowledge of size and political clout Maria Csanadi analysed seven types of preferential access to resources available to engineering enterprises in the 1970-1979 period:

(1) First came subsidies of various sorts, including tax reliefs (of which a multitude exists in reformed STEs).

(2) Since the 1968 reforms, long-term investment credits became the main method of affecting industrial investment by the centre. Enterprises compete vigorously for these credits characterized by low (sometimes negative) real interest rates. The repayment of principal may even be written off altogether after a few years.

(3) Certain enterprises were deemed by the centre to be important enough to get a priority access to material inputs. It was assured through the right of these enterprises to buy some inputs directly from producers rather than wholesalers. They not only obtained them first, an important advantage in a Kornai's shortage economy, but also obtained them cheaper (prices did not include wholesalers' margin, i.e. 12 per cent in the period under consideration).

(4) During the period of retreat from reforms (1972-1973) a group of large enterprises obtained formally a special status, conferring upon them an unspecified priority: a useful bargaining chip in every effort to extract privileges (something Hegedus, an already quoted Hungarian economist, fulminated against).

(5) Another way of increasing the probability to obtain scarce resources was to be included into a group of - again almost exclusively large - enterprises which were formally involved in the preparation of the national plan by the central planning board. Both routine plans and expansion programmes of these enterprises had in these cases greater probability to be realised once their needs were recognized by the centre and written into, say, import plans.

(6) Yet another preferential access - primarily to foreign exchange - resulted from having one's projects approved and included into national technological development plans.

(7) The last type of analysed preferences concerned approved requests for mergers, in fact for absorption of smaller by large enterprises. Pressure for absorbing independent enterprises (often own suppliers) stems from the enterprises' tendency towards self-sufficiency in the face of the high uncertainty generated by the system [14].

The study in question reveals a highly significant pattern of preferences. First of all, large enterprises obtained preferences much more often than medium-sized or small ones. The pattern is no less significant if the political clout becomes the discriminating variable.

Table 1.3 shows the participation of enterprises with or without the political clout in all types of preferences in percentage terms. Enterprises with political clout obtained subsidies and investment credits in about 90 per cent of cases, while in the figures for those without it is barely 20-25 per cent of cases.

Table 1.3
Share of enterprises with and without political clout having preferential access to resources (classified by type of access), in percentages

Type of preference	With political clout [a]	Without political clout [b]
Subsidies (incl. tax relief)	93.6	22.9
Long-term investments credits	87.2	24.3
Preferred supply of inputs (bypassing wholesalers and paying less)	78.7	15.5
Special status (priority formally conferred)	48.9	6.1
Coordination of plans with central planners	51.1	1.7
Participation in technological change programmes (i.e. preferential access to foreign exchange)	53.2	2.4
Accepted requests for absorbing smaller enterprises	48.9	0.7

[a] 47 enterprises with political clout
[b] 407 enterprises without political clout

Source: M. Csanadi (1984), p. 228

The ratio between 'haves' and 'have-nots', already about 4:1 for subsidies and investment credits, becomes even more disadvantageous for the latter with respect to other preferences. According to yet another calculation, out of 47 enterprises with political clout only two did not obtain any preferences (but 12 obtained all seven types of preferences), while out of 407 enterprises without political clout only one obtained all preferences (but 268 obtained none) [15].

Categories of large enterprises (43 according to Csanadi classification) and enterprises with political clout (47 according to her classification) are not identical but overlap to a large extent. In the case of one 'priority' industry, as in the study in question, this stems from the territorial distribution of enterprises. Usually the largest enterprises in a given territory (a region or Budapest district) is formally linked to communist party body at a given level (a regional or district committee). But if a region or district does not have a large enterprise it may confer the formal political importance to a medium-sized one and *vice versa* - the existence of a few large enterprises in another territory deprived some of them of the formal status of political importance.

Let it be noted, however, that the territorial distribution explains differences between size and political clout in the case of that particularly important industrial branch. Where all industry is taken into account another factor has an even greater impact in this respect. It is central planners and the political masters' obsession with heavy industry. Thus, say, a medium-sized engineering enterprise may have the formal status of political importance while a large textile enterprise may not (and higher salaries and 'perks' may be allocated to the former).

Nonetheless in the case of a 'priority' industrial branch heavy industry obsession did not affect preferential access and large enterprises without political clout, as measured by Maria Csanadi, did well in terms of their ability to enjoy preferential access to resources. According to the study in question, a large enterprise that did not possess formal status of political importance obtained on the average the preferential access in 64.3 per cent of cases. At the same time a medium-sized enterprise with the said status obtained on average preferential access in 44.4 per cent of cases [16]. Thus, the latter did less well in relative terms.

As I stressed already, the measure of political clout used by Maria Csanadi excludes the possibility of measuring aggregate political clout by degree. Therefore, a relatively smaller middle-sized enterprise from, say, a district where there were no large enterprises appeared in her dichotomous classification as the one that has the political clout, while a large enterprise from another district with a few large enterprises appeared as the one that has not. The data quoted in the preceding paragraph point to a different ranking according to the aggregate political clout as defined by this author. Links of a great number of managers with many levels of *nomenklatura* (often up to the central committee level) in a large enterprise proved to be more efficient in rent-seeking terms than links of a smaller number of managers with fewer levels of *nomenklatura* in middle-sized enterprises within the same industrial branch.

Csanadi study reveals a highly significant effect of the symbiosis of politics and economics on preferential access to resources. Wherever enterprises are simultaneously both politically important and large, the probability of obtaining preferential access becomes certainty in the case of subsidies and long-term investment credits and increases sharply with respect to all the remaining types of privileges. Table 1.4 shows unambiguously the results of such synergy.

Table 1.4
Share of large enterprises with political clout having preferential access to resources (classified by type of access), in percentages

Type of preference	Share
Subsidies (incl. tax relief)	100.0
Long-term investments credits	100.0
Preferred supply of inputs (bypassing wholesalers and paying less)	92.0
Special status (priority formally conferred)	72.0
Coordination of plans with central planners	76.0
Participation in technological change programmes (i.e. preferential access to foreign exchange)	84.0
Accepted requests for absorbing smaller enterprises	92.2

Source: M. Csanadi (1984), Annex Tables

However, the generalizations formulated by Maria Csanadi are less ambiguous than results. She clearly sees the complementarity of general rules and individualized decisions creating together a highly interventionist mechanism of hands-on management. This mechanism is working within the interlinked political and economic power structure, with the dominant role of the political component.

This author agrees with the descriptive aspects of the model outlined by Maria Csanadi but not with its motivational aspects. It is not completely clear why apparatchiks intervene in the affairs of enterprises. In an article generalizing the results of her study [17], she explains interventions in terms of both the superior motive of trying to correct the outcomes of an inefficient economic system and the ulterior motive of exercising their power over enterprises (showing 'who is the boss'). This exercise of power forces enterprise managers to conform to the unlimited relativism of their bosses. Nor is it clear which of the two motives prevail.

Of course, the belief in being able to correct the increasingly unwieldy economic system through individualized decisions may linger on among bureaucrats and apparatchiks. However, the fact that it is more or less the same enterprises in the same industries that are favoured by these interventions year by year casts serious doubts upon the validity of this explanation. Since corrections are systematic, it should not be difficult to modify the system accordingly.

Thus, it must be the exercise of power that really motivates the party apparatus. But even this explanation is not wholly satisfactory. Maria Csanadi points out that throughout the whole post-1968 period the communist party never loosened control over enterprises (a view shared by many of her compatriots).This statement, however true, begs the question why the control has been so important to them? Surely it could not be only for the fun of it!

Seen from the vantage point of property rights the answer is clear. Control over enterprises enables those in the ruling stratum who exercise control over the inefficient economic system to appropriate rent. The rent is mainly appropriated in large enterprises in 'priority' industries. Therefore it is these enterprises that are accorded not only higher salaries and 'perks' for managers (as a part of their pecuniary rent) but also various preferences with respect to scarce resources (as a part of their non-pecuniary leisure-on-the-job kind of rent).

Managers who overwhelmingly are a part and parcel of the ruling stratum do not need to be forced to conform to the hands-on management. They play the loyalty (read: obedience) game not only because it is the only game in town, as Maria Csanadi rightly suggests, but also because this is the only game most of them are able to play. Thus, bureaucrats, apparatchiks and their colleagues who switched to managing enterprises all stand to loose from the substitution of efficiency for loyalty game. The structure of property rights would change, then, to their disadvantage.

Soft budget constraint and aggregate political clout. A reinterpretation

Managers who are reasonably sure they will be able to obtain inputs they need due to their political clout cease, with time, to regard resources as scarce. They demand more and more - and get what they want most of the time. In consequence, they can afford to use resources inefficiently, wastefully even, for their immediate benefit. Thus, the author arrived - via another route - at the famous soft budget constraint formulated by Janos Kornai [18].

Kornai stated that repeated interventions of bureaucrats (he was less explicit about apparatchiks), which alleviate difficulties encountered by enterprises, give managers an idea that such behaviour is by and large a norm. Enterprise managers become convinced that the state, paternalistically helping every enterprise (both good and bad), is a general insurance agency of sort. This in turn gives rise to near insatiable demand of enterprises for input of all kinds facilitating the implementation of plan targets. Kornai's lucid analysis outlines vividly the mechanism of soft budget constraint. It is much more vague with respect to the rationale of the phenomenon in question.

Kornai points to paternalistic attitudes of bureaucrats towards the enterprises they guide. In case of difficulties enterprises will be helped with subsidies, credits and/or permission to raise prices. Why? Because, according to Kornai, the multi-level bureaucracy identifies itself strongly with the roles it plays and, consequently, intervenes benevolently in the affairs of subordinate enterprises. Bureaucrats seem to maximize their utility through the sheer fun of giving. Non-pecuniary benefits of that sort are the only ones that appear in Kornai's rationale.

The main weakness of his rationale lies in the fact that it is able to explain any allocational pattern, not only the real one outlined in the preceding section. It does not explain preferential access of 'priority' industries, large firms within these industries, etc. A closer look at Kornai's rationale reveals that it is not a rationale at all.

Some other East European economists who accept the basics of the shortage economy with its corollary, i.e. soft budget constraint and near insatiable demand, suggest another rationale. Tamas Bauer [19] points to the mistaken calculus of central planners and their political masters, who are ready to accept output realised at any cost ('after all, we need lathes, tractors, houses...'). Therefore they are ready to validate excessive costs of realised output through subsidies, tax relief, etc.

This author agrees that the economic illiteracy in STEs is endemic among bureaucrats and apparatchiks (and each year party schools and economics schools turn out new economically illiterate alumni!) but this is not the only, may be not even the main explanation. If output is so important, then all producing enterprises should have equal access to resources, say, in proportion to their size. This is not the case, as Maria Csanadi study tells us in no uncertain terms.

This author's approach suggests that bureaucrats and apparatchiks accord privileged access to scarce resources to those enterprises with the highest aggregate political clout, i.e. overwhelmingly to large enterprises in priority industries. The rationale for such a pattern of resource allocation is that it is in their own interest to do so. Their colleagues, representatives of the same ruling stratum, who were appointed managers, benefit materially from their position directly (best paid jobs, 'perks' associated with their position) and indirectly (acquisition of goods and services in short supply at below market prices), while bureaucrats and apparatchiks benefit from having their colleagues there indirectly (from the flow of these goods and services arranged by their colleagues-managers). Let us add in passing that both managers and bureaucrats and apparatchiks benefit also from the former ability to appoint their relatives to relatively well-paying non-*nomenklatura* jobs with a large capacity for shirking.

In this way bureaucrats and apparatchiks maximize pecuniary benefits in their utility function, apart from maximizing non-pecuniary benefits (the fun of meddling). The pattern of resource allocation outlined above has yet another advantage. It does not contradict the one explained by the economic illiteracy. The allocational pattern stemming from the property rights structure favourable to powerful segments of the ruling stratum is superimposed upon that based on the inability to apply fundamental microeconomic criteria of efficiency. While the latter spreads scarce resources more or less at random, the former spreads them in accordance with the rent-seeking principle outlined earlier.

The pattern of resource allocation based upon rent-seeking is stable and changes only slowly over time. Lazslo Csaba [20] stressed that after the introduction of 1968 reforms in Hungary a group of enterprises emerged that were perpetual loss-makers. Similar lists were drawn in 1979 and 1982 and they were near identical, consisting of the same large enterprises that traditionaly received a lion's share of scarce resources. According to another source [21] they are in the same loss-making condition now. Similarly, lists of the 500 largest manufacturing enterprises published in Poland since 1983 [22] show year by year highest subsidies for largest enterprises.

Maria Csanadi's calculations give the same picture - and more systematically at that: 43 large enterprises obtained over the 1970-1979 decade 79 per cent of the value of all subsidies and 76.5 per cent of the value of all preferential credits allocated for 454 engineering enterprises. This pattern changed only marginally over the 1970s, e.g. the largest 43 enterprises in question obtained 83.6 per cent of the value of subsidies in 1970 and 79 per cent in 1979 [23].

Soft budget constraint is typical for all STEs, not only for persistent tinkerers with the economic system such as Hungary and Poland. In traditional STEs, however, the range of preferences is somewhat different. Rather than give subsidies afterwards, plan targets are revised downwards during the year so that managers obtain the expected bonuses for plan fulfilment.

According to a Soviet source [24], bureaucrats changed enterprise plan targets in 1980 in 57 per cent of all industrial enterprises. Moreover, in every third of these plans revision took place in December. It was a retroactive validation of lower than planned effects at planned (or above planned) costs. And the year 1980 was not unusual in this respect. 'The practice of (downward - J.W.) plan revision within a planned period continued in 1981 and was widespread' - said the same source [25]. Although the above mentioned figures are unrelated to the size of enterprises, it is assumed that those with the high aggregate political clout are the ones that obtain downward plan revisions most easily.

Closely related to the reinterpretation of soft budget constraint proposed here is another reinterpretation, i.e. one of Kornai's near insatiable demand of STE enterprises. This author, who accepts the thesis, used standard neoclassical price/quantity space to present it [26]. The vertical demand line in Figure 1.2a indicates that demand of enterprises is completely price inelastic.

The question arises how that explanation accords with the rent-seeking perspective outlined and evidenced so far. Another look at Table 1.4 tells us that large enterprises with the political clout operate in an environment where they have near-certain preferential access to scarce resources. The management there does not need to concern itself with prices for demanded inputs. Their purchases at

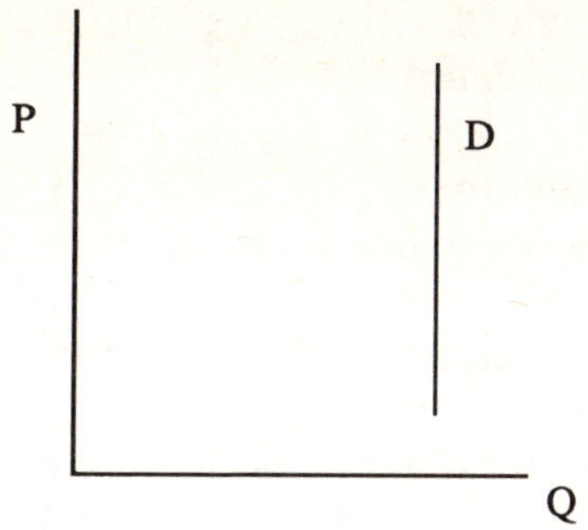

1.2a: Vertical aggregate demand line under 'standard' Kornai-type insatiable demand explanation

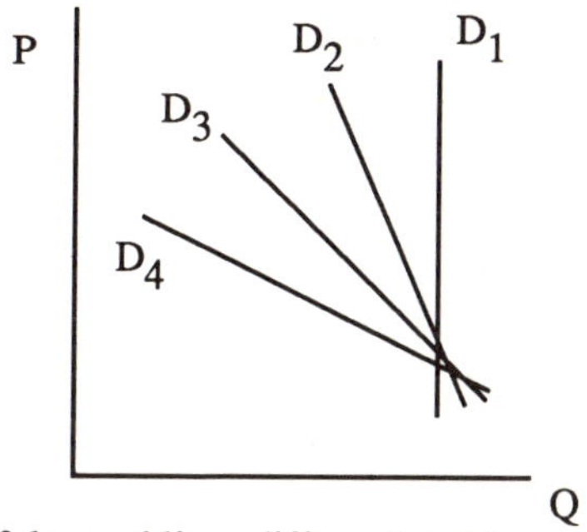

1.2b: A set of demand lines differentiated by a varying political clout of enterprise managers under a property rights approach

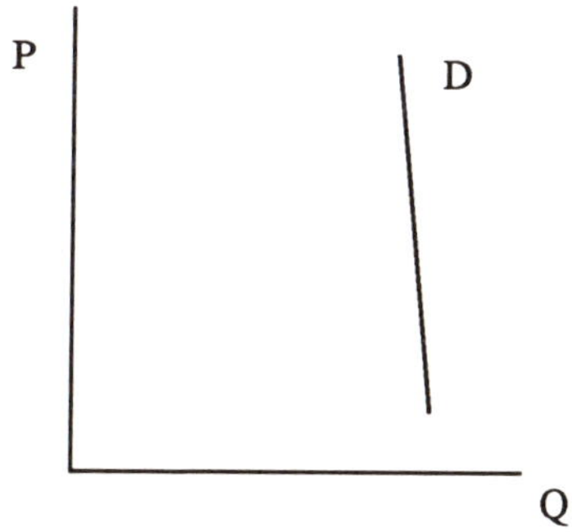

1.2c: Near-vertical aggregate demand line under a property rights approach

Fig.1.2 Property rights approach to insatiable demand: a diagrammatical presentation

whatever price will be validated ex post one way or another. The demand function of these enterprises is vertical, i.e. price independent. It is reflected by the D_1 line in Figure 1.2b.

Other categories of enterprises in the revealing study by Maria Csanadi present a different picture, though. Large enterprises that enjoy no political priority or medium-sized enterprises with the political clout have both relatively high probabilities of such ex post validation but no certainty. Thus, under certain circumstances, they may face a budget constraint that makes their demand price elastic to some extent. This is reflected by D_2 and D_3 demand lines in Figure 1.2b.

Finally, medium-sized and small enterprises without the political clout can only rarely count upon the *largesse* of bureaucrats and apparatchiks. They count for little from the rent-seeking perspective.

The rare subsidies they obtain are due to the economic illiteracy of their superiors or their (randomly applied) fun meddling rather than rent-seeking manoeuvres of the latter. The budget constraint of this last group of enterprises is relatively price elastic, i.e. its slope does not differ much from that on a neoclassical diagram in economic textbooks. It is reflected by the D_4 demand line in Figure 1.2b.

Differing degrees of softness of STE enterprises budget constraint diagrammatically presented above apparently require some modifications of the completely price inelastic demand line reflected in Figure 1.2a. Collapsing all four demand lines from Figure 1.2b into one results in a very steeply sloping demand line, such as in Figure 1.2c, but nonetheless not a vertical one. Thus, a rent-seeking perspective, by differentiating softness of budget constraint, suggests modifications in the concept of near insatiable demand.

However, the need for modifications is - in the view of this author - more apparent than real. Privileged access to scarce resources is an important but not the only factor determining the soft budget constraint of STE enterprises. Given the exorbitant transaction costs of monitoring enterprises under the distinctly non-exclusive property rights, managers are able to soften their budget constraint in other ways as well.

One such way is hidden inflation [27]. Changing output mix towards higher-priced goods, lowering quality on inputs without the commensurate reduction in price and, finally, pseudo-innovations that rise prices without commensurate improvement in product quality - all loosen enterprises' budget constraint. They enable enterprise managers to cover costs without subsidies.

No less importantly, the ability of enterprises to loosen their budget constraint through price manipulation is by and large the greater, the more varied is its product mix and the less control is exercised over changes in that mix. Since large enterprises in 'priority' heavy industries usually turn out homogeneous or at best moderately differentiated products, other smaller enterprises producing a wide range of differentiated products and having greater ease of changing their product mix have correspondingly greater room for manoeuvre. Contrary to the privileged access factor, the price manipulation factor compensates to some extent smaller, underprivileged enterprises for their lack of political clout. Thus, the aggregate demand line for all STE enterprises becomes near vertical again, almost as in the original explanation reflected in Figure 1.2a.

Generalizing the reinterpretation made in this section, it is the rationale for soft budget constraint and near insatiable demand that was substantially modified. The phenomenon itself represented by a vertical, price independent demand line in the price/quantity space withstood the reinterpretation very well, requiring only marginal modifications (if any).

Thus, we know by now <u>why</u> bureaucrats and apparatchiks defend the patently inefficient Soviet-type system particularly strongly with respect to the industrial sector and within that sector with respect to the large enterprises - their main rent-seeking area. The property rights approach explains that well enough. We also know <u>how</u> the rent-seeking is affecting the allocation of resources to maximize both the pecuniary and non-pecuniary benefits of bureaucrats, apparatchiks and their colleagues appointed to managerial positions. This shift of emphasis from the traditional critique of the Soviet-type economic system to a neo-institutional property rights-based critique did not require substantial changes in explanations of the mechanics of distortions generated by the system.

As it often happens, real-world situations can be explained by more than one theory. A rationale supplied by the property rights approach is, however, more coherent and explains more of the real-world (or rather unreal world, as many would have it!) than competing rationales.

Concluding remarks

This author tried to explain why the resistance to change in the property rights structure is the strongest with respect to industry and within industry to large enterprises that offer greatest opportunities for appropriating the rent by bureaucrats and apparatchiks. He also explained why political clout of nomenklatura nominees affects resource allocation and how politically-determined resource allocation is translated into pecuniary and non-pecuniary benefits of bureaucrats and apparatchiks together with their colleagues appointed to managerial positions. The property rights approach was shown to be in accord with the widely accepted description of the mechanism of the Soviet-type economy while supplying a markedly more coherent rationale for its continuing existence.

Notes

[1] Winiecki, J., 'Pourquoi les réformes economiques échouent-elles dans les systémes de type soviétique?', *Revue d'études comparatives Est-Ouest*, vol. 18, 1987, n.3; Winiecki, J., 'Why Economc Reforms Fail in the Soviet System? A property rights-based approach', *Economic Inquiry*, 1989.

[2] For 1965 data, see Winiecki, J., *The distorted world of Soviet-type economies*, Routledge, London, 1988, p. 161; for 1985, own calculations from OECD statistics.

[3] See e.g. North, D.C., 'A Framework for Analysing the State in Economic History', *Explorations in Economic History*, vol. 31, March 1979.

[4] See the articles quoted in 1 but also: Szymanderski, J. - Winiecki, J., 'Dissipation de la rente, managers et travailleurs dans le systéme soviétique: les implications pour un changement du systéme', *Revue d'études comparatives Est-Ouest*, 1989; Winiecki, J., *Gorbachev's Way Out?*, Centre for Research into Communist Economies, London 1988.

[5] See Winiecki, J., The Distorted World..., op.cit., chapter III.

[6] Actually four branches of manufacturing: electrical and non-electrical machinery, textile, clothing, and footwear and food industries. For the source, see the next note.

[7] *Zarzadzanie*, 1985, n.11, p.27 (in Polish).

[8] According to a survey covering 404 general managers and their deputies: Kasten, M., 'Professional Careers of the Winners of Competitive Managerial Appointments (A Sociological Survey)', *Materiały i Studia IPPS*, n.14, Warsaw 1986, p.12 (in Polish).

[9] Gorynia, M. - Otta, W.J., 'Do Enterprise Have to Export?', *Zycie Gospodarcze*, 1988, n.9 (in Polish).

[10] See Szymanderski, J. - Winiecki, J., op.cit.

[11] Hegedus, A.,'Large Enterprises and Socialism', *Közgazdasagi Szemle*, vol.31, 1984, n.1 (in Hungarian)? These were, in fact, Hegedus' considerations on the book by Erzebet Szalar (also in Hungarian) about the investment preferences accorded to large enterprises.

[12] Wieczorkowski, A., 'Guiltless Galley Slaves', *Zarzadzanie*, 1984, n.12, p.24 (in Polish).

[13] Csanadi, M., 'Dependence, consensus and selection. The relationship between economics and politics in the decision-making system', Institute of Financial Research, Study n.3, Budapest, 1984, mimeo (in Hungarian).

[14] See Winiecki,J., The Distorted World..., op.cit., chapters I and III.

[15] See Csanadi, M., Dependence, consensus and selection, op.cit., p.227.

[16] See Csanadi, M., 'On the Mechanism of Decision-Making', *Tarsadalomikutatas*, 1987, n.4 (in Hungarian), on the basis of data from her study quoted earlier.

[17] See Csanadi, M., On the Mechanism of Decision-Making..., op.cit.

[18] See, first of all: Kornai, J., 'Resource-Constrained versus Demand-Constrained Systems', *Econometrica*, vol.47; July 1979, n.4.

[19] Bauer, T. (1978), 'Investment Cycles in Planned Economies', *Acta Œconomica*, vol. 21, n. 3.

[20] Csaba, L., 'New Features of the Hungarian Economic Mechanism in the Mid-Eighties', *The New Hungarian Quarterly*, vol.24, Summer 1983, n. 90.

[21] *Zycie Gospodarcze*, 1988, n.52 (Eugeniusz Mozejko's report on Hungarian Reforms)?

[22] *Zarzadzanie*, June issues each year since 1984.

[23] See Csanadi, M., Dependence, consensus and selection, op.cit., p.232 and Annex Table 8 and 20.

[24] See the report of the deputy of the Committee of National Control (i.e. the Office of the Comptroller General), A. Shitov, 'Raising the Discipline of the Plan: the Requirement of Our Times', *Planovoe Khozyaistvo*, 1981, n.11, p.17 (in Russian).

[25] Ibid., loc.cit.; see also *Planovoe Khozyaistvo*, 1980, n.6, p.22, where another author shows the numbers of enterprises that had their plan targets changed in the last month of the year in 1977 (up to 2.3 thousand enterprises), 1978 (up to 2.5 thousand) and 1979 (up to 3.8 thousand).

[26] See Winiecki, J., The Distorted World..., op.cit., chapter I.

[27] See i.a. See Winiecki, J., ibid., chapter II and the literature quoted therein..

2 The ten commandments of economic reform

RUUD KNAACK

Introduction

The abortive coup d'état launched on August 19, 1991 by the eight members of the State Committee for the State of Emergency in the USSR forms a decisive demarcation line in the history of the USSR. From a political point of view it marked the end of political dictatorship, the organization of society on the basis of a mono-hierarchical system and the existence of a socialist world. From an economic point of view the coup marks the transition from four decades of a reform process, which granted the persistence of a number of crucial elements of the traditional model, to a replacement of the traditional model by a quite different model of economic organization, characterized not only by large scale market relations but also by private ownership, liberal democracy and a full membership of the international economic community.

The coup d'état was caused by immediate political and economic factors (Mann, 1991). Chief among the political factors was the impending conclusion of the new Union treaty, that would have granted de facto recognition of the secession of six republics from the USSR and stripped the central government of nearly all its powers. Chief among the economic factors was the failure of the economic reform process under Gorbachev resulting in the decline over a long period of most economic indicators.

Economic reform under Gorbachev must be understood as a part of his efforts to revive and modernize the Soviet economy following 10 years of stagnation. In order to improve the economic situation Gorbachev changed economic policy as well as the economic system. The former comprised the changes in the investment policy, the 'non-labour incomes' campaign, the anti-alcohol campaign. The system related changes comprised both changes within the traditional economic model like a variety of administrative reorganizations, and changes of the traditional economic model. The most important changes so far concern individual economic activity, state enterprises, producer cooperatives, family contracts and leases in agriculture, joint ventures and the expansion of the rights of enterprises in foreign trade (Ellman, 1989).

The results of the Twelfth Five-Year Plan (12th FYP) (1986-1990) were disappointing. Soviet economic performance in 1986-90 has not been better then in 1981-85. At the end of 1988 a deep depression started. The net material product decreased by 9 per cent in the period 1989-90, compared with an increase of 11 per cent during the period 1983-88 (Khanin, 1992). Moreover, the depression is accelerating. In the first half of 1991 the net material product decreased already by 12 per cent. The USSR is also entering the stage of hyperinflation. While inflation in the period 1988-90 was in average 14 per cent, in June 1991 the yearly inflation was already 95 per cent [1].

In this paper we will ask ourselves the question whether or not the reform process can be blamed for the depression starting at the end of the last decade. More generally we will discuss the relationship between the reform process and the outcome of the economic process in order to find the conditions for a successful economic reform. This is not only interesting from an economic history point of view but also, as we will see, because the factors hampering the reform process will in large part also be influential during the transition period.

Economic conditions

The outcome of an economic system (o) depends basically on the components of the environment (e), the policies pursued by the participants in the system (p), and the system structure (s) (Montias, 1976, p. 31). In general we may write

$$o = f(e, p, s)$$

The reforms of the systems structure fall into two groups, reforms which only want to change the organizational structure and hence are within the traditional economic model and reforms which change the traditional economic model. With respect to the last group we can distinguish between reforms which change the relations between the organizations in the state sector and reforms which give more freedom for the cooperative and private sector in and outside agriculture. Let us look to all these elements in turn.

1. Congenial environment

The disappointing results of FYPXII so far cannot be blamed totally on the Soviet authorities. They stem, partly, from unfavourable environmental circumstances. For example, since 1986 the terms of trade both with the non-socialist and the socialist countries deteriorated. The terms of trade with the non-socialist countries deteriorated by 23 per cent in 1986 and 13 per cent in 1988 [2]. The fall in the terms of trade reflected a decrease in average dollar export prices (solely due to the huge fall in average energy export prices) and an increase in average import prices (mostly due to an increase in average food import prices). This was a major blow for the USSR since in 1985 almost 60 per cent of its non-socialist export earnings came from energy. The terms of trade with the socialist countries deteriorated also. After falling by 5 per cent, in 1987, Soviet rouble terms of trade with socialist countries are estimated to have fallen with another 6 per cent in 1988.

The Soviet Union reacted immediately by increasing the volume of its energy exports to the West. Soviet oil exports in volume terms rose by 23 per cent in 1986, 6 per cent in 1987 and 24 per cent in 1988. Simultaneously imports were reduced. Soviet imports in volume terms fell by 19 per cent in 1986 and by a further 10 per cent in 1987. However, in 1988 the non-socialist import rose by 12 per cent in quantity terms. This partly reflected the large increase in the quantity of crude oil imported from the Middle East for re-export to Western Europe. With the CMEA Six the trade stagnated more or less. Both export and import increased scarcely. The export to the developing countries increased slowly. Worthwhile mentioning is the still huge share of arms (about 55.5 per cent) in Soviet export to the Third World. As a result of all these developments, first, the trade balance with both the socialist and the non-socialist countries deteriorated. The trade balance with the socialist countries for the first time since 1973 showed in 1988 a trade deficit. With the Western countries the trade balance decreased from 8.4 billion dollar to 4.2 billion, being composed of a trade deficit of 2.8 billion dollar with the developed West and a surplus of 7.0 with the developing countries. It is not clear how the Soviet Union can afford this mountain of paper claims given the poor shape of its domestic economy. Secondly, given the contrast between the development of the Soviet trade with the socialist and non-socialist countries, the overall Soviet dependence on trade with non-socialist countries has dramatically risen and the relative importance of trade with socialist countries has fallen correspondingly.

The worsening of the terms of trade was a serious blow for the USSR. Given the large increase in the quantity of crude oil imported from the Middle-East for re-exporting to the West and the necessary grain and food imports to compensate for the poor 1988 harvest, it is clear that non-socialist imports of machinery and equipment, non-food raw materials and industrial consumer goods declined significantly in real terms. It both delayed industrial modernization and exacerbated domestic shortages. Moreover, the loss by the budget of the income which would have been earned from the high prices at which many imported consumer goods can be sold in the USSR, and the inability of consumers to buy these goods, worsened the deficit on the state budget and the financial disequilibrium on the consumer goods market at the same time.

2. *Macroeconomic consistency*

The most informative source for the intended economic policy of Gorbachev is the Guidelines of FYPXII. The draft of FYPXII has been the focus of a very heated debate between Gorbachev and the planning bureaucracy. Rejecting three times a draft version of the Plan, based on conservative low efficiency growth rates, a very ambitious fourth draft was published. The FYPXII called for an acceleration in economic growth. In effect the Plan intended to 'replay' the national income growth record of the 1970s, but backwards: achieving growth rates characteristic of 1976-80 during 1986-

90, and then accelerating to growth rates characteristic of the first half of the 1970s in the 1990s (Hewett 1985, p. 288).

The acceleration of the growth figures was not to come from an increase of the labour force and/or the capital stock. The growth of the labour force, 1.8 per cent during the 1970s, was falling steadily during the 1980s to 0.5 per cent. In addition, labour productivity was falling steadily from 6 per cent in the first half of the 1970s to 3 per cent in the first half of the 1980s. Also the growth rates of capital stock were falling from 8.7 per cent in the beginning of the 1970s to 5.5 per cent in the second half of the 1980s. In addition, the capital costs of Soviet raw materials and fuels have begun to rise very rapidly, particularly in the 1970s as the geographic centre of Soviet fuel and raw material production began to shift eastwards at an increasing pace. Moreover, in the period 1970-85 capital productivity declined by roughly one half. Therefore it is only through reversing the decline in labour and capital productivity that the growth acceleration can be accomplished.

How could Gorbachev achieve this reversal? First, he wanted to exploit the 'human factor'. Basically, this refers to the possibility of significantly enhancing economic performance by inducing the labour force to work at rates closer to its potential. The increase of labour-productivity was not stimulated by an increase of real wages. In the FYPXII real per capita income was intended to grow only by 2.8 per cent compared with 3.3 per cent in 1981-85 and 4.4 per cent in 1976-80. The most important element of the 'human factor' strategy was the entire range of discipline measures, including the drunkenness and anti-alcohol campaign from the summer of 1985 and a lot of personnel changes and dismissals throughout the system.

Secondly, the FYPXII placed a strong emphasis on renovation of the old-fashioned capital stock. FYPXII specified that it was not necessary to speed up investment over the whole 1986-90 plan period; the plan held down the growth of investment to 4.3 per cent compared with the 3.5 per cent in the period 1981-85. More importantly, on the one hand the investment growth was divided unequally over the plan period, with planned total investment increasing by 7.6 per cent in 1986 and decreasing accordingly in the remaining part of the period, and on the other hand more investment were to go to renovating enterprises than before. As a consequence most notable in FYPXII was the very substantial shift in investment resources to machine-building industry. According to the modernization programme, the mass-produced output of the civilian machine-building industries, which in 1985 met 'world standards' only by 29 per cent, in 1990 was to meet the world standard in the range from 80 to 95 per cent. In order to accomplish this target it was necessary to replace immediately the capital stock in machine-building with new modern equipment to allow the new mass-produced products to find their way into the system. For this reason the plan called for a 12.5 per cent increase of investment in machine-building industry in average and an increase of 30 per cent in 1986.

In fact, the plan did not work out as was hoped for. From a policy point of view there are several reasons. First, because FYPXII was from the beginning not feasible (Hewett, Roberts & Vanous, 1987, p. 32). The rapid shift of resources to machine-building industry implied that other sectors should give up substantial resources, for example the energy sector and agriculture and the nonproductive sectors. This contradicted explicit formulated social goals of the FYPXII: an increase of 50 per cent of the production and sale of consumer goods over the five-year period and the promise that nearly every family should have an apartment or individual house by the year 2000. The too tight FYPXII naturally led, *ceteris paribus*, to an aggravation of the already existing shortages in the economy, as was noticeable in the last years.

Secondly, the participants in the economy behaved differently from what was anticipated. This was most noticeable with the anti-alcohol campaign. The idea was to reduce alcohol abuse and thus increase labour productivity. The result was that the sales of alcohol in the state system dropped by 37 bn. roubles in 1985-1987, or almost a quarter of 1985 food sales, with also devastating effects for the state budget. On the other hand, it was not clear whether or not alcohol abuse diminished; the drop in the sales of vodka, for example, was partially offset by an increase of the illegally brewed *samogon*. With a similarly unexpected development, the high targets for investment growth led to an excessive growth of money wages.

Thirdly, it was not clear whether or not the budget deficit of 183 billion roubles in the period 1986-88 was planned for. A significant proportion of the budget deficit was financed by monetary expansion. That in turn led to an excess money supply, which allowed excess purchasing power to be created.

Altogether, the increased purchasing power in pursuit of consumer goods, coupled with problems in the supply of both domestic production and imports to the state shops, led to a fall of the stocks in the distributive sector by about 17 bn. roubles in 1985-1988, or by about 5 per cent of 1985 sales.

Shortages and in general macroeconomic inconsistency is one of the most dangerous threats for the reform process. Shortages have a direct negative impact on labour productivity, and they undermine the belief in the possibility of the reform's successful implementation. Consumer goods have to be readily available, otherwise material incentives are largely meaningless. Producer goods also have to be readily available, otherwise the autonomy of enterprises is largely meaningless.

3. Institutional reforms

The formula for the organizational restructuring of the state sector was the 'union of centralism and the independence of economic organizations'. Central control should been strengthened in some respects and reduced in others (Berliner, 1987, p. 74). It has been strengthened by the creation of new Central Organizations to coordinate the agro-industrial, engineering, foreign trade and social sectors analogous to the Military-Industrial Commission which has long coordinated the military industrial complex. Central control was strengthened, secondly, by redefining the division of tasks between the centre and the ministries by concentrating central effort on major issues of general policy and the coordination of activities that cut across ministry boundaries. Gosplan, for example, was released from work on current economic questions and dealt instead only with long-run planning problems and major allocation issues. On the other hand, central control was reduced by putting operational control in the hands of the ministries.

Also the ministry-enterprise relations changed more or less in the same way. The ministries position is strengthened by the coordination of its efforts on matters of ministry-wide policy, like the direction of technological change, and is reduced by the cessation of its involvement in the enterprises' internal activities. The enterprises became responsible for the economic use of their own assets. Their ability to produce salable output directly determined funds available for wages, bonuses, and new capital projects. This was called 'self-financing' (*samofinansirovanie*).

In spite of all these changes the ministerial system as such was retained. The old power relation between the enterprises and the ministries did not fundamentally change. In this respect Gorbachev's *perestroika* did not learn from Kosygin's abortive 1965 reform and from the experiences with the Hungarian reform process. One of the reasons of the disappointing results of the Hungarian reforms in the seventies was the lack of institutional reforms (Kornai, 1986). If enterprises are given the formal rights to set prices and output, they will not exercise those rights freely so long as each enterprise has over it a branch ministry responsible for the overall performance of 'its' industry. Such a ministry cannot but intervene in the operations of its enterprises if it is held responsible for the sum total of their activities. Meetings in the Central Committee continue to produce calls to the branch ministries to put this or that problem in this or that industry to rights.

This problem cannot be solved completely by abolishing the branch ministries. Experiences in Hungary and Poland make clear that the abolition of branch ministries is a necessary but not a sufficient condition for genuine enterprise autonomy. What is necessary is the creation of a competitive environment and the formal abolition of the right of state organs to intervene. In this respect it was a progressive measure that for example the *Ispolkomy* had no formal powers any more to intervene in the creation of a cooperative. However, as long as they had any say in the supply system in a shortage economy, they had more than enough informal powers (Knaack & Stolker, 1989).

4. Microeconomic consistency

On the microeconomic level, the reform intended to replace the information system based on obligatory targets with one that relied primarily on economic instruments and flexible prices. The goal for the planning system was a familiar one: a shift to five year plans, in which the most important decision variables for planners were norms, fixed for five years. But there were also two more conventional routes for conveying central desires to the enterprises. First, Gosplan, the branch ministries and republican authorities had the right to issue orders (*goszakazy*) for the fulfilment of the state's highest-priority needs, like defence.

Secondly, central planners were also able to convey a considerable amount of information to enterprises through control figures, none of them being officially obligatory. The excess demand for consumer goods was linked to price control.

To the extent that *goszakazy* took up only a modest share of total output and control figures are truly no more than information for the enterprises, the role of the price system loomed large in determining the success of the reform. A revision of prices was to be completed in 1988 and a reform of the price-setting mechanism at the end of the decade.

The absence of a reform of the price system can also be seen as a source of shortages. Subsidies are not only necessary from an income policy point of view, but they all stimulate the demand for a product. The demand for heavily subsidized meat is exceptionally high in the East compared with the West. Moreover, if the state were able to reform the retail prices so as to reduce sharply the food price subsidies, without returning all the saved subsidies to the population, it would be able to eliminate the monetary financing of the state budget. In 1989 the food subsidy was in the order of 88 bn. roubles compared with an estimated budget deficit of 100 bn. roubles [3].

The need for microeconomic consistency as a prerequisite for a successful economic reform is evident. In order to make the profit rate an indicator of the overall working of an enterprise, working conditions have to be equalized as much as possible. To achieve this, the three parts of the stimulation system (the price system, the incentive system and the calculation system) have to form a harmonious whole. For example the price structure has to be reconsidered: in the old situation the profit rates before taxation show too wide a dispersion. (The profit rates after taxation reflect the subsidy-obtaining capacity of the firm). To harmonize the stimulation system is not an easy task, not only because it transforms the hidden inflation into an open one, but also because it strikes against provincial interests.

5. Agricultural reform

The experiences of China and Hungary show that a bold package of agricultural reforms can play a major role in rising living standards and making economic reform a success and irreversible. This potential has not been realized up till now in the USSR. Not because there is no potential. Also in the Soviet Union there are huge possibilities to improve the agricultural situation by efficiency gains in agriculture itself as well as in its upwards and downwards linkages. The availability of food can be tremendously increased by 'reinstating the peasants as the masters of the land' and by diminishing the huge harvest and post-harvest losses (Wädekin, 1989).

Gorbachev's approach to agriculture was in line with his approach to industry. First, he wanted to streamline the bureaucracy. In November 1985 the five ministries and one state committee which had previously administered agriculture were abolished and replaced by one new body, the State Agro-Industrial Committee (Gosagroprom). Secondly, he directed more investment to the downstream linkages of agriculture. The growth in the processing industry was 16 per cent in 1988, compared with the overall growth in the agro-industrial complex of 3 per cent. Thirdly, he gave more incentives to farms by increasing procurement prices by 50 per cent in 1986 on major commodities for production in excess of the average for 1981-85. Furthermore, the farms were allowed to market freely 30 per cent of their planned output of fruit and vegetables and the whole of their output of all products in excess of the plan. Measures have also been taken to enhance the autonomy of the farms. The new law on cooperatives was also valid for the collective farms. This law gave also a legal basis for experiments with 'family commitments', 'individual commitments' and 'leasing contracts'.

All these measures did not appear to be very successful. For example, the farms did not take advantage of the possibilities to sell the above-plan production on the free market, because it was safer under conditions of shortages of supply to 'please' the local leadership by fulfilling their non-obligatory demands (Avon & Shironin, 1988, p. 36). Although the family contracts were reported in the Soviet press to spread all over the country with good results, in reality most of them proved to be just part of the brigade contract under a new name. The amount of people really involved in it was relatively very small and concentrated mostly in the Baltic and Central Asian republics. Several reasons explain this lack of success. First, it seemed that the traditions of family organization in agriculture have been lost after 60 years of collectivization (Nikoforov, 1989, p. 71). Secondly, the overwhelming majority of contracts were for one year, reflecting the lack of legal regulation. Thirdly, there was a lot of social and ideological mistrust regarding small-group forms. Fourthly, the family contract specified a task, to be implemented basically with inputs made available by the collective under conditions of the collective. With the exception of the Baltic *khutory* this form of family contract differed fundamentally from the highly successfully Chinese form of peasant household operating on leased land.

Some of the dangers for a reform in a bureaucratic environment were understood by Gorbachev. Others were not. The bureaucratization, inefficiency and high costs of Gosagroprom and its regional branches were much criticized at the party conference of June 1988. At the March 1989 Central Committee plenum on agriculture

Gosagroprom was abolished and replaced by a new State Committee. Negative was, that the 'Law on Leasing' did not emerge before the end of 1989. It became also clear that the right to grant leases would remain primarily in the hands of the *kolkhozy* and *sovkhozy* and the Party and state apparatus. This was not an auspicious prospect for lessees. The *kolkhozy* and *sovkhozy* were criticized in the Soviet press for refusing to cooperate and for concluding contracts on unfavourable terms that exploit their partners (Whitlock, 1989, p. 5).

6. Legalization of the second economy

Another area where quick results could be achieved was the individual, family and small group business. Since the party congress in March 1986, a variety of initiatives have been taken by the government. The new law on individual economic activity from November 1986 permitted housewives, students, pensioners and state employees working in their free time to become self-employed. In May 1988 a very radical law was adopted providing an authoritative legal framework for cooperatives in all branches of the economy. This law came into force on July 1, 1988. The cooperatives were given a considerable amount of freedom to operate within the law. State organizations were forbidden to issue extra-legal orders on them. The cooperatives could set their prices freely, unless they were producing for state orders or using state supplied materials. In May 1986 regulations were issued which gave explicit legal sanction to *shabashniki*, brigades of workers, mainly in rural areas, who hire themselves out to farms to perform construction work or field work. These laws were supplemented, by a law on 'unearned income', aimed at corruption by officials and ordinary citizens and at theft and corruption associated with underground activities.

At the end of 1988 almost 2 million people were registered as working in this new legal sector. The birth of this new sector had a favourable effect on the variety, availability and quality of services and goods available to the public.

Unfortunately, there were also numerous difficulties already confronting this sector. First, persons other than pensioners, students and housewives who chose to earn their living from full-time self-employment rather than to work in the state sector would potentially risk prosecution under the state's 'anti-parasite' laws, which remained in effect. Secondly, although local authorities under the new law were forbidden from interfering in the cooperatives, they still had a responsibility for assisting individual and cooperative business in finding sources of supply, tools, and transportation and in selling their products. This gave them a huge informal power under conditions of scarcity (Knaack & Stolker, 1989). Thirdly, while the regulations on *shabashniki* made an end to the ambiguous legal status of the brigades, they may made their work less attractive by putting strict controls on operations and limiting payments to rates paid for comparable work in the state sector. Fourthly, the measures about 'unearned income' provoked much debate about what should or should not be considered as 'unearned'. In some regions, party and law enforcement authorities interpreted the decrees as a mandate for an across-the-board crackdown on private activity, driving such activity further underground and reducing the availability of goods and services produced privately (Blough, Muratore & Berk, 1987, p. 265).

Evidently, the conditions under which private business could flourish were still not fully accepted in all sectors of the decision making system. Many party officials and local authorities felt that the expansion of the legal private sector would create opportunities for individual enrichment that were incompatible with socialist egalitarian principles. From this point of view one of the obstacles to the further development of this sector was the already mentioned macroeconomic and microeconomic disequilibria which made high prices and short-term profits so easy.

Ideological conditions

In the preceding section the economic conditions for a successful economic reform were described and analysed. It became clear that these conditions are not fulfilled for a variety of reasons. The reforms were opposed because they threatened socialism, or the interests of social groups like local authorities; or the reforms had unexpected outcomes, which had to be corrected. Obviously the authorities had an insufficient insight in the working of the economy and in the content of the political 'Pandora's box'. Let us look at these ideological and theoretical conditions in more detail.

7. *Ideological barriers*

The economic reforms had been obviously constrained by ideological barriers. Gorbachev's economic reform process could be criticized from the viewpoint of traditional Marxist-Leninist orthodoxy. The most important theses of traditional Marxist-Leninist orthodoxy can be summarized as follows. First, a socialist economy should be based on state ownership and central planning. Secondly, ex-ante planning and the absence of antagonistic relations in society will guarantee that a socialist economy will be enormously more efficient than the anarchy of production under capitalism.

Given these theses, the only 'economic reforms' that are possible are those aiming at the realization of the ideal type of socialism. For example, the transformation of collective farms into state farms, the abolition of private plots, the replacement of the remaining value relations between enterprises by 'direct product exchange' on the basis of plan instructions, and a reduction of the part of national income destined for 'product for themselves' in favour of an increase of the part of 'product for society' (Knaack, 1980, pp. 394-397). Hence, what is nowadays known as economic reform appears in this framework as 'the restoration of capitalism', a very serious and extremely risky criminal offence (Ellman, 1989, p. 3).

Precisely because of its negative effect on the elaboration of reform proposals, the Marxist-Leninist orthodoxy came under strong attack. On May 6 1988 *Pravda* published a radical article denouncing the traditional formulations of the political economy of socialism. The article criticized *Economic Problems of Socialism in the USSR*, the 1954 textbook, and all the succeeding textbooks and literature. However, the attack was not on the political economy of socialism in general, but just on its Stalinist formulation. Therefore, although some of the traditional doctrines were declared to be unscientific, an improved political economy was commended.

Of course, a reformulation of political economy backing Gorbachev's reform process had to start with a reformulation of the concept of socialist property. From a Marxist-Leninist point of view property realizes itself through the appropriation of the surplus product. In socialism the mode of appropriation characterized by exploitation and hired labour is excluded by definition. From this follows that the theoretically possible forms of property in socialism are state property, cooperative property and property based on individual labour activity. However, in the Soviet practice the state ownership of the means of production has been treated as the main criterion of socialism. Cooperative property had in fact lost their objectively inherent right to possess, use, and dispose of their own money, produce and means of production at their own discretion and individual property of the means of production had up till now nearly no significance at all.

The narrowing of socialist property to state property has been made possible by the Marxist-Leninist thesis of the identity of state ownership and social ownership. This identity is connected with the view that each individual person is in direct relationship with society or with the state because he is the 'coproprietor' of all state means of production regardless of where he works.

This axiom has been criticized both by intellectuals and by the authorities themselves. According to Shkredov (1989, p. 10), this view downgraded the role of the enterprise and its work collective as an objective necessary binding link between each individual working person and the state. The difference between state ownership and social ownership had been implicitly recognized by the law on the state enterprise. The law characterized the work collective of enterprises as the 'boss' (*Khoziain*) who used public property.

The new way of thinking about property was also reflected in a renewed attention for cooperative and individual property. The law on the state enterprise had been supplemented by a law on Cooperatives and a law on individual labour.

However, in spite of all these changes the authorities adhered to their standpoint that the hiring of non-household labour by individuals constituted exploitation and was undesirable, that cooperatives were preferable to private enterprises, and that the overwhelming majority of economic activities should take place in state owned enterprises. These major relics of the traditional view remained constraints on the reform process.

Of course, changes in the concept of socialist property had consequences for the concept of socialist planning. The realization of socialist property depends, inter alia, on the conditions under which decisions are made to use public property, on who makes the decision, on what kind of economic authority is centrally concentrated, on what kind of authority is transferred to the middle-level managers and on what is retained directly by the work collective.

In the traditional Marxist-Leninist orthodoxy, a plan is a set of binding instructions for the participants in the economy. As Stalin once put it, 'our plans are not forecasts but instructions'. Hence in the traditional model, 'planning' is identified with the bureaucratic allocation of resources. This conception of planning has been criticized. First, it has been argued that the traditional model was not a planned economy. What has been referred to for decades as 'socialist planning' became commonly referred to from 1985 onwards as the 'administrative-command' system. This terminology implicitly rejected the notion that the traditional model could be considered as planned. Yakovlev went one step further by saying that the traditional system functioned as a braking mechanism, behind which also hide the most experienced opponents of *perestroika* (Yakovlev, 1989, p. 6).

The idea that real planning did not exist, but would have to be introduced as part of a radical economic reform, had been put forward already by TSEMI in the 1960s but failed to find adequate political support at that time. In the 1980s it was revived. According to Abalkin (1988), in the reformed economic system the conception of 'centralism' must be radically different from that in the 'administrative-command' system. It should cover only two functions. First, it includes those questions that cannot be successfully resolved by the independent actions of lower-level economic links. Among them are the development of the strategy of economic growth, and the implementation of a unified scientific-technological, structural and investment policy. Secondly, it consists in the creation of conditions for effective, independent and responsible actions of the basic links of the national economy. For example, the realization of general, universal balance in the economy and the elimination of the monopolistic position of individual producers. The methods to be employed in attaining these goals and strategic objectives must be economic methods instead of methods based on commands and orders. In the new methods 'economic norms' and 'state orders', as an expression of the most strategic important and socially significant targets of the state, play a key role. This is basically a description not of a regulated market economy but of an indirectly bureaucratically controlled economy of the Hungarian NEM type as described for example by Kornai (1986).

According to Marxist-Leninist orthodoxy, in a socialist society there are only two classes, the working class and the peasants, and one stratum, the intellectuals. Between the working class and peasants and between both classes and the intellectuals there are no antagonistic relations.

'The intellectuals are recruited from the ranks of the workers and the farmers, hence they are serving the interests of both, fraternally linked classes' (Lehrbuch, 1972, p. 101). In general traditional Marxist-Leninist orthodoxy denies the existence in socialism of deep, even antagonistic contradictions between personal, group and social interests, as between the interests of different classes and social groups.

This point of view has been criticized by Soviet economists and sociologists. For example, Zaslavskaia (1986, p. 36) argued 'that the actual development of the production relations is not only and not so much the result of occupational activity of workers engaged therein as it is the complex interaction of socioeconomic groups that occupy different levels in social production and that pursue contradictory interests'.

The thesis about the non-existence of antagonistic relations in socialism was not without practical meaning. It could explain the ambivalent attitude of the authorities against the phenomenon of strikes. On the one hand it was possible that Gorbachev welcomed the strikes of the coal miners in Siberia as an expression of real problems, on the other hand in the past strikes were often condemned as behaviour of lunatics acting against their own interests and therefore ripe for locking up in a mental hospital.

Looking at Soviet discussions about the ideological important theses with regard to socialist ownership, planning, and social classes, we can see that a few years of *glasnost* have been sweeping away a lot of ideological barriers. However, most authors tried to reformulate the content of the concepts to make them less contradictory with the actual reform process. As a consequence, important ideological barriers for the reform process remained. The authorities adhered to their standpoint that the hiring of non-household labour by individuals constituted exploitation and was undesirable, that cooperatives were preferable to private enterprises and that the overwhelming majority of economic activity should take place in state owned enterprises.

8. Partial ignorance

Strongly related to the ideological barriers as a constraint for a successful economic reform process, is the constraint of the lack of knowledge by the authorities of the functioning of the real economy. These partial ignorance has two sources: conceptional ignorance and informational ignorance.

By conceptional ignorance we mean the lack of understanding by the authorities about the functioning of the real economic system. The conception of the Soviet economy as a rational, planned economy, in which people are viewed as 'labour resources', which can be 'formed', 'distributed' and 'used' by someone else on the basis of interests that are external to their own, is highly incorrect. As a result, people's reactions to policy measures prove often to be different than expected. For example, the high labour turnover in the northern regions of Siberia in the late 1960s highly detrimental to production was thought to be caused by an insufficient level of earnings. Hence, the authorities raised the wage coefficient in order to stabilize the workforce. However, following the wage increase, personnel turnover did not diminish but actually increased. The reason was that a large number of workers went north with the aim to save money to buy a house, car etc. Under the new conditions they achieved this aim in a shorter period of time. This example shows that the effective management of economic and social development requires reliable knowledge of the behavioural patterns (motivations, interests, conditions) of the managed groups (Zaslavskaia, 1987).

As already said before, the USSR was not a rational, centrally planned economy. There is a huge literature on economic planning explaining why the enterprise plans turned out very often to be inadequate, inaccurate and partial. Hence, the enterprises were caught in a decision trap: they were supposed to fulfil nonfulfillable plans (Knaack, 1984, p. 116). Given this trap, the enterprises had to develop alternative strategies in order to meet the demands on them. These strategies could remain between the limits of the planning system, but often they went over the borderline. An important part of the required inputs, for example, had to be obtained through unofficial channels. These channels were most of the time characterized by personal relationships. The structural circumstances of central planning based on partial ignorance and complexity made mutual trust a scarce and highly valued commodity which could be obtained through the exchange of personal favours extended at personal risk. From this it followed that the success of the enterprise director was largely determined by his ability to use the resources of his office for exchanging favours with key officials in the institutions constituting his organizational environment. Thus, there emerged cross-institutional cliques whose members disposed of their respective official prerogatives to mutual advantage. It was through and by these informal relations that plans were (partly) implemented and modified. For these reasons the Soviet economy, could be better characterized as a 'bargaining' economy instead of a 'planned' economy (Aven & Shironin, 1988).

Considering the Soviet economy as a bargaining economy it was not surprising that under conditions of scarcity and a situation in which central allocation was the main control, current attempts at introducing material incentives were ending in failure. Given the primary significance of the centrally allocated material-technical resources the farms not surprisingly fulfilled the claims of the local authorities in exchange for future help in the distribution of material-technical supply (Avon & Shironin, 1988, p. 36).

The lack of knowledge by the central authorities about the functioning of the real economy was also caused by the absence of reliable statistical information. This phenomenon was not new. For ideological reasons the Soviet leadership needed the creation of myth about the successes of the Soviet economy in order to 'prove' its superiority over capitalism.

The two most important myth about the past in the pre-*perestroika* period concern the success of the collectivization process and the rate of growth achieved since the late 1920s (Ellman, 1989, p. 6 onwards). With the advent of *glasnost*, however, the situation changed dramatically. According to the interview with Danilov and Teptsov in *Pravda* (19.9.1988) the estimate of 3-4 million famine death by Western Sovietologists was admitted to be 'objective'.

In spite of *glasnost*, this habit of mythmaking continued during the Gorbachev-period. For example, undoubtedly the most dubious claim made in the official 1988 plan fulfilment report was the 7.1 per cent increase in retail trade turnover in real (comparable price) terms. Given the 7.2 per cent increase in retail trade turnover in nominal rouble terms, this would have implied a mere 0.1 per cent increase in the average retail price level. With 8 per cent growth in wages on a yearly basis registered during April-December 1988 and, at most, 2 per cent growth in labour productivity, the official implicit claim of price stability insulted the intelligence of most Soviet citizens. An authoritative Soviet government figure explained once to a group of visiting Western economists as to why key monetary statistics in the Soviet Union could not be published because they would cause 'social instability'. We can see that the same reasoning could apply to deliberate manipulation and distortion of politically sensitive statistics such as inflation rate, growth of national income, and changes in living standard [4].

9. *Social interests*

Describing the Soviet economy in terms of a 'bargaining' economy we must recognize the fact that the actual development of production relations is the result of the complex interaction of socioeconomic groups that occupy different levels in social production and that pursue contradictory interests. Hence, the success of any reform is possible only when the social forces interested in the reform outweigh the forces interested in stagnation. And this means that in order for a reform to be successful, it is necessary not only to analyse the array of social forces, but also to make provisions in the restructuring programme for winning over those who are opposed to it.

The subjective attitude of social groups towards the projected economic reforms has been more and more studied by economists and sociologists, both in the West and the East. In the West, for example, Nove (1979) argued that the retention of aspects of the old system after the economic reforms in the sixties was partly caused by the sociological fact that most strata in the Soviet Union were against the reform. The aged leadership was intensively conservative and disliked risks. Furthermore, the reform was against the interests of those particularly concerned with military and other top-priority sectors. The regional and republican officials were opposed because the Kosygin reform abolished the regional economic councils and replaced them by central ministries. The local officials disliked the reform because a strengthening of the intermanagerial ties, of their nature, crossed all kinds of regional boundaries. The reform did not meet the favour of the planning and the financial bureaucracy because the use of automatic criteria for an optimal plan might liquidate directive planning. The workers were against the reform because they valued greatly security of employment, and the strive for higher labour productivity by transferring surplus labour to where it was needed might be inconsistent with this goal. Even without this, the jobs done would have to change and there would have to be some training and retraining. The workers might also be against one possible outcome of the reform, namely a more unequal income distribution. Nove concludes: 'the political pressures for the reform are unlikely to issue from any powerful group. The pressures for changes arises from circumstances, from the consciousness that the old way will not, or does not, work. Will this overcome the well-integrated habits and self-interest of so large and well-entrenched a party-State apparatus?' (Nove, 1979, p. 165).

Nove's analysis of the impact of the social interest constraint on the fate of the Kosygin reforms in the sixties is surprisingly topical also with respect to the Gorbachev reforms. On the main lines it fits in with Zaslavskaia's (Zaslavskaia, 1989) analysis about the impact of the social factors on the outcome of the Gorbachev reform. However, her analysis is a little bit more sophisticated than Nove's, insofar as she points out that social groups are not homogeneous with respect of their support for *perestroika*. In nearly all social groups it is possible to make a division between supporters and opponents of economic reforms. For example, the position of the economic management depends on their place in the hierarchy. The hierarchy consists of (a) interdepartmental management of the national economy, (b) branch ministries and departments and their territorial administrations, and (c) associations and enterprises. Differences in the attitudes of these groups toward the economic reform are to a considerable degree associated with the fact that prestige and social status in the first and third groups rise as a result of the reform, whereas they decline in the second group.

From the above analysis we can draw some conclusions. First, that a reform must be embedded in a politically stable and supportive environment. An in-depth, comprehensive reform that represents a sharp departure from the existing system requires a strong government which will have enough experience and confidence to prepare the proper grounds for the reform and enough patience to wait out an occasionally lengthy gestation period before the reform comes to fruition (Knaack, 1984). It can also explain on the one hand the already mentioned necessity of winning over the support of the working class by a sufficient supply of consumer goods and immaterial improvements in the way of life and on the other hand the sensitive reactions of the government on nationality problems.

Secondly, given the different outcomes of the economic reform for the social groups and their expected reactions to it, it is necessary to have a 'feedback' system, which can value and damp the opposed interests. The question then rises, whether or not the political system can fulfil this role.

10. Political democracy

For a long period of time many economists in the East and the West advocated political reforms as a prerequisite for a successful economic reform. This is a very delicate question. Who will deny the need for political reform in East Europe? However, being well aware that political democracy has a 'consumption' aspect, at this place we have to restrict ourselves to the 'production' aspect, namely, whether or not a reform of the political system is needed to raise economic efficiency (Gomulka, 1977, p. 394).

This question was answered affirmatively already in the seventies by the Polish economist Brus. Basically he argued that under central planning the existence of a highly motivated group of employees requires their meaningful participation in forming economic policy at higher levels of decision-making structure, particularly at the central level. A higher degree of political democracy is also thought to increase the probability that the policies adopted are close to the social optimum, and that the cadres employed are better selected to carry these policies out. This proposition is not confirmed by the study of Adelman & Harris (1967). Studying which variables could explain variations in the level of per capita GNP in 1961 in 74 less developed countries, they found that the form of government, whether democratic or authoritarian, has little or no systematic effect on economic performance at any level of development.

However, political democracy has more aspects than the form of government. It includes also concepts of 'legal society' and 'civil society'. Let us look to these concepts first before returning to the question of the form of government.

The success of an economic reform requires that not only the various decrees to give economic independence to the participants are followed by legislative acts, but also that their practical observance will be secured. Conditions must be created such that the enterprises would be able to make actual use of rights granted to them. The building of a 'Rechtsstaat' in which people can work according to rules and manage according to the law, is seen as a first step in the democratization of economic life (Roundtable discussion, 1989, p. 36).

The second step is the forming of a civil society. In the economic reform process the activation of people is uneven, and people are also differently affected by the outcomes of the reform process. Under conditions that one cannot speak the truth, or discuss urgent problems inside the official structures, the need rises for parallel structures. Those parallel structures can become a definite counterweight to the state. This was also understood by Gorbachev. In July 1989, he proposed on a meeting of the Central Committee that it must be possible to form committees in defence of *perestroika* [5].

Returning to the form of government, we have argued already that a successful reform requires a strong government, that can convert the economy to self-regulation against the existing system of interests. Does this require a 'authoritarian stage' in the reform process? History on the one hand gives a lot of examples of very efficient authoritarian societies. On the other hand, the Polish example makes clear that the Party can be an obstacle in the reform process because it has no credit any more. Hence, which form of government suits best the progress of the reform process depends on the historical circumstances of that particular country.

Evaluation

So far we have analysed *perestroika* from a static perspective. We were mainly concerned with the question which of the described conditions could explain the negative outcomes of *perestroika*. We have seen that all the conditions had their impact on the negative outcomes. However, in the absence of the possibility of factor analysis it looks like we cannot be sure of which one had the biggest impact.

This conclusion might be too negative. According to Kontorovich (Kontorovich, 1988) the negative outcome of the reform process is not a surprise. Any institutional change *must* have a negative effect on the economy because it unbalances the economy as the logical outcome of the decentralization of economic decision-making. For example, the Law of State Enterprise, announced in 1987 and implemented in 1988, increased the scope of independent decision-making of the state enterprises. It was hoped for that this would improve the efficiency of the enterprises and that more attention would be paid to the wishes of the customer. However, under conditions of macroeconomic unbalances the enterprises behaved differently. In practice it led to sharp increases in prices, changes in the product assortment, decreases in the level of production, extraordinary increases in wages. More important was that Gorbachev ruined the traditional supply system (Ellman, 1991a, p. 862). By attacking bureaucracy, Gorbachev eliminated the economic role of the party. The party committees on all levels informally functioned as a coordination mechanism by using their contacts if something went wrong. After their elimination the enterprises felt in an empty space which was not yet filled by the creation of markets and the building of new formal and informal relations with suppliers and consumers. As a result it became very difficult to obtain the required materials and spare parts. In this respect bureaucratic resistance to the reform is not necessarily one of the causes of the reform failure, but more the logical behaviour of bureaucrats to restore order.

On top of the disturbances caused by institutional change came the disturbances reflecting environmental and policy related circumstances. For example, the large budget deficits under Gorbachev reflect the Chernobyl disaster, the decline in world energy prices, the anti-alcohol policy, the acceleration of investment and the centrally determined income increases. None of them are related to institutional changes and hence none of them have anything to do with economic reform. The first two factors are wholly environmental, and the last three policy related. From this story we can conclude that an economic reform or transition process which is not accompanied by a corresponding and consistent economic policy is doomed to fail.

More generally we can say that the negative outcomes of *perestroika* are mainly caused by too much reform instead of too little reform. Gorbachev destroyed the old system without creating at the same time a new system. That he could not create a new system is, according to Popper (Popper, 1991), not surprising. Any economic system constitutes an organic whole. The behaviour of economic actors is learned behaviour. It will take time for the system and the actors to adapt to new circumstances. Seventy years of communism constitute a difficult heritage to get rid of even if you are absolutely determined to get rid of it. To think that you can do this in 500 days is an ideological fallacy. Hence, the design of social institutions should be carried out not in accordance with some 'grand design', but on a cautious, trial-and-error basis. Those who try to remodel society in accordance with a 'definite plan or blueprint' run the risk of building a deformed social structure whose flaws can be corrected only with greatest delay and difficulty. The people in the East and the West who think that you can do that have an attitude similar to that of early generations of communists anxious to 'build communism' regardless of the 'short run' consequences (Ellman, 1991b). They tend to ignore the system-specific features of those countries and are surprised when the outcome of the policies they support is quite different from what they anticipated.

The fact that the socio-political-economic transformation of the Soviet Union will be a long and difficult process has important consequences for the *sequence* of the measures to be taken in the reform and transition process. A reform is fundamentally a social process, one of learning by doing, trial and error. What is needed is 'piecemeal social engineering', incremental improvements which can be continually improved upon. Hence, the one thing the leadership in the Soviet Union must not do is to dismantle their industrial system abruptly. In contrary, before taking other measures, the Soviet economy must be stabilized. Only after this policy has succeeded, one can go further on the road of institutional change.

It is important to note that there are three objects of a stabilization policy, namely the stabilization of the foreign debt, the monetary system and the real economy. With respect to the foreign debt problem, the Soviet Union cannot serve its debt and interest obligations without help at the end of 1991. At that moment the foreign debt will be roughly 60 billion dollars and the necessary debt and interest payments 17 billion dollars, compared with 35 billion dollars of export earnings.

With respect to the monetary system, the Soviet Union has both a 'stock' and a 'flow' problem. The amount of roubles that cannot be spent in the state shops is 1.1 times the value of one year production of consumer goods. One way of 'confiscating' the monetary overhang is to privatize the economy by selling state property, apartments, enterprise stocks, etc.. Also price increases might be unavoidable. However this will cause tremendous social unrest with the Soviet people, who prefer rationing over price increases. The solution of the flow-problem is strongly related to the budgetary deficit of both the Union and the republics. Without a sharp reduction of the deficit, it is difficult to overcome inflation. Positive is that after the coup there is a political climate favourable to cutting down expenses on the military-industrial complex and the agricultural lobby. Less positive is the breaking down of the Union. In the future also the collection of taxes will be decentralized. Experiences in China indicate that this situation will be a permanent source of conflict and a built-in mechanism for macroeconomic instability (Oksenberg and Tong, 1991).

In the Soviet Union there is also a real stabilization problem. A part of the problems in the Soviet Union is not caused by a lack of production, but by a lack of transport and communication, or - in comparison with West - too much consumption. For example, a huge part of the yearly agricultural production is lost by a lack of transport and storage capacity. An improvement of the transport system is also needed for the solution of the energy problem. Leaking oil pipes are causing tremendous losses. The Soviet energy problem is also caused by its huge energy consumption. On average Soviet enterprises are consuming twice as much energy as in the West. Stabilization of the transport and energy sector might improve the economic situation in a short period of time.

Only when the economy is stabilized, the institutional reforms may continue. But also in this field some 'fine tuning' is required. Experiences in China and Hungary make it clear that it is much easier to stimulate the private sector in agriculture and small-scale industry than to reform the state sector in industry. In China, for example, during the period 1978-83 grain production grew by 5 per cent a year, and the production of products like cotton and meat increased in the same period by 10-15 per cent [6]. The eighties showed also a spectacular growth of the rural industry. In 1989 the rural industry produced 840 billion yuan, equal to the value of production of state enterprises. Moreover, the positive developments in agriculture and the cooperative and private sector have a positive effect on the performance in the state sector. Material incentives will have more impact, when people can really buy something with their money. And finally, the improvements in the food and service supply will give the political leadership the legitimacy to implement the more difficult reforms in industry.

This is not to say that in the short run nothing might change with respect to the state enterprises. It is important that some minimum requirements are met: to give up compulsory indicators, to introduce wholesale trade in place of the system of material-technical supply, and the institutional separation of at least the financial, if not the career fortunes of enterprise management from the hierarchy (Scaba, 1989, p. 30). These conditions correspond to what we have called microeconomic consistency and institutional reform. However, it is an illusion to think that the state sector might be profitable in the short run. Only when the state enterprises are imbedded in a sea of small scale enterprises, the time might be ready to free the state enterprises completely (Kornai, 190, p. 57).

Notes

[*] The author is lecturer in economics at the Economics Department of the University of Amsterdam. He is indebted to Michael Ellman for valuable comments on this first draft of the paper.

[1] *Ekonomika i Zhizn*, n. 30, July 1991.
[2] *PlanEcon*, 7 April 1989.
[3] *PlanEcon*, 17 February 1989, p. 2.
[4] *PlanEcon*, 17 February 1989.
[5] *Pravda*, 23 August 1989.
[6] *Beijing Review*, 28 April 1984

References

Abalkin, L. (1988), 'A New Conception of Centralism', *Problem of Economics*, May.

Adelman, I., and C. Harris (1967), *Society, Politics and Economic Development: A Quantitative Approach*, Baltimore.

Avon, P.O., and V.M. Shironin (1988), 'The Reform of the Economic Mechanism, *Problems of Economics*, June.

Berliner, J.S. (1987), 'Organizational Restructuring of the Soviet Economy', Joint Economic Committee, *Gorbachev's Economic Plans*, Washington.

Blough, R., J. Muratore, and S. Berk (1987), 'Gorbachev's Policy on the Private Sector: Two Steps Forward, One Step Backward', Joint Economic Committee, *Gorbachev's Economic Plans*, vol. II, Washington.

Ellman, M. (1989), *The USSR in the 1990s. Struggling out of Stagnation*, London.

Ellman, M. (1989), *Intellectual and Ideological Barriers to economic reform in the USSR*, (mimeographed), Amsterdam.

Ellman, M. (1991 a), 'De economische crisis in de Sovjetunie', *Economisch Statistische Berichten*, August 28.

Ellman, M. (1991 b), 'General Aspects of Transition', *Discussion Paper*, University of Amsterdam, (mimeographed).

Gomulka, S. (1977), 'Economic Factors in the Democratization of Socialism and the Socialization of Capitalism', *Journal of Comparative Economics*.

Hewett, E.A. (1985), 'Gorbachev's Economic Strategy: A Preliminary Assessment', *Soviet Economy*, n. 2.

Hewett, E.A., B. Roberts, and J. Vanous (1987), 'On the Feasibility of Key Targets in the Soviet Twelfth Five Year Plan (1986-90), Joint Economic Committee, *Gorbachev's Economic Plans*, Washington.

Khanin, G. (1992), 'Economic Growth in the 1980s', in M. Ellman - V. Kontorovich (eds), *The Disintegration of the Soviet Economic System*, London and New York.
Knaack, R. (1980), 'The Role of Profit in the Soviet Economy', *De Economist*, n. 3.
Knaack, R. (1984), 'Dynamic Comparative Economics: Lessons from Socialist Planning', in A. Zimbalist (ed.), *Comparative Economic Systems: Present Views*, Boston.
Knaack, R., and J. Stolker (1989), 'Cooperaties in the Sovjetunie', *Internationale Spectator*, January.
Kontorovich, V. (1988), 'Lesson of the 1965 Soviet Economic Reform', *Soviet Studies*, vol. XL, April.
Kornai, J. (1980), 'The Dilemmas of a socialist economy: the Hungarian experience', *Cambridge Journal of Economics*, n. 4.
Kornai, J. (1986), 'The Hungarian Reform Process', *Journal of Comparative Economics*, vol. XXIV, December.
Kornai, J., (1991), *The Road to a Free Economy*, Cambridge.
Lehrbuch Politische Okonomie, (1972), Berlin.
Montias, J.M. (1976), *The Structure of Economic Systems*, New Haven and London.
Nikoforov, L. (1989), Roundtable, 'Problems and Prospects for the Family Contract in Agriculture, *Problems of Economics*, January.
Nove, A. (1979), *Political Economy and Soviet Socialism*, London.
Oksenberg, M. and Tong, J. (1991), 'The evolution of central-provincial fiscal relations in China, 1971-1984: the formal system', *The China Quarterly*, March.
Popper, K. (1991), 'The Best World We Have Yet Had', *Report on the USSR*, vol. 3, n. 22, May 31.
Nuti, M. (1979), 'The contradictions of socialist economies: A Marxist interpretation' in R. Milliband and J. Saville (eds), *The Socialist Register*.
Roundtable Discussion, (1989), 'Is Economic Reform Possible Without Restructuring in Politics?', *Problems of Economics*, February.
Scaba, L. (1989), 'Some Lessons from Two Decades of Economic reform in Hungary', *Communist Economies*, vol. I.
Shkredov, V.P. (1989), 'Socialism and Property', *Problems of Economics*, April.
Wädekin, K.E. (1989), 'Prospects for Soviet Agriculture: some less noticed Aspects, Nato Colloquium, *Soviet Economic Reforms: Implementations under Way*, Brussels.

Whitlock, E. (1989), 'Soviet Agriculture after the March Plenum', *Report on the USSR*, April 28.

Yakovlev, A. (1989), 'Otvet-v nas samikh', *Voprosy ekonomiki*, n. 2.

Zaslavskaia, T.I. (1986), 'Economics Through the Prism of Sociology', *Problems of Economics*, September.

Zaslavskaia, T.I. (1987), 'Social Justice and the Human Factor in Economic Development', *Problems of Economics*, May.

Zaslavskaia, T.I. (1988), 'O strategii sotsial'nogo upravleniya perestroikoi', in Y.N. Afanas'ev (ed.) *Inogo he dano*, Moscow.

3 Is there a role for macroeconomic planning in Eastern Europe ?

BRUNO DALLAGO

Introduction *

Central administrative planning has been for some sixty years the main and almost only coordinating mechanism first in the Soviet Union and later in Central and Eastern European countries. It has also been the main means to impose over the economy preferences and decisions of central governments and, as a consequence, of communist-type parties in power. Throughout this period there were ups and downs in the role and direct intervention of central government over economic agents: a wave of centralization was often followed by a wave of decentralization [1]. The role and content of central planning changed accordingly. In debates preceding and accompanying economic reforms, role and content of central planning were discussed, but its central role in the economy was never seriously challenged.

However, in recent years, and in particular since 1989, the situation has radically changed, and central planning has inevitably ceased to exist. The present situation in those countries is showing that - in spite of the results of theoretical debates and the experience of various Western countries [2] - among policy makers, the public at large and also a part of scholars, macroeconomic plan and market are still seen as mutually incompatible.

To be sure, an incredible variety of programmes, plans, recipes have been proposed by various organs - there comprising governments - to lead transition. However, these usually concentrate on institutional transformation and leave uncoordinated the government intervention in the economy. A case by case and short-run perspective dominates in the economy. This is probably inevitable during the first period of transition. It may also be correct, because planning may be impossible when the economic system and agents' behaviour are subject to rapid and radical transformation. However, in the medium- and long-run macroeconomic planning should gain a fundamental role.

The aim of this paper is to challenge the widespread wisdom that macroeconomic planning is not necessary and harmful by showing that in transition economies it will be necessary - together with market - to drive the direction (if not the measure) of the transformation of the economic system and to solve structural distortions left by the old system. However, it has to radically change its nature. An attempt will be made to delineate the fundamental prerequisite and features of such a planning. We shall also see that much misunderstanding arises from the identification of one particular type of planning (namely the directive or administrative planning, often defined simply as central planning), traditional in Soviet-type economies, with macroeconomic planning tout court, while attributing to it a political value of an instrument of implementing communist or socialist policies.

In what follows the word planning will be used in a political value-free meaning as a set of coordinated instruments and activities which serve to work out and implement the government's decisions, whatever they may be. Planning shall be analysed as a coordinating mechanism, i.e. without reference to a specific system. However, we shall have in mind the reality of Central and Eastern Europe when discussing the utilization of planning in a real context.

In the next section we shall briefly discuss the major types of economic decisions and the role for macroeconomic planning. The aim is to show how macroeconomic planning is not a universal mechanism, because it cannot by its very nature extend its scope to all the different types of decisions, and how different coordinating mechanisms are required to efficiently deal with different types of decisions. In the third section we shall briefly review the major criticisms of macroeconomic planning, as they are stressed by the relevant literature. In the fourth section four different types of macroeconomic planning are discussed, with the aim of showing that directive (central) planning is not the only type of macroeconomic planning. The fifth section of the paper shall be devoted to present and discuss a theoretical approach that appears to be particularly useful in order to analyse the role of macroeconomic planning, namely the heterogeneity hypothesis. In the following sixth section an attempt is made to answer the question of the usefulness and relevance of macroeconomic planning for transition in former Soviet-type economies and for their change into a new type of socio-economic system. The answer is positive, provided that a radical change of planning nature is implemented, and some ideas for the development of a new paradigm are worked out.

Types of economic decisions and the role for macroeconomic (nation-wide) planning

By the term 'planning' different people mean different things, so a clear definition and a specification of the components of such an activity are due before its role is analysed. First, it is necessary to distinguish planning from similar, but still different types of activities, such as simple forecasts, policies, government intervention [3]. Planning and plans usually comprise such activities, but these may exist also without planning. Macroeconomic (nation-wide or national economic) planning is defined here as a conscious and coordinated government activity, whose purpose is to bring about a desired situation of the entire national economy after a given period of time. This activity includes socio-political control (by the society's representatives: government, parliament, political parties, etc.) over the economy, the preparation of studies over the present situation of the economy and its 'spontaneous' evolution, the elaboration of a picture of a desired state of the economy at a future point in time, and the utilization of some means (instruments, policies, orders, etc.) to bring about this desired state [4]. Such a definition permits to comprise various types of planning activity, defined according to the degree of compulsoriness of the plan itself for microeconomic agents and to its relationship with market. The plan is the result of the planning activity and has usually the form of a publicized document.

It should be noted at this point that plan and market are not freely interchangeable: a little bit more of this may be compensated by a little less of that and vice versa [5]. On the contrary, there are rather precise rules governing the role and scope of activity of both plan and market. If they are not kept, economic efficiency suffers and the system may become unstable and incapable of working. We shall return later to this point.

It may be seen that planning involves a wide and coordinated decision-making activity, which can be considered its basic characteristic. Therefore, it is important to discuss briefly the main types of economic decisions. Two broad different types of economic decisions can be distinguished [6] [7]:

1. microeconomic decisions, based on the specific economic interest of individual agents (individuals, households, firms), on government orders or preferences broken down among economic agents or on the basis of different considerations (traditions, education, social ties, etc.);

2. macroeconomic decisions, concerning the major proportions of an economy, such as the investment ratio, the level of aggregate demand, the rate of growth. They may be the result of decisions directly taken by the central government or can be more properly defined as (intermediate) goals of government policy. In the latter case direct decisions are taken concerning certain crucial variables of the economy (such as tax rates, interest rates, state investments) in view of their macroeconomic effects.

A further classification of economic decisions is based on the temporal relation between decision-making and the resulting action. More exactly, because we are dealing here with macroeconomic (nation-wide) decisions, we consider ex-ante and ex-post decisions relative to the macroeconomic state of the economy: (macroeconomic) decision-making is said to be ex-ante when the macroeconomic situation of the economy is consciously planned before the action takes place. It is said to be ex-post in the opposite case, namely when it is the unforeseen (unplanned, not consciously projected) result of conscious or routine microeconomic decisions.

In this sense the following four theoretical situations can be distinguished:

a. Microeconomic coordination of decisions, which determines ex-ante the macroeconomic situation of the economy. An example of such an economic system is an economy based on free oligopolistic enterprises which take all the relevant decisions. Another example is a corporative economy, where guilds take all relevant decisions and where a central government may not even exist.

b. Microeconomic decisions taken by isolated agents, which react to impersonal parameters (prices) in a competitive environment. Individual agents have only the choice between adapting to those parameters or go bankrupt. The macroeconomic configuration of the economy is the ex-post result of that process of adaptation and competition. Here the best known example is the neoclassical competitive economy.

c. Ex-ante macroeconomic decisions taken by some central agency (government) which also determines, as a consequence, the microeconomic situation for the economy. In this case, individual agents (enterprises) cannot be but mere executors of the central agency's decisions. The main example here is a centrally planned (better: administered) economy in the traditional Soviet-type economic system.

d. Ex-ante macroeconomic configuration of the economy which is the direct result of operative decisions, concerning specific instruments of economic policy, taken by a central agency in order to pursue precisely that macroeconomic situation in the economy. Microeconomic decisions are taken (ex-post) by individual economic agents performing their aims (profit or other) in a competitive or cooperative environment. Examples of this system are market economies with planning, like so-called mixed economies, and market socialism.

It appears from what has been said so far that only type 1 (individual) decisions can have a direct market character, while type 2 (macroeconomic) decisions involve in some way the government - if they exist at all in a specific situation. Moreover, the macroeconomic is not the simple sum of microeconomic decisions [8] and also ex-ante and ex-post decisions (in the sense used above) are truly different types of decisions and not simply a different way to take the same decisions. Therefore, if the government pursues a certain situation of the economy there is no theoretical reason to consider plan and market as mutually incompatible. However, a more precise statement is the following: between certain types of plan and of market there is incompatibility, but an incompatibility also exists both between certain types of market and between certain types of plan. Obviously, there is incompatibility between central planning discussed sub c. and any type of market and also between market discussed sub b. and any type of plan. In any other case (decisions type a. and d. and in all intermediate cases) there is an asymmetry between plan and market, which makes their cooperation not only possible, but also desirable. Therefore, the real problem is not to determine whether market is better than plan or vice versa, but what combination between them and with what specific characteristics is the most efficient in each particular situation [9].

In order to better assess this statement in the case of Central and Eastern European countries in the present period of transition it is necessary to briefly discuss first the most relevant general criticisms to planning and the most important types of planning. Advantages of planning shall not be discussed here, because the aim of the present paper is to see whether, in spite of a widespread opinion in Central and Eastern Europe and also in the West and notwithstanding planning weaknesses, there may still be a role for it. In a sense, therefore, I take the advantages for granted.

Criticisms of macroeconomic planning

The balance between limits and advantages of planning as a mechanism for the coordination of decision making depends on the type and role of planning in the economy, on the specific features (scientific basis, institutional framework, coordination among the various agencies involved in planning, relevance of the incentives utilized to its implementation, etc.) of the plan, and on the relationship (cooperative or conflictual) between government and economic agents. Moreover, as we shall see, much depends also on whether planning activity is limited to those fields where it is more powerful and efficient than market or otherwise covers also areas which should be left to market. Looking at the role of planning in Soviet-type economies, two different problems have to be stressed. The first is a theoretical one: planning is a coordinating mechanism whose role and validity are not absolute or general. It is very important and may be even irreplaceable for solving certain allocative and decisional problems and for helping to overcome certain structural and development (long-term) questions. However, in other cases its dominance is clearly counterproductive while market or tradition can be more effective. The first problem lies, therefore, in locating those fields and actions where planning can be the most effective coordinating mechanism.

The second problem consists of the custom, prevalent in Soviet-type economies, of assigning to planning an almost exclusive administrative character. This practice caused a bureaucratization of the behaviour of economic agents and assigned the government unsolvable problems and duties.

Returning to the theoretical examination of planning (reference to reality shall be made in the last section), its limits are as follows.

a. Economic calculation, information and control

The Austrian school (von Mises, Hayek and others) pointed out in different ways that planning of the economy based on public ownership is suboptimal and irrational. According to the traditional interpretation of L. von Mises' thought, socialism is theoretically impossible because it would be in the realm of irrationality. In fact, a rational economic calculation is only possible when prices reflect relative scarcities, but such prices are lacking in socialism. This is due to the fact that in the market of production goods both demand and supply come from the state. Therefore, due to public ownership, prices are fixed arbitrarily by the state and this prevents an economically rational allocation of resources [10].

On the other side, the advantages of planning were already stressed by many classics of the socialist thought. However, in the celebrated socialist calculation debate of the 1930s the accent was more on the capability of planning to imitate the working of the free competitive market than on the intrinsic advantages of planning. In fact, F.M. Taylor and H.D. Dickinson, further developing E. Barone's classical argument (published in 1908), proved the theoretical feasibility of socialism [11]. They were followed soon by O. Lange and others. Lange demonstrated that the Ministry of production can lead the economy to establish equilibrium prices through a process of 'trials and errors' - by varying prices in order to always keep in the market an equilibrium between demand and supply - thus playing the role of the walrasian auctioneer. In this he has to assert two general rules: first, the combination of production factors must equalize, in the case of each factor, the ratio among marginal productivities to the ratio among prices; second, marginal cost must equalize price for each good [12].

Since then the argument of the theoretical unfeasibility was no further supported. However, F.A. Hayek challenged, with various contributions [13], not the theoretical feasibility but the practicability of socialism. In his view, even if theoretically possible through a process of trials and errors, the rational use of resources in socialism is impracticable because central planners should collect and elaborate an enormous amount of informations that no office could afford. To this new challenge O. Lange and others opposed the use of computers, that could drastically speed up the process of information elaboration and make easier decision-making [14]. However, even this idea proved to be illusory.

The Austrian criticism regards socialism - intended as a socio-economic system based on state ownership of production means - and not planning in itself. However, because in their view it is interference with the unconstrained working of a free market that prevents the economy from reaching its optimum position, the argument can easily be extended to planning.

In the 1960s the Soviet school of linear programming and optimal planning [15] applied linear programming not only to the problem of combining available productive resources in a factory to maximize production, but also to the problem of optimal macroeconomic planning in a socialist economy. According to them, a successful centrally planned economy should utilize a system of prices - the so-called 'shadow prices' - derived from solving linear programming problems, including a social rate of discount similar to an interest rate.

In favour of planning is also one fundamental criticism made to market: that it solves only private calculation. Welfare economics and economic policy in general have proposed various correctives to the working of market (taxes, subsidies). However, planning is per se, even in its indicative form, a mechanism for social calculation which creates a general framework within which ex-post intervention can take place in a coordinated and orderly way in order to better implement the plan goals. It should also be stressed that planning helps the collection, elaboration, coordination and circulation of information: therefore, it greatly facilitates the formation of a macroeconomic vision of the economy and reduces transaction costs connected to it.

b. Motivations, incentives, coordination

According to M. Dobb [16], Hayek's 'retreat' from von Mises' position moved the accent onto a very different set of questions: the institutional structures of a socialist economy, the systems of information and control, motivation and incentives to the economic activity. These are all largely unsolved problems in planning. As pointed out by Hayek [17], the practicability of socialism is not merely a technical question but a genuinely political-economic one, connected with the nature of motivations of economic agents. These are often unwilling to cooperate with the planning agency and transmit false or wrong informations to avoid risk and to defend their autonomy and the pursuit of specific interests. Moreover, in a planned economy the collection of informations, because it is not left to the free working of a competitive market, is organized in a bureaucratic way and is by its very nature slow. All these points have been corroborated by the actual experience of Eastern European countries.

The problem of a contrast of interests within the centre and between this and economic agents and the lack of incentives to production and work have been stressed, among others, by O. Sik [18]. Moreover, if the plan gives priority to a certain sector or activity, economic agents operating in it become easily aware of the relevance of their activity for the government. Lacking risks for agents because of the adopted institutional solutions, this may give them an opportunity to reach extra advantages through ways not foreseen in the plan (bargaining, lobbying, etc.). As a consequence, the flow of informations from enterprises to planners is easily distorted and incomplete. In this sense, planning in all its forms is not free from a well-known set of problems typical of economic policy: that the behaviour of agents and, as a consequence, the working itself of the economic system change following the announcement of planning decisions and their implementation. If planning fails to take this fact into account, it is bound to failure.

However, planning has also well-known advantages in the sense that it may help to coordinate the economic agents' activity and may stimulate cooperation among economic agents and between them and government agencies; it may favour a rational and efficient allocation of centralized (state) resources and a coordinated state intervention in the economy in order to increase welfare; it helps to better coordinate and forecast the long-run economic processes (e.g. educational training, development of energy sources, coordination of research activity). All these facts and potentialities may represent an additional source of motivation and incentives (e.g. through a demand-pull effect or by guaranteeing energy sources) for economic agents, private, co-operative and state-owned alike. Once again, the final result depends on the institutional framework of planning and its relation to the market and not only on the intrinsic characteristics of planning.

c. Rivalry and competition

D. Lavoie [19], a follower of the Austrian school, resolutely criticized the standard account of the socialist calculation debate and has pointed out that the most detrimental consequence of planning is to eliminate rivalry (intended as a dynamic, dialectical competition - distinguished from the nonrivalrous, static notion of neoclassical economists) among economic agents. He stresses correctly that this has negative consequences on both the transmission of information and the efficiency of production. Therefore, contrary to the conclusions reached by the neoclassical 'market socialism' position (F. Taylor, O. Lange, and others), planning is actually incompatible with the market and they are fundamentally alternative coordination mechanisms. The attempt to combine them would subvert the operation of each one.

Of course, Lavoie disregards that competition may sometimes be harmful, in particular when associated to an oligopolistic structure of the market (e.g. certain types of oligopolistic price or non-price competition to reach a stronger control of the market) or when competition prevents economic agents from fully exploiting economies of scale. In various cases competition may also be less efficient than co-operation [20]: in all these cases its limitation through planning can be of great utility in regulating the market. However, the major point here is that Lavoie identifies central (administrative) planning with planning tout court and therefore attributes to planning a feature (the elimination of competition) which should be more accurately imputed to the (centralized) economic system - which often utilizes central planning, but also other means, like unplanned orders and political pressure - to eliminate competition.

d. Entrepreneurship, uncertainty, expectations

A further problem has been pointed out indirectly by J.A. Schumpeter [21]. He stressed the relevance of entrepreneurship and predicted the fall of capitalism and the rise of socialism due to the routinization of innovation, which implies the vanishing of the role of the entrepreneur. However, his idea of socialism was one of a bureaucratic society directed by the centre [22]. The recent experience of both the Western countries (mostly in positive) and the Eastern

European countries (mostly in negative) has shown the fundamental importance of entrepreneurship even in today's economies. The process of economic development is in reality unbalanced (non-equilibrating), but planning tends for its nature to balance and equilibrium. Therefore, it can be inferred that planning is incapable to direct innovation and effectively replace entrepreneurship.

This criticism is a relevant one and stresses a fundamental problem which especially some Central and Eastern European countries are presently confronted with. However, if planning cannot and should not try to plan innovation and entrepreneurship, it can usefully contribute to improve the environment for entrepreneurship. In particular, by working out and advertising a general institutional and policy framework for the economy in the next period, it helps the formation of expectations and reduces uncertainty.

e. Budget constraint

From J. Kornai's work it may be inferred that planning contributes - together with other factors - to the softening of the budget constraint [23]. Through the consequences this has for motivations and the behaviour of economic agents a situation of shortage is generated. In such a situation not only economic calculation becomes difficult: incentives become largely ineffective, production inefficient and 'perverse' behaviour of economic agents is widespread. However, Kornai's criticism appears to concern directive planning in a Soviet-type economy and not other types. Moreover, it seems to concern more precisely the lack of economic and financial discipline of enterprises, which leads to their lack of responsibility and to the absence of any risk for the consequences deriving from their activity [24].

However, it can be maintained that planning may become a powerful instrument for implementing a general hardening of the economic agents' budget constraint through an announcement effect of a new, hard government policy (e.g. through planning the adoption of a hard credit and fiscal policy) which can modify the agents' expectation.

f. Type of goods

One problem implicit in applied analyses of planning - but rarely touched upon in theoretical debates - is the efficacy of planning according to the types of goods considered. The role of planning can be more direct and is less disputed in the case of public goods. Different is the situation with private goods, where the role of the market appears fundamental and where 'planning failure' is most evident. However, as was seen above, even here planning has an important role to play in moulding the economic environment, forming expectations, promoting circulation of information and the like [25].

g. Freedom and democracy

Last but not least, there may be consequences for freedom and democracy. As pointed out by various authors [26], the decision to work out plans gives rise to a group of specialists and bureaucrats, who may become very powerful and whose democratic control by the rest of society may be difficult. If this is the case, that group may impose on the rest of society its allocation, production and consumption preferences.

However, planning may also introduce in the economy and the society a more general and better coordinated perspective ('social preferences') which gives a fairer (greater) weight to the economically disadvantaged people and reduces the economic and political power of monopolies and oligopolies. It may also contribute to stabilize the political situation and favour freedom of the society's members and democracy by reducing or eliminating unemployment and by favouring economic and socio-political equality.

Types of macroeconomic planning

The validity of the above mentioned criticisms, as we have seen, varies according to the type of planning considered. According to their nature and relation to the market, four main types of planning can be distinguished [27] [28]. They are discussed in order of a decreasing role for the planning agency (government):

a. Directive (administrative, dirigist, command) planning

The state is the owner of the production means and the plan is the document embodying the government's strategy and priorities regarding resources allocation, the growth of production through time and income distribution, the instruments (generally administrative orders) to implement them. To facilitate the issuing of plan orders and the control of their implementation, plan targets may be expressed in physical units. Plan implementation is compulsory for enterprises: to this end the government can use both economic and administrative (orders) and also political means. If economic agents fulfil the plan targets, they receive economic or moral rewards. However, if they do not implement the plan, they are punished in economic or other terms. Therefore, directive planning not only is meant to completely eliminate the market, but also subdues any microeconomic decision to macroeconomic ones. The former has no autonomy in itself and therefore it has no direct relevance in the decision making-process. Criticisms reviewed in section 3 fully apply to directive planning.

b. Indirect planning

The state is the owner of the production means and the government embodies its goals, strategy and priorities in a plan and works out the means to actively induce economic agents (enterprises) to implement it. Not only the allocation of centralized resources is tied to the plan implementation, but also the establishment of government controlled ('market') parameters (formulas and coefficients for price formation, interest rate, exchange rate, investment coefficients, etc.) serves the same purpose. No administrative punishment is foreseen for those agents which do not implement the plan; however, in such a case they have to give up the (usually economic) advantages deriving from plan implementation (bonuses for managers and employees; priorities in state resources allocation for those enterprises which implement or overimplement plan targets, etc.). In order to be successfully implemented, such a type of plan requires not only that economic agents actively cooperate, but also that economic parameters established by the government have the right values to keep the economy in equilibrium and to incentivate agents to implement the plan. If enterprises are under financial discipline (if their budget constraint is hard), this type of planning coexists with a simulated market. Therefore, because the market is only simulated, criticisms seen above have a substantial force against this type of planning, even if the result is not as destructive as for the previous type.

c. Regulative planning

The economy is a mixed one. The explicit aim of planning activity is not only to allocate state resources and to direct the activity of the state sector, but also to actively influence decisions and activity of the private sector. In order to implement such a target, the government gives incentives to independent private and public agents in order to induce them to cooperate in the plan implementation. On some occasions, the government and enterprises stipulate contracts. In such a planning activity, the government acts as a supreme coordinator of the nation's economic activity. Here plan and market are on a level of parity and perform different goals. However, the market is completely free to determine the private and public sectors decisions and this compels the state to base its own economic decisions on the results of market activity. However, the plan can impose its decisions on the market, where this appears desirable for the society's interest (e.g. in the case of externalities). Criticisms to planning discussed in the previous section do not apply here, because there exists a true division of labour between plan and market, where each one is able to compensate (to a certain extent) the other's 'failures'.

d. Indicative planning

The economy is a mixed one as in the previous case and the aim of planning activity is to work out documents (plans) outlining the forecast of the government about the desired development of the economy and containing decisions about government expenditure and investment and current expenditure of state-owned enterprises. Therefore, the direct target of the plan is to coordinate the allocation of state resources to the above-mentioned end. There is no direct attempt to determine the decisions of private economic agents. However, the announcement of macroeconomic and growth targets, and of targets concerning the activity of state agencies and state-owned enterprises, is intended to create an environment influencing decisions of private enterprises. Overall, indicative planning may be said to influence a private economy through a demand-pull effect and only indirectly - due to state expenses - through a supply-push effect. Here, there is no real division of labour between plan and market: the role of planning is modest and subordinated to that of the market. Therefore, there is no meaning in considering the above criticisms in relation to this type of planning.

The heterogeneity hypothesis: a neoinstitutionalist approach

From what has been said so far, it appears that the problems and questions with planning discussed above lie not so much in planning as a coordinating mechanism, but in the institutional environment and democratic control [29]. However, a further problem arises: can plan and market really coexist, so that they can mutually reinforce their advantages and correct their weaknesses? This leads to a brief discussion of the heterogeneity hypothesis, which is the most fruitful theoretical explanation of the necessity of this coexistence [30].

In economics, as in other social sciences, two broad different views of the nature of economic systems exist. According to the first one, dominant in economic theory, the economic system is the sum of rational economic agents trying to maximize utility and the economy naturally tends toward full employment equilibrium. Every interference with this state of affairs - e.g. by the state through planning - takes the economy away from its optimum. Therefore, only a free competitive market is efficient and planning is incompatible with it.

More sophisticated versions of this theoretical approach, in particular welfare economics and linear programming, stress that a market economy can hardly reach such an optimum and that a centrally planned economy can more easily approach it. In fact, only a centrally planned economy is capable to impose the marginal principle in price formation. Common to the various versions of this approach is that plan and market are symmetric, that is they operate on the same level in order to perform the same goal: the coordination of the same decisions. There is no theoretical possibility of a cooperation between them. This aspect is even more strongly stressed by the Austrian school, as seen above.

According to the other view of the nature of economic systems, these do not tend naturally towards full employment equilibrium. The best known approach of this type is the Keynesian one, but also - as far as Soviet-type economies are concerned - J. Kornai's analysis can be ascribed to this group. Also the classical and Marxian approaches are of this type. Here really existing economies are unable to reach any optimum (however defined) because of the real goals of economic agents. The necessity for private enterprises to make a profit in a competitive environment (hard budget constraint) or for state enterprises to implement plan targets (soft budget constraint) leads inevitably to waste of resources: to unemployment in the former case, to shortage in the second.

This second view does not stress openly the existence of a heterogeneity or an asymmetry between plan and market. In fact, generally it treats theoretical economic systems as homogeneous, that is based on only one (dominant) coordinating mechanism: plan or market.

However, this view opens the way to the question of the asymmetry between plan and market: given that a coordinating mechanism alone - whatever its nature - is unable to guarantee an efficient working of a modern economy, can plan and market cooperate to that end? Or maybe they even must cooperate, because each one performs a task different from - but interdependent with - the other's? This question has not yet been answered by orthodox economic theory and only some institutionalist and neoinstitutionalist economists have treated it. Moreover, it has been extensively treated by applied economists. However, the radical changes under way in Central and Eastern Europe call for a restatement of traditional views.

According to the heterogeneity approach, and contrary to the orthodox approach to economic systems, these cannot be 'pure'. Instead, all the existing systems are heterogeneous: this is due not only to the accidents of everyday's life, but to a precise theoretical requirement, which is known under the name of 'impurity principle' [31]. This principle is derived from systems theory or cybernetics, according to which '...to minimize the chances of disruption an open system has to contain sufficient variety to deal with all the potential variation in its environment. Complexity and variety within the system is necessary so that the system can survive and deal with complexity, variety and unforeseeable shocks in the real world' [32].

The impurity principle is derived as a special - narrower and at the same time more general - case of this corollary. It is narrower because it refers only to socio-economic systems: it states that '...there must always be a plurality of economic structures, so that the socio-economic formation as a whole has requisite variety to promote and cope with change. Thus if one type of structure is to prevail (e.g. central planning), other structures (e.g. markets, private firms) are necessary to enable the system to function' [33]. However, the impurity principle is also more general than the 'law of requisite variety' stated by cybernetics in the sense that the former stresses the necessity of variety not only to cope with variety in the environment external to the system, but also within the system itself. In fact, social systems differ from physical or mechanistic ones in the sense that they have a further dimension, not present in the latter: internal potential variety which derives from partially indeterminate human acts.

Once established that plan and market must coexist to have an efficient management of the economy, one has also to decide what criteria are relevant in determining the appropriate mix between market and plan. On this point two relevant positions can be distinguished. In reality, they are mutually compatible and stress two different components of the choice process.

According to the first position, asserted by J. Kornai and A. Nove [38], technical reasons determine the above mentioned mix. In particular, according to Kornai, where industrial concentration, essential indivisibilities, increasing returns and longer time horizons prevail and when decisions involving major structural transformations are involved a favourable ground exists for overall (macroeconomic) planning. Where these conditions are lacking the market is more efficient and advantageous. Similarly, Nove stresses 'plannability' in case of measurability and homogeneity of the product.

The second position stresses that more than a simple technical question is involved [35]. In fact, the choice between plan and market has various, fundamental consequences in terms of power relations, democracy, social and individual priorities. According to this approach, the major problems that beset many of the leading industrial nations need radical and new solutions. These questions can be solved neither by unconstrained market, nor by administrative intervention. Only a (planned) combination of different methods of action and intervention, of different coordinating mechanisms can bring such problems to a solution. This requires not only a wide use of the market mechanism, but also of a planning system comprising different types of intervention [36].

Therefore, it seems reasonable to conclude that plan and market not only can, but must coexist in order to bring about an efficient management of the economy. Their relationship is defined - besides political, social, and historical factors - by both technical and institutional reasons. However, a further problem exists, which is not touched upon by the above mentioned positions. It concerns incentives: if the strongest and most efficient incentive to economic performance is profit, can ex-ante coordination made through planning attenuate or eliminate its strength? The heterogeneity approach advocates a stringent incomes policy [37]. May such a policy be dangerous for the efficacy of the (material) incentive system? After all, one could easily argue that one of the basic reasons of the failure of the Soviet-type economic system has been that it was unable to work out an effective incentive system and that egalitarianism was one of the major causes of the poor performance of that system.

Even leaving aside highly debated and still basically unresolved questions [38], this statement would be simplistic at the least. In fact, an incentive system is a complex one. In the first place, it is made not only of incomes, but comprises also moral aspects and components (such as professional ethics, love for one's own job, career prospects, self-realization, national proud, political and ideological belief). In the second place, the incentive role of incomes can never be separated from the use that can be made of these incomes. Therefore, a highly differentiated income distribution or a high profit rate give no incentive if the incomes cannot be utilized to buy goods or production means to reinvest (e.g. when the market is constrained or in a situation of shortage). The poor performance of the incentive system of the Soviet-type economies was due to this concurrence of events and not to egalitarianism alone. A further reason has been that in the irregular economy incomes have traditionally been much higher than in the regular one [39]: as a consequence, incomes in the latter were bound to loose their strength in any case. Therefore, a relatively egalitarian income distribution can have a strong incentive effect, if combined with a well organized market where those incomes can be utilized to buy goods desired by income receivers, with moral incentives and, in Kornai's words, a hard budget constraint of income receivers.

The present and future of planning in Central and Eastern European countries

Most reforms attempted from the sixties to the late eighties were clearly unsuccessful as far as the management of the economy is concerned. A really working market existed nowhere in Central and Eastern Europe and planning, once lost its directive character, has been unable to find a really new and effective role [40]. In the meantime, most Central and Eastern European countries started to transform their economies into market economies with a dramatic increase of the integration into the world economy.

From the point of view of the topic discussed here, these developments pose two orders of problems. First, we have seen above that for an efficient and effective management of the economy, market and plan must coexist. But this, one could maintain, refers to the most developed and complex economies and may not be the case for the less developed and less complex economies of Central and East Europe. May be that, for practical reasons, in those countries is it better to leave the job of transformation to the market alone? Isn't the reforms' failure to introduce a well functioning and balanced market a proof that the maintenance of planning is an unsurmountable obstacle for the market?

The second order of problems regards integration into the world economy, which comprises acceleration of foreign trade and international financial activity on the world market, and convertibility. The fundamental question involved here is the following: is domestic planning compatible with the integration into the (supposed) largely unplanned world economy?

As far as the first question - concerning the fruitful coexistence of plan and market in Central and Eastern European countries - is concerned and apart from theoretical reasons reviewed in the previous sections, there are also practical motives why these countries should implement a mixed coordinating mechanism with both market and a strong nation-wide planning - albeit radically changed in its nature and content. On the one side there are the positive experiences with planning of many western countries [41]. On the other side, there are various practical reasons within the Central and Eastern European countries themselves. The most relevant such reasons appear to be the following.

A first reason is that these countries are affording a large and deep structural transformation in their economies. The private sector is too small, weak, and backward to be ready to manage such a transformation. Domestic and foreign private capital for implementing a large-scale privatization is by far insufficient and is showing to be unwilling to bind itself to a long-term undertaking with an uncertain perspective and could be more profitably utilized to start new enterprises instead of privatizing already existing ones.

Alternative privatization schemes, such as through coupons, have still to prove to be really viable. Experience gathered with privatization - albeit on a much smaller scale - in already well functioning market economies also rises many doubts concerning the actual feasibility of a rapid, massive privatization programme. Popular attitudes as measured by opinion polls are also progressively becoming less favourable to massive privatization. Entrepreneurial spirit is growing, but it is far from being already the dominating and driving economic force in society. Moreover, in many of these countries historical traditions are not very favourable in this sense either. Disappointment with the first two years of transition are creating in various countries an increasing consensus among policy makers and population that the state sector should continue to keep a strong, maybe even dominant position. In sum, there is a necessity to carefully steer the transformation process. All this requires a decisive role for macroeconomic planning mostly regulative in character. After all, also in Western countries the period of reconstruction following the war was largely planned by central authorities (often they were occupation authorities) with excellent results, and the present situation in Eastern Europe resembles a reconstruction period from many points of view.

A second major reason is that these countries have accumulated many scientific and practical experiences in planning. True, much work was concentrated on microeconomic and short-term planning, which now becomes less useful if not superfluous or even dangerous for the smooth working of the market. However, these competence and knowledge can be fruitfully utilized by keeping the relevance of planning in a new context and with a new content and role.

A third fundamental reason is that these economies need very much new and clear 'rules of the game'. One major reason for their economic troubles has been the medley and unclear border between central administration and economic agents [42]. Planning may become a powerful instrument - if coupled with a clear political will in that direction - to establish new, 'hard' rules for microeconomic agents and central administrators alike and publicize the new policy, thus giving a decisive push to the formation of new, clear, and 'hard' expectations.

As to the second group of questions, the integration into the world economy, one (apparently) reasonable position could be that planning may be useful in domestic affairs, but not when a country pursues a deeper and more consistent integration into the world economy. However, planning has a fundamental role to play also in this case, provided that its competence and coordination with market is clearly defined and that it does not attempt to curb or divert the influence of the world economy onto the domestic one. Basically, planning should concentrate on the definition and coordination of long-term issues of industrial and trade strategy, such as the role and specific content of a policy of export-led development, whether and where to utilize a policy of import substitution, whether and where it is necessary to defend infant industry, and the promotion of technical progress. It can also try to coordinate export activity of enterprises and favour their integration into the world economy. It should also plan the pace of the integration process so as to form expectations and utilize indirect and, if necessary, also direct instruments to implement the government's integration policy preferences. Therefore, the plan should define the long-term, strategic lines of the government's trade policy, without entering into short-run, particular operations. These should be left to the enterprises' autonomous decisions and to the competence of ad hoc trade policy bodies interested in managing the country's trade balance.

It is sometimes maintained that domestic currency convertibility is incompatible with planning [43], in particular under a system of flexible exchange rates. Of course, this situation is incompatible with directive planning of the exchange rate. However, it seems particularly important for Central and Eastern European countries to carefully plan all the strategic questions (such as industrial and trade strategy, long-term international financial relations, regional agreements) that may have a substantial long-term influence on the convertibility and the exchange rate. Instead, daily operations should be left to the market and the activity of the Central Bank.

Last, but not least, comes the problem of regional integration. The CMEA was largely inefficient [44] and its dissolution has left almost no regret among Central and Eastern European member countries. However, this fact is no proof that these countries should try to become integrated in loose order into the world economy and the EC. Their economic system is still far from a developed market economy, they share many common problems and have some complementarities in their economies. Therefore, if Eastern European countries want to keep a certain weight in the world economy, avoid a new dependence on Western countries, and start a process of true economic development, they should try to develop an efficient regional integration parallel with an increasing integration into the world economy [45]. Obviously it would be more rational if it would comprise only a limited number of countries with similar characteristics: this means at least a regional integration without the Soviet Union (or what will remain of it) as a full member. Such an integration should be based on world prices and convertible currencies and it should be connected as strictly as possible with the European Community and be considered as a first, necessary step towards a full integration into the latter. It should promote industrial cooperation and trade among its members, based on long-term framework agreements, leaving its implementation to autonomous, both private and state, enterprises, influenced when necessary through economic policy. In this sense too strategic planning could do a lot in promoting such an integration. This is not only in the interest of Central and Eastern European

Countries, but of the European Community herself, because it would guarantee a smooth and better coordinated transition towards a new set of international economic relations in Europe.

Conclusions

From what has been said above, it appears that the dilemma between plan and market is a false one. In the case of Eastern European countries plan and market must coexist to implement the transition in the most effective way, namely if these economies want to proceed rapidly on the path towards a developed market economy, without experiencing disruptive and dangerous shocks. Of course, between plan and market there must be a clear division of roles. In particular, directive planning has to be completely eliminated and administrative intervention reduced as much as possible and limited to a few special cases. The dominating character of the plan should become a regulative one. In general, the plan has to fix for a certain (possibly long) period of time the rules within which the market must be free to work and establish the fundamental parameters of the economy. Of course, there may be the necessity to change the nature and content of planning itself through time, as the economic system changes: in particular, as entrepreneurship grows, as international integration proceeds, as the new rules are accepted by and become natural for everybody.

It is necessary to stress once again the falseness of the contraposition of plan and market. This conception is wrong, because it hides the real problems of the transition in Central and Eastern Europe. These are the medley of politics and the economy, the lack of separation between enterprises and central administration, the still weak financial discipline of enterprises, the lack of confidence of investors, the difficulty of balancing the market without depressing for a long time the economy, high inflation rates, low labour productivity, low quality of production, difficulties in increasing exports to the West and the persisting collapse of the Eastern European market, high indebtedness. As I have tried to prove, a different type of planning may become a powerful means for a radical change, if coupled by political will and backed by social support.

Notes

[*] Department of Economics, University of Trento, Italy. The author has benefited from helpful comments by László Csaba, Kopint-Datorg, Budapest and by Alberto Chilosi, University of Pisa, on an earlier version of this paper. However, the usual disclaimers apply. The research on which the present work is based has been financially supported by the Ministero della Pubblica Istruzione and by the Department of Economics, University of Trento.

[1] See, for instance, on Hungary A. Ungvárszki, 1989

[2] On the experience of various countries with planning, see, e.g., M. Bornstein, 1975a; J. Kovács and B. Dallago, 1990. The best known theoretical debate on plan and market was that on market socialism, which reached its climax in the thirties. The classical account of that debate is A. Bergson (1967). See also B. Jossa (1975) and D. Lavoie (1985).

[3] M. Bornstein, 1975b, pp. 1-3.

[4] See also H.S. Levine, 1971, p. 140.

[5] This was the dominating point of view in the debate over economic reforms in socialist countries which took place during the 1960s in various countries. See, e.g., the classic work by W. Brus (1961).

[6] For different classifications see A. Etzioni, 1988; G.M. Hodgson, 1988, pp. 123-134; E. Neuberger and W.J. Duffy, 1976. Most scholars distinguish three different types of economic decisions, because they isolate traditional and other decisions of a non-economic nature (e.g. motivated by education, moral values, social ties, etc.). However, I prefer here to concentrate the attention on the scope of the decision and the decision-making agent. As a consequence, traditional decisions can be split between the two other types.

[7] Each one of these types of decision may consist of both automatic (non-conscious) and rational (conscious) choices. In the former case decisions are taken without a rational calculation on the basis of routines and habits, i.e. based on repetitive, settled ways of thought and behaviour (A. Etzioni, 1988, pp. 157-163; G.M. Hodgson, 1988, pp. 124-134; see also the classical works by Katona, Knight, and Veblen). In the latter case, decisions are taken on the basis of a rational calculation - individual or group or nation-wide, economic or non-economic in nature.

Macroeconomic planning comprises much rational calculation, but certainly routinization is not of secondary importance in it. However, in the present paper we shall concentrate on the rational decisions involved in planning activity, because they are the most distinguished feature of planning and because they play the most fundamental role in defining the place of planning itself in the economy.

[8] This fact has been proved in a most convincing way by J.M. Keynes' theory of effective demand. However, various previous classical authors proved the same point, when they stressed that the sole microeconomic agents' decisions may be insufficient to guarantee full employment and may lead the economy in a crisis (cf. in particular, Malthus, Marx and the marxists).

[9] This point has been clearly stressed by neoinstitutionalist economists: 'The market functions through a web of institutions which are inevitably entwined with the state and government ...Consequently, the main argument is not really between intervention and non-intervention, but which type of intervention is to be carried out, and for which ends.' (G.M. Hodgson, 1988, p.253)

[10] Cf. L. von Mises, 1920, 1922.

[11] Cf. E. Barone, 1908; H.D. Dickinson, 1933, 1939; F.M. Taylor, 1929.

[12] O. Lange, 1936.

[13] Cf. F.A. Hayek, 1935a, 1935b, 1945.

[14] 'The market process with its cumbersome tâtonnements appears old-fashioned. Indeed, it may be considered as a computing device of the pre-electronic age' (O. Lange, 1967, p. 158). In Lange's view, the computer would give the Planning Board a decisive advantage over market as far as information is concerned. Various other economists shared this conviction: for an excellent review cf. D. Lavoie, 1985, especially pp. 94-98.

[15] L.V. Kantorovich, 1965; V.V. Novozhilov, 1969; and others.

[16] M. Dobb, 1969, pp. 204-205 of the Italian edition.

[17] Cf. F.A. Hayek, 1935b.

[18] O. Sik, 1967.

[19] D. Lavoie, 1985.

[20] R. Axelrod, 1984.

[21] J.A. Schumpeter, 1942.

[22] A. Vercelli, 1989.

[23] J. Kornai, 1980.

[24] To be sure, this point has not been completely explained yet. In J. Kornai's works the soft budget constraint appears to be a structural feature of the economic system of Eastern European countries. However, P. Murrel (1990) observes that financial discipline was mainly undermined by reform attempts, and this corresponds to the historical experience. However, the traditional Soviet-type system was so inefficient that economic reforms were inevitable. Lacking a market which could implement financial discipline, the softening of the budget constraint was inevitable. In this sense it was an immanent feature even of the traditional Soviet-type system.

[25] A supposed contradiction to this analysis comes from the observation of Central and Eastern European planned economies, where one can easily observe failures and poor results also in the field of public goods. The analysis of the economic development of these countries easily demonstrates that behind this poor performance there is not planning in itself, but administrative interference, which often made use of directive planning.

[26] See e.g. C. Bettelheim, 1975; F. Hayek, 1960 pp. 45-46, 1944; S. Ricossa, 1989.

[27] For a rather similar classification see E.S. Kirschen, 1974, pp. 299-306.

[28] There are some similarities among the different types of planning, such as in the procedures of construction of plans and in their reliance on the collection and publication of information. However, among them there also are substantial differences, on which the specific content of each type of planning depends: these are in particular the systemic environment, the mode of implementation (e.g. via incentives or orders) and the microeconomic behaviour on which planning relies and which is generated by the plan implementation process (D.M. Nuti, 1986, pp. 243-244). These basic differences mean that the utilization of each type of planning is limited by various factors, in particular by systemic ones. Planning can also be used - as an element of major reforms - to change or transform the economic system itself. However, it is true that historically and once implemented planning has proved to be more powerful as a factor of conservation of the existing economic system than as a means for its reform.

[29] In relation to the question of democracy it has been correctly stressed that '...it is not simply a question of markets and the

state; it is also a matter of enhancing democracy within society so that this educative process [of needs] can flourish.' (G.M. Hodgson, 1988, p. 252)

[30] An approach which leads to similar conclusions, defined as the asymmetry hypothesis has been recently restated by R. Dietz (1990): '...Plan and market are not coordination mechanisms capable of being symmetrically mixed - a little less of the one, a little more of the other; they are systems which - ... - execute completely different, yet mutually interdependent tasks' (p. 420).

[31] '...what is involved is more than an empirical observation that different structures and systems have co-existed through history. What is involved is an assertion that some of these economic structures were necessary for the socio-economic system to function over time... The idea that they are essential for the system as a whole to function is called the impurity principle.' (G.M. Hodgson, 1988, p. 256).

[32] G.M. Hodgson, 1988, p. 258.

[33] G.M. Hodgson, 1988, p. 258.

[34] J. Kornai, 1971; A. Nove, 1983.

[35] G.M. Hodgson, 1988, pp. 271-3.

[36] 'As well as substantial political and economic decentralization, with widespread use of the market mechanism where appropriate, structural and institutional intervention on this scale is likely to take place in the context of national and supra-national planning which is partly indicative, partly regulatory and partly directive in character' (G.M. Hodgson, 1988, pp. 273).

[37] 'The determination of wages has to be done outside the "free market", in part to establish norms of fairness; but the consequent incomes policy has itself to have a strong egalitarian ethos for it to be regarded as fair and to be accepted on a more permanent basis' G.M. Hodgson, 1988, pp. 272.

[38] Such as the prevalence of an income or a·substitution effect or the existence and relevance of a demonstration effect among consumers belonging to different income echelons.

[39] Cf. B. Dallago, 1990 and the literature there cited.

[40] Cf. J. Kornai, 1986a; J. Kovács, B. Dallago, 1990; E. Szalai, 1989.

[41] Cf. J. Kovács, B. Dallago, 1990.

[42] This situation has been analysed by J. Kornai and summarized by the concept of soft budget constrained. See J. Kornai, 1980a, 1980b, 1986b.

[43] See, for instance, C. Schioppa, 1988: 'currency convertibility and socialist economic planning must be considered antithetical concepts' (p. 516).

[44] See, e.g., L. Csaba, 1990.

[45] For a stimulating analysis of this point, see M. Lavigne, 1990. Some tentative steps in this direction have been undertaken by Poland, Czechoslovakia and Hungary.

References

Axelrod, R. (1984), *The Evolution of Cooperation*, Basic Books, New York.

Barone, E. (1908), 'Il ministro della produzione nello stato collettivista', *Giornale degli economisti*, September, pp. 267-93 and October, pp. 391-414 (Engl. transl. 'The Ministry of Production in the Collectivist State', in Hayek, F.A., 1935c, pp. 245-90).

Bergson, A. (1967), 'Market Socialism Revisited', *Journal of Political Economy*, n. 5, pp. 655-73.

Bettelheim, C. (1975), Economic Calculation and Forms of Property: An Essay on the Transition between Capitalism and Socialism, *Monthly Review Press*, New York.

Bornstein, M. (1975a) (ed.), *Economic Planning, East and West*, Ballinger, Cambridge, Mass.

Bornstein, M. (1975b), 'Introduction', in Bornstein, M. (1975a), pp. 1-21.

Brus, W. (1961), *The Market in the Socialist Economy*, Routledge and Kegan Paul, London.

Csaba, L. (1990), *Eastern Europe in the World Economy*, Cambridge University Press, Cambridge.

Dallago, B. (1988), 'The Role of the Non-Socialized Sector in Hungary and Poland', in R. Weichhardt (1988), pp. 190-216.

Dallago, B. (1990), *The Irregular Economy*, Dartmouth, Aldershot.

Dickinson, H.D. (1933), 'Price Formation in a Socialist Community', *Economic Journal*, June, pp. 237-50.

Dickinson, H.D. (1939), *Economics of Socialism*, Oxford University Press, Oxford.

Dietz, R. (1990), 'The Reform of Soviet Socialism as a Search for Systemic Rationality: a Systems Theoretical View', *Communist Economies*, vol. 2, n. 4.

Dobb, M. (1969), *Welfare Economics and the Economics of Socialism*, Cambridge University Press, Cambridge.

Eckstein, A. (1971) (ed.), *Comparison of Economic Systems. Theoretical and Methodological Approaches*, University of California Press, Berkeley.

Etzioni, A. (1988), *The Moral Dimension. Toward a New Economics*, The Free Press.

Feinstein, C.H. (1967) (ed.), *Socialism, Capitalism and Economic Growth: Essays Presented to Maurice Dobb*, Cambridge University Press, Cambridge.

Hayek, F. (1935a), 'The Nature and History of the Problem', reprinted in Hayek, F. (1948), pp. 119-47.

Hayek, F. (1935b), 'The Present State of the Debate', reprinted in Hayek, F. (1948), pp. 148-80.

Hayek, F. (1935c) (ed.), *Collectivist Economic Planning: Critical Studies on the Possibilities of Socialism*, Routledge & Sons, London.

Hayek, F. (1944), *The Road to Serfdom*, University of Chicago Press, Chicago.

Hayek, F. (1945), 'The Use of Knowledge in Society', *American Economic Review*, vol. 35, September, pp. 519-30, reprinted in Hayek, F. (1948), pp. 77-91.

Hayek, F. (1948), *Individualism and Economic Order*, University of Chicago Press, Chicago.

Hayek, F. (1960), *The Constitution of Liberty*, The University of Chicago Press, Chicago.

Hayek, F. (1971), The Road to Serfdom, London.

Hodgson, G.M. (1988) *Economics and Institutions. A Manifesto for a Modern Institutional Economics*, Polity Press, Cambridge.

Jossa, B. (1975), *Lezioni sulla teoria economica del Socialismo*, Cooperativa editrice di Economia e Commercio, Napoli.

Jossa, B. (1989) (ed.), *Teoria dei sistemi economici*, UTET, Turin.

Kantorovich, L.V. (1965), *The Best Use of Economic Resources*, Harvard University Press, Cambridge (Mass.).

Kirschen, E.S. (1974) (ed.), *Economic Policies Compared. West and East*, North-Holland, Amsterdam - American Elsevier, New York, vol. 1.

Kornai, J. (1971), *Anti-Equilibrium: On Economic Systems Theory and the Tasks of Research*, North Holland, Amsterdam.
Kornai, J. (1980a), *A hiány*, KJK, Budapest (Engl. trans. Economics of Shortage, North Holland, Amsterdam, 1980).
Kornai, J. (1980b), '"Hard" and "Soft" Budget Constraint', *Acta Oeconomica*, pp. 231-45.
Kornai, J. (1986a), 'The Hungarian Reform Process: Visions, Hopes, and Reality', *Journal of Economic Literature*, December, pp. 1687-737.
Kornai, J. (1986b), 'The Soft Budget Constraint', *Kyklos*, pp. 3-30.
Kovács, J., Dallago, B. (1990) (eds.), *Socio-Economic Development and Planning*, Dartmouth, Aldershot (forthcoming).
Lange, O. (1936), 'On the Economic Theory of Socialism', *The Review of Economic Studies*, October 1936 and February 1937, reprinted with modifications in Lippincott, B.E. (1938).
Lange, O. (1967), 'The Computer and the Market', in C.H. Feinstein (1967), pp. 158-61.
Lavigne, M. (1990), 'Economic Relations Between Eastern Europe and the USSR: Bilateral Ties vs. Multilateral Cooperation', paper presented to the NATO Colloquium 1990: 'The Central and East European Economies in the 1990s: Prospects and Constraints', Brussels, 4-6 April.
Lavoie, D. (1985), *Rivalry and Central Planning. The Socialist Calculation Debate Reconsidered*, Cambridge U.P., Cambridge.
Levine, H.S. (1971), 'On Comparing Planned Economies (A Methodological Inquiry)', in Eckstein, A. (1971), pp. 137-60.
Lippincott, B.E. (1938) (ed.), *On the Economic Theory of Socialism*, McGraw-Hill, Philadelphia and New York, 1964, pp. 55-143.
Mises, L. von (1920), 'Die Wirtschaftsrechnung in sozialistischen Gemeinwesen', *Archiv für Sozialwissenschaft und Sozialpolitik*, vol. 47, April, pp. 86-121 (Engl. translation: 'Economic Calculation in the Socialist Commonwealth' in Hayek, F. (1935c), pp. 87-103.
Mises, L. von (1922), *Die Gemeinwirtschaft*, G. Fischer, Jena (Engl. translation: Socialism: An Economic and Sociological Analysis, Jonathan Cape, London, 1936; 2nd ed.: Yale University Press, New Haven, Conn., 1951).
Mises, L. von (1949), *Human Action: A Treatise on Economics*, William Hodge, London.

Murrell, P. (1990), 'Big Bang versus Evolution: East European Economic Reforms in the Light of Recent Economic History', *PlanEcon Report*, n. 26, June 29.

Neuberger, E. and Duffy, W.J. (1976), *Comparative Economic Systems: A Decision-Making Approach*, Allyn and Bacon, Boston.

Nove, A. (1983), *The Economics of Feasible Socialism*, George Allen & Unwin, London.

Novozhilov, V.V. (1969), *Problems of Measuring Outlays and Results under Optimal Planning*, International Arts and Sciences Press, New York.

Nuti, D.M. (1986), 'Information, Expectations and Economic planning', in AISSEC, III Convegno scientifico annuale, Nuova immagine editrice, Siena, pp. 231-50.

Ricossa, S. (1989), 'Socialismo, liberalismo e liberismo', in Jossa, B. (1989), pp. 53-76.

Schioppa, C. (1988), Review of 'Adjustment, Structural Change, and Economic Efficiency. Aspects of Monetary Coordination in Eastern Europe' by J.M. van Brabant, *Giornale degli Economisti*, n. 9-10, pp. 516-17.

Schumpeter, J.A. (1942), *Capitalism, Socialism and Democracy*, Harper & Brothers, New York.

Sik, O. (1967), *Plan and Market under Socialism*, International Arts and Sciences Press, White Plains (N.Y.).

Szalai, E. (1989), 'Tervalku napjainkban. Az 1989. évi népgazdasági terv döntési mechanizmusa' (Plan bargaining in our days. The decision-making mechanism of the 1989 annual plan), *Közgazdasági Szemle*, n. 12, pp. 1413-44.

Taylor, F.M. (1929), 'The Guidance of Production in a Socialist State', in *American Economic Review*, March, reprinted in Lippincott, B.E. (1938), pp. 41-54.

Tinbergen, J. (1952), *On the Theory of Economic Policy*, North Holland, Amsterdam.

Tinbergen, J. (1961), 'Do Communist and Free Economies show a Converging Pattern?', *Soviet Studies*, vol. XII, n. 4, pp. 333-41.

Ungvárszki, A. (1989), *Gazdaság-politikai ciklusok Magyarországon (1948-1988)*, KJK, Budapest.

Vercelli, A. (1989), 'Un riesame critico della teoria schumpeteriana della "transizione" al socialismo', in Jossa, B. (1989), pp. 265-93.

Weichhardt, R. (1988) (ed.), *The Economies of Eastern Europe under Gorbachev's Influence*, NATO Colloquium, Brussels.

4 Labour redeployment and cooperatives in the Soviet Union

SILVANA MALLE

Introduction *

Soviet economic reforms are presently focusing on methods and means capable of rapidly increasing the efficiency of labour. It is acknowledged that higher efficiency needs a great deal of reallocation of labour within the state sector and between the state economy and other forms of management, such as the cooperatives and individual activity. Soviet economic performance has been much dependent on the so-called extensive model of growth and has been affected by the progressive exhaustion of labour reserves. Within the *perestroika* approach, emphasis has gradually shifted towards social priorities. Material production branches should release labour for the expansion of services. In the next decade the state economy as a whole is expected to release 16 million manual workers and to redeploy to other jobs some 50 million workers [1]. This programme is not without opposition. Only a minority among the Soviet economists maintains that some unemployment is necessary. That the transformation of the economy will entail a considerable amount of frictional unemployment is in general a source of concern. Moreover, the phenomenon of excess-labour in Central Asia, which existed well before Gorbachev's modernizing drive, is increasingly discussed as a form of involuntary unemployment [2].

The Soviet 'conservatives' fear the appearance of open unemployment, the 'reformists' urge technological change and the release of excess-labour from state enterprises. Labour is to be redeployed from the material branches to services, culture and education and from the upper state apparatus to direct production. One of the forms of labour redeployment, which State statistics have started monitoring, is from the state economy to legally approved cooperative and individual activities.

Campaigns for the intensification of growth have been recurrent in Soviet history long before *perestroika*. How original is the present campaign? Are targets implemented? Is the release of labour under control? Does labour redeployment within the state sphere give evidence of economic priorities moving towards the social sphere? Four years cannot offer the horizon which would be necessary to appreciate the results of radical changes. This time span, however, offers some insights into the difficulties encountered by *perestroika*.

This paper examines labour redeployment within the state sector and from the state sphere into other forms of economic enterprise. The question is raised of whether cooperative and individual activities, which may be considered the embryo of a developing private sector, are presently recipient of unemployed or redundant labour or compete for workers in a still taut labour market. Art. 4 of the law on cooperatives states that 'cooperatives increase people's employment in socially useful occupations and attract additional labour resources into production of goods and services. They also create conditions enabling citizens who are not cooperative members to take part in the cooperative activity on a contractual basis in the time not devoted to their primary occupation.' No approval is needed from the state institution where the primary job is performed. Cooperatives are therefore supposed to offer additional work opportunities both to employed and unemployed. The planned redeployment of state workers to cooperatives and individual activities could help to smooth the process of transformation of the state sphere. This seems to be envisaged by the State Planning Committee [3]. Within a taut labour market, however, competition for highly skilled workers could hinder the performance of state enterprises. The function of cooperatives in labour redeployment needs to be explored, taking into account the differences of republican labour markets.

This paper tries an assessment of the relative tautness of republican labour markets, examines the results obtained so far in the field of labour redeployment and discusses some possible options in this field. Some aspects of the traditional employment policy are outlined in order to put emphasis on present alternatives.

Labour release: from conventional release to overfull employment

From the beginning of Soviet planning 'extensive growth' (in J. Kornai's meaning of 'resource constrained growth') [4] laid the foundations for the steady expansion of the state economy thanks to underutilized rural and home labour. The problem of labour redeployment on a mass scale is a new one for the Soviet Union. State labour redeployment in the past was, by and large, a gradual process, which did not entail significant social frictions as long as additional labour (new entrants and labour reserves 'stored' in the non-state economy) was available.

In the practice of planning, labour productivity growth used to be planned under the aspect of relative and conventional labour release (*vysvobozhdenie)*[5]. These indicators are still used, although nowadays the focus is falling on absolute release. Under the assumption that the output volume increases, labour release does not entail redundancies, but only lower labour cost per unit of output. Thus, each plan foresees the *relative* labour release to be obtained from the saving of labour time (or wage cost) with respect to the base-indicators due to organizational measures. *Conventional* labour release is expected from the introduction of new technology and of so-called technical measures. That is to say, labour productivity growth is planned to be obtained from lower current cost in the short-run and from technical progress in the long-run.

With stable or raising prices and with increasing output targets, enterprises can reduce the cost of labour per unit of output, whilst *de facto* increasing their demand for labour. A physical indicator showing the expected saving of time (or wage) costs is attached to each organizational or technical measure. One negative consequence of this method is that the effects of labour-release may be double-counted, since some measures are at the same time technical and organizational. In practice, state enterprises claim high labour productivity gains, even though labour costs are increasing. If wage rates increases are ruled out by some financial constraint, additional worktime may be rewarded by lessening the intensity of output norm.

It would be self-deceiving to believe that the Soviet model of growth is a full-employment model. Its main foundation, indeed, is the existence of labour reserves outside the sphere of the state economy [6]. These resources, stored in the household and rural economy, have always provided a necessary buffer against the negative effects of demographic trends on growth, under the disputable assumption that labour resources outside the state economy and cooperative farming (*kolkhoz* economy) were non-productive and that peasants' worktime was underutilized [7]. As long as the demand for labour from industry, construction and transport could be satisfied by rural labour reserves, indeed, this model produced growth, in spite of its negative effects on the rural economy and society.

Redeployment of labour from other spheres to the state economy rested on the following axioms: 1. the state economy was more efficient than other forms of economic organization; 2. underutilized labour of the *kolkhozy,* a lower form of organization, could be transferred with no damage for the economy to the state sphere; 3. any other economic activity, whether artisanal or domestic, could be promoted or squeezed, depending on the needs of the state economy. In principle, then, intersectoral labour redeployment did not entail worse earnings or labour conditions, but, on the contrary, their improvement. One of the latest manifestations of this approach was the law on unearned incomes approved in 1986, often used by local Soviets to fight small private business, such as the selling of flowers, wool and foodstuffs [8].

In the past, interbranch labour redistribution in the Soviet Union occurred occasionally under the impact of 'exogenous' factors, such as, in the late sixties, the closure of some coal mines due to their exhaustion. As Table 4.1 shows, the branch proportions changed slowly until the end of the sixties, when the rate of growth of the working age population started decreasing and major structural changes took place. After then, branch proportions remained almost stable. Only in the late seventies and early eighties, under the joint impact of the exhaustion of the net inflow of new entrants in the labour market and military strains, plans were made to discharge labour in transport and in some industrial branches.

To appreciate the approach to employment characterizing *perestroika,* one needs to outline the labour-saving policies adopted in the early eighties. This information is also useful to draw the attention to

Table 4.1
The Soviet employment branch structure, 1960-85.

Years	Industry	Construction	Agriculture	Transport & Communic.	OMB+	Trade°	Other*

Employment as a percentage of total national employment

1960	26.8	7.5	34.7	8.3	0.6	5.5	16.3
1965	28.6	7.6	29.0	8.6	0.7	6.3	18.8
1970	29.5	8.4	24.6	8.7	0.9	7.0	20.4
1975	29.0	9.0	22.1	9.1	1.1	7.5	21.9
1980	29.3	8.9	19.9	9.5	1.1	7.7	23.0
1985	29.2	8.8	19.1	9.6	1.2	7.7	24.0

Rates of change of employment between the two years

1960-65	121.3	115.3	94.9	117.5		128.5	130.8
1965-70	115.1	124.3	95.0	113.0		125.4	121.2
1970-75	107.8	116.8	98.1	115.3		117.5	117.7
1975-80	108.3	106.3	96.9	111.3		109.4	113.5
1980-85	103.3	102.2	99.6	104.9		103.5	107.3

Absolute change in employment, thousand of workers

	I	C	A	SA**	T&C	OMB	T	Other
1960-65	4,827	966	-1,500	1,964	1,226	298	1,334	4,246
1965-70	4,146	1,767	-1,400	491	1,072	223	1,528	3,891
1970-75	2,461	1,522	-0,500	1,102	1,428	252	1,320	3,869
1975-80	2,837	666	-0,800	1,129	1,215	186	837	3,463
1980-85	1,212	252	-0,100	590	591	186	337	2,134

Share of branch employment on the increment of employment in the state economy

	I	C	SA	T&C	OMB	T	Other	TOTAL
1960-65	32.4	6.5	13.2	8.2	2.0	9.0	28.5	99.8
1965-70	31.2	13.3	3.7	8.1	1.7	11.5	28.8	98.3
1970-75	20.6	12.7	9.2	11.9	2.1	11.0	32.3	99.8
1975-80	27.4	6.4	10.9	11.7	1.8	8.1	33.5	99.9
1980-85	22.9	4.7	11.1	11.1	6.4	3.5	40.3	100.0

\+ OMB means other material branches which official statistics do not specify.
° includes also social catering, material-technical supply and delivery, state purchase.
* includes communal housing, everyday services, health, physical culture and social services, education, culture, art, science, credit and state insurance, administration.
** SA means state agriculture which comprehends *sovkhozy* and other productive agriculture enterprises.

Source: *Narodnoe khoziaistvo SSSR v 1985 g.*, Moskva: Finansy i statistika, 1986, p.304, 391 and *Narodnoe khoziaistvo SSSR v 1970 g.*, Moskva: Finansy i statistika, 1971, pp.404 and 550-1.

policies and outcomes during Gorbachev's era which do not seem consistent with the 'new conception' and are probably the effect of traditional mental frameworks and institutional behaviours.

The first reaction of planners to growing intensity of labour shortage [9] was, predictably, the rationing of labour resources by fixing branch and territorial limits to additional manpower. In the meantime, extraordinary labour reserves were sought in the work of pensioners, housewives, invalids, better use of working time and in the reduction of absenteeism and work breaks [10]. Chasing social parasites became a honourable activity. Additional net investment was subordinated to the attainment of the planned targets of existing capacity utilization. The focus shifted from the expansion of capacity to restructuring and reequipment. Higher targets for capacity utilization were approved, following the instruction to dispose of unused (or unusable) capacity. Similar policies had already been adopted in other socialist countries with mixed results [11]. From the economic point of view, this policy represented the effort to sustain growth by reducing the slack within the state economy, in the apparent belief that unused worktime was conspicuous and could be easily mobilized. The State Planning Committee claimed that the hoarding of capacity was the main cause of the excessive demand for labour. Enterprises and ministries were given tasks of inspection, assessment and rationalization of the installed capacity. The screening of the production equipment was supposed to bring about the upgrading of some capacity and the discharge of unusable machinery and premises. Indicators used to plan new investments were changed in such a way as to contribute to increase the capital intensity in labour-intensive branches. Tauter capital-labour proportions, in general, were supposed to make the production process more regular, by reducing the enterprise reserves for storming, thereby improving macroeconomic balances.

From the point of view of labour, this course entailed emphasis on multi-shift work regimes filled by factory workers redeployed from 'non-production' workshops to production lines particularly in branches of industry, such as machine-building, the capacity utilization of which was considered to be much below its potential rated on a two-shift regime [12]. In order to direct labour redeployment according to plans the focus fell on labour discipline, since decreasing productivity rates did not leave scope for manoeuvring wage differentials. Severe regulations restricting spontaneous labour turnover were approved [13]. The attempt was made to turn some job placement bureaux into monopsonistic labour exchanges. This campaign produced some results, since the basic economic indicators improved after 1983, but, not surprisingly, improvements were short-lived. The *uskorenie* campaign in the first years of Gorbachev's leadership was still very much dependent on this policy approach. The anti-alcohol campaign and the law on unearned incomes, criticized nowadays by the reformers, marked the beginning of Gorbachev's leadership and can hardly be distinguished from the other measures directed to increase work discipline and effective work time in the state economy.

In principle, the advantage of this policy of 'intensification' is that redundancies can be avoided, while raising the exploitation of capacity and the output volume. The 'rationalization' of the production process (monitored through physical indicators, such as mechanization, number and types of brigades, shift rates, etc.) is expected to be based on a tauter capital-labour ratio and a lower capital-output ratio. The gradual process of transformation permits the retraining of part of labour within the factory and the redeployment of excess-labour to unfilled vacancies either in production or non-production sections (catering, social and everyday services, etc.).

Rationalization based on intra-factory labour redeployment, however, does not meet the requirements of important technological change. It is not accidental that plans of technical reequipment and restructuring in the early eighties were based mainly on indicators of mechanization. Automated technology and numerically controlled production programmes, which had already started dramatically changing the production scene in the West, remained confined by and large to the realm of discussion among few experts. While in the West computerization was transforming rapidly not only the production process, but also managerial and clerical work as well as the industrial relations, bringing about mass-scale labour mobility, technical innovation in the Soviet Union lagged almost hopelessy behind.

Was stagnation the result of job rights incorporated into the very planning model, as argued by David Granick, [14] or the by-product of the shortage economy, as maintained with distinct arguments by J. Kornai and P.Hanson [15]? Both theses offer interesting insights into Soviet employment policy, which this paper does not discuss. There are ideological implications in each thesis, which, however, need to be taken into account in order to understand the present approach to employment and redeployment. The job-rights approach implies that full employment is the result of a conscious policy based on labour-intensive technology. Consequently, capital-intensive technology could be planned and introduced on a macro scale as a result of changing labour balances. Arguments developed along the lines of the 'resource constrained economy' imply that full employment is obtained by default. Systemic changes are needed to grow further.

Empirical evidence shows that technological competition with the West has been one of the main targets from the beginning of planning [16]. Labour balances are imperfect and are not used in planning production, but only to check the macro plan consistency. The actual demand for labour is planned by ministries which do not take into account local labour resources. Capital-intensive branches (extractive industry, metallurgy and other branches of the heavy industry) have been developed in the excess-labour areas (causing, among else, shortage of skilled labour and low capacity utilization rates) [17]. The actual labour intensity of capital equipment is usually higher than the technical intensity because of defective construction, delays in installation and inefficient organization. Information failures need to be overcome with rather expensive (labour-intensive) adjustments.

Experience shows also that all socialist countries failed to sustain output and productivity growth when efforts were made to substitute capital for labour. This failure seems to reflect not only the scarce adaptability of centrally planned systems to exogenous constraints, but also the lack of motivation for change among the protagonists of the economic scene.

Economic reforms and employment: the 'new conception' and performance

The implication of the 'resource-constrained economy' approach, shared by many outstanding Soviet reformers, is that high participation rates in the state economy have been attained *in spite of plans and regardless of social preferences*. They are the result of inefficiencies inherent in the planning system. As long as planning based on physical indicators rather than price signals remains unchanged, the labour market will remain taut. One can argue, consequently, that Soviet society will not resist, by and large, economic changes directed to *reduce* the level of employment, increase leisure time and offer old-age pensioners a decent retirement allowance as an alternative to on-going work [18]. All these goals seem to belong to the alternative package of socio-economic measures worked out by some of Gorbachev's experts [19].

The fact that this policy has not yet been implemented casts some doubts on the strength of support for reforms as well as on the consistency of the socio-economic programme. Nonetheless, one needs to emphasize the importance of the socio-political revolution brought about by the recognition that the socialist model of growth has deeply rooted shortcomings and that initiative and entrepreneurship are not compatible with what even eminent Soviet scholars interpret as a pre-capitalist and pre-socialist *state mode of production* [20].

That the mid-eighties have marked a qualitatively new stage under the impact of Gorbachev's leadership is by now a trivial assessment. Started with an emphasis on acceleration of growth, labour-saving technological change and quick productivity gains, broader financial autonomy and responsibility, i.e. with a programme the borderlines of which are not easily distinguishable from the early eighties policies, the programme of economic transformation is evolved rapidly into a manifesto of social and political claims which bears the characteristics of a revolution.

As in any revolutionary situation, new policies and institutions develop within the hostile surviving network of personal and institutional relationships. Albeit institutional changes may not be correctly implemented, they deserve attention for their possible role in the dynamics of economic reforms. Within the scope of this paper, four aspects need to be stressed in so far as they help identifying the foundations of a new policy approach in the field of employment.

Firstly, the increase of state employment is interpreted as a sign of inefficiency, rather than as evidence of mature socialism. Hence, state employment must be curtailed, particularly, but not only, in material production branches. This entails interbranch labour-redistribution and in the short-run some amount of registered unemployment. Unemployment needs to be defined in legal terms, taking into account individual preferences, in order to establish appropriate unemployment benefits [21].

Secondly, the external diseconomies of excessive participation rates are taken into account for their psychological and social impact. High rates of female employment are considered to have a negative impact on marriage, fertility, female leisure time and child health and discipline [22]. Overtime used for 'storming' affects the regularity of production. Increasing state employment drawing resources out of the personal economy (private plots) reduces the availability of vegetables and other foodstuffs [23].

Thirdly, individual motivations are recognized to be crucial elements of economic performance and positive factors in social development. This appreciation is not only at the basis of demand for higher earnings differentials, but also the argument for the introduction of market tools, leasing, shares and eventually other forms of participation to economic profit and risk [24].

Last but not least, the right of economic enterprise and property outside the state sector is discussed as a possible contribution to the modernization of the economic organization. The law on individual activity legalizes a wide range of formerly illegal activities and the law on cooperatives provides grounds for the development of private enterprise [25].

All these elements, of course, are exposed to contamination and corruption when they are transplanted into a socio-economic organization which is unhealthy, but resistant to treatment. Some changes receive support from different motivations and contrasting interests. Statistical manipulations are still used. Price increases boast productivity figures. Leasing is hampered by arbitrary estimates of capital costs. Private enterprise, whether individual or cooperative, does not receive institutional and financial support. The comparison between intentions and deeds justifies a critical assessment of *perestroika*.

The 1985-88 changes in state employment do not give evidence that labour redeployment policies are implemented, although, as a whole, the state economy releases 298,000 workers (i.e. legal work-time equivalents). Firstly, the release of labour is accompanied by the worse performance of the state economy, in the terms of lower rates of growth, unfulfilment of delivery contracts and increasing shortages. Secondly, the volume of state labour redeployment has been overrated statistically by reclassifying some branch aggregates. About 400,000 workers, formerly included in the administrative apparatus branch, have now been statistically transferred to 'production enterprises', thus helping the administration employment figures to appear more compatible with present policies, although functions and performance of the reclassified workers remain unchanged [26]. Thirdly, labour is released from branches which should expand and jeopardizes structural changes.

Industry, agriculture, forestry, transport and communications together released 2,508,000 workers. The other branches altogether added 2,230,000 workers[27]. Interbranch redeployment offers some insights into labour mobility flows (see Table 4.2). Labour redeployment occurs in two main directions. First, within the production sphere, from industry and agriculture towards construction. Second,

Table 4.2
Labour redistribution in the state economy, 1985-1988

Branches		Thousands	Percentage change in the total labour release (-) or in the total additional employment (+)
State economy	-	298	
Labour-releasing branches:			
Industry	-	553	22.0
Agriculture	-	490	19.5
Forestry	-	41	1.6
Transport	-	1,328	52.9
Communications	-	96	3.8
Labour- receiving branches:			
Construction	+	1,273	57.1
Trade	+	144	6.5
Inf-computer*	+	106	4.7
OMB	+	103	4.6
Other branches	+	604	27.1

Source: Estimates from *SSSR v tsyfrakh v 1988 godu*, Moskva: 1989.
Note: The branch classification is the same as in Table 4.1. Only a branch of information-computer services have recently been added to the usual classification.

from the production sphere towards the non-productive branches. Construction receives more than half the total increase of employment in the expanding branches, while redeployment to non-productive branches occurs also as a consequence of labour movements from branches, such as banking and insurance, whose staff one would have expected to increase following the present focus on financial policy tools. Science and banking-insurance release altogether 358,000 workers [28]. On the other hand, trade and catering get only 6.5 per cent of total additional employment, in spite of official emphasis on the need to expand the service sector. Lower employment in some branches does not seem to spring out of rapid increases in labour productivity. The decreasing volume of employment in light industry is accompanied by lower rates of growth of this branch, which, instead, should expand if the volume of consumer goods must increase and the supply of excess-labour in the Asian Republics must find an outlet in labour-intensive activities [29].

The increase of employment in construction, related in part to the large-scale territorial plans of development in the Far East and other economic regions, reflects pressures to shorten the time of installation of new capacity. However, this is an indication that the productive sphere, according to Soviet classification, cannot release the necessary labour to develop the social sector and that the volume of slack is, indeed, lower than estimated by planners. The conversion of military industry to civilian production is hampered not only by institutional frictions, but also by labour resistance to redeployment to less rewarding jobs [30]. The state economy, by and large, seems to be still short of labour, as suggested also by the liberal regulations on second jobs (*sovmestitel'stvo*) in the state economy, approved in September 1988 [31].

Mixed economic results obtained so far in the field of state employment are accompanied by labour laws which do not always reflect the preference for the 'fellow' (*chelovek*) factor, an aspect of industrial relations developed by T. Zaslavskaia and skillfully utilized by M.S. Gorbachev in his speeches, compared with the resource approach to labour which has been a constant in Soviet planning.

Soviet industrial relations have been shaped under the pressure of the expansion of the state economy and economic growth at the price of individual choice and social development. In the traditional Soviet model based on state ownership and one-man management, labour has a subordinate role [32]. Redundancies in the case of planned shutdown of enterprises and for production necessity have always been authorized. Factory regulations make individual dismissal the last resort in the case of violation of labour discipline, but give management much power in allocating labour within the enterprise [33]. In general, management rights in redeploying workers within the enterprise, without violating the labour contract, are broad. These rights are consistent with the view that labour is, first of all, a production factor (resource) which must be mobilized on command and that worktime losses, such as the three weeks out of work authorized in the case of dismissals, must be minimized. In the late eighties, new laws have been approved to make it easier for managers to redeploy workers within their factory to different jobs and work regimes, with no need for workers' consent even in the case of the application of lower wages and night shifts [34]. Mass scale redundancies are also authorized if they are necessary to award higher wage rates to the remaining workforce [35].

Labour redeployment, therefore, does not find obstacles in Soviet labour law. The workers' councils have been introduced before Gorbachev's appointment as Party Secretary and do not interfere with hiring and firing or with intra-factory labour redeployment [36]. Neither workers' councils, nor the factory trade union committees, on the other hand, are truly representative of workers' interests, as it appears once again from the springing of different bodies entrusted with the representation of coal miners' and transport workers' demands [37].

There is no information on mass scale redundancies due to shutdown of capacity or to wage increases, although these may have occurred and not been reported. The number of transfers, instead, seems to be increasing in some areas [38].

These considerations seem relevant to the issue of labour redeployment from state jobs to other forms of economic enterprise. Do individual and cooperative activities offer an alternative to workers made redundant from state enterprises or do they attract new entrants in the labour market? Is private enterprise an attractive alternative to Soviet workers or is it feared by them?

Cooperative and individual enterprise: an outlet for redundant labour or competitors in a taut labour market?

The number of cooperatives has been rapidly growing in the last few years and is constantly monitored by official labour and financial statistics. In 1989, cooperatives produced 27 per cent of total everyday services, but still only 2 per cent of the total volume of consumer goods [39]. By 2000 cooperatives are expected to produce 25-30 per cent of national output [40]. Cooperatives are authorized in all types of activities except in those specifically forbidden by USSR or Republican laws. Cooperatives may employ hired labour. There does not seem to be, however, a parallel development of financial institutions suggesting active support by the government to these forms of economic organization.

To draw any tentative assessment on the nature of labour redeployment in cooperatives one must take into account republican differences, separating labour-deficit from excess-labour areas. The shrinking of state employment does not only mean redeployment of existing workforce, but also less job opportunities for new entrants. The demographic outburst of Central Asia in the seventies is reflected now in the concentration of young able-bodied cohorts in less developed regions. The notion of *nezaniatost'*, used so far to separate labour resources not employed in the state economy and cooperative farming and considered to be occupied at home or in their private subsidiary economy (PSE), is not useful to identify the actual rate of unemployment. This explains why the number of non-employed labour resources is by no means agreed upon by Soviet experts. As predictable, the estimates reflect conflicting policy approaches of different institutions. According to the president of the State Committee for Labour, V. Shcherbakov, the number of regularly non-employed people is estimated between 7 and 15 million, part of whom only could be included among involuntary unemployment [41]. Estimates by some State Planning Committee officials bring down to 3 million the number of non-employed in excess-labour republics, 20 per cent of whom are mothers of many children, whilst the Vice president of Gosplan, S. Sitarian gives a 1,2 million unemployment estimate [42]. A recent western study has estimated over 8 million unemployed [43].

According to A.E. Kotliar, there are about 6 million non employed workers of working age in Central Asia. One cannot assimilate de facto non-employed with unemployed, i.e., with people actively looking for a job. Firstly, one needs considering that part of the non-employed do, indeed, work permanently or sporadically in the underground economy [44]. Secondly, for the country as a whole the number of vacancies is higher than the number of job seekers [45]. However, low propensity to interregional mobility creates unemployment *de facto*. Recent nationalistic unrest, in part related to conflicts with immigrant workers, also suggests that macro-equilibrium considerations are meaningless from the practical point of view.

The publication of data on number, membership, annual turnover and field of activity of cooperatives provides some information on the performance of cooperatives and their possible development as an outlet for excess-labour or labour made redundant in labour-deficit areas. The usual caveat is needed. The data are subject to the flaws of Soviet statistics. Interrepublican differences may be affected by uneven statistical errors. The number and importance of unreported activities and earnings may be different across republics. Comments and preliminary conclusions based on such data, therefore, cannot but be tentative.

The trends in 1987-89 show for the country as a whole the accelerating growth of the number of cooperatives (see Table 4.3). From about 14,000 in 1988 cooperatives increased to 133,000 in one and a half years. In only six months the number of cooperative members more than doubled reaching 2.9 million, (including 1,350,000 second

Table 4.3
Cooperatives: number, membership and revenue (thousand roubles) at 1 January 1988 and 1988-89 percentage growth.

	Cooperatives	% change 1988-9	members per coop.	% change 1988-9	revenue per coop.	% change 1988-9	revenue per member	% change 1988-9
USSR	13,921	457	11.2	61	25,120	211	2,243	93
RSFSR	7,326	431	9.5	91	22,120	287	2,417	94
Ukraine	1,843	634	13.0	41	25,936	157	1,995	81
Belorussia	787	220	10.4	66	14,231	299	1,368	140
Uzbekistan	550	486	18.4	21	35,636	99	1,937	65
Kazakhstan	452	911	11.7	36	25,442	137	2,174	74
Georgia	594	252	12.4	25	32,997	196	2,661	137
Azerbaidzhan	320	303	8.1	51	25,312	111	3,125	40
Lithuania	503	212	11.7	38	25,248	198	2,158	115
Moldavia	286	475	13.3	76	24,475	293	1,840	123
Latvia	246	384	21.1	14	39,431	306	1,869	255
Kirghizia	199	536	9.5	31	20,100	150	2,116	90
Tadzhikistan	177.	308	10.2	69	23,729	106	2,326	11
Armenia	263	1275	16.3	- 4	57,414	8	3,522	12
Turkmenia	119	276	9.2	16	22,689	126	2,466	93
Estonia	256	278	17.6	26	32,422	223	1,842	157

Source: *SSSR v tsifrakh v 1987 godu*, Moskva: Finansy i statistika, 1988, p. 232 and *SSSR v tsifrakh v 1988 godu*, Moskva: Finansy i statistika, 1989, p. 38.

job holders). Total worktime spent in cooperative work in January 1989 is estimated equal to that of 1 million full-time workers [46]. Cooperative revenue increases more rapidly than that of individual members, but with republican differences which suggest considerable productivity differentials. Higher increases accrue to the Russian Federation, Belorussia and Moldavia. These need to be explained probably with the nature of goods and services provided rather than with particular labour skills. Republican rates of growth in the number of cooperatives do not suggest that private initiative is more dynamic in developed areas compared with others. In one year the number of cooperatives multiplies tenfold in Kazakhstan and 14 times in Armenia, while in Latvia and Estonia it increased 4-5 times. At the same time the rate of increase in membership per cooperative suggest that there can be objective barriers, probably of institutional nature, to the expansion of scale. In republics, where cooperatives started with a relatively higher membership, this number increases moderately compared with others.

Most cooperative members in the labour-deficit republics work in condition of *sovmestitel'stvo,* i.e. as second job holders. The opposite occurs in the excess-labour republics, particularly of Central Asia, where from two thirds to four fifths of the cooperative members are full-time participants. Individual earnings in the more backward areas

Table 4.4
Cooperatives in the USSR: number, membership and revenue (roubles), 1 January 1989.

Republics	Cooperatives number	Member ave/coop	Part-time %	Revenue annual ave/coop	Revenue annual ave/member	Earnings annual ave/member
USSR	77,548	18.0	46.8	78,153	4,334	1,547
RSFSR	38,895	18.2	47.0	85,507	4,696	1,668
Ukraine	13,534	18.4	50.2	66,543	3,620	1,389
Belorussia	2,518	17.3	53.8	56,831	3,290	1,271
Uzbekistan	3,226	22.2	35.7	71,079	3,202	1,179
Kazakhstan	4,572	15.9	35.7	60,236	3,793	1,358
Georgia	2,089	15.5	40.2	97,654	6,316	1,718
Azerbaidzhan	1,291	12.2	32.3	53,447	4,367	1,051
Lithuania	1,569	16.2	61.2	75,335	4,635	2,078
Moldavia	1,644	23.4	61.0	96,168	4,106	1,748
Latvia	1,190	24.1	67.6	160,084	6,638	1,780
Kirghizia	1,265	12.5	37.3	50,198	4,019	1,462
Tadzhikistan	723	17.3	36.0	48,824	2,584	984
Armenia	3,616	15.6	25.9	61,753	3,959	1,378
Turkmenia	447	10.7	18.7	51,230	4,771	1,354
Estonia	969	22.2	68.4	104,850	4,726	1,507

Source: *SSSSR v Tsifrakh v 1988 godu*, Moskva: Finansy i statistika, 1989, p.178.

range from less than a half to two thirds of the earnings in more advanced republics (see Table 4.4), whilst there is about 20 per cent difference between average republican wages.

From the point of view of organization, it seems interesting that the average number of members per cooperative is higher in the labour-deficit republics. Overall, with the exception of Uzbekistan, the number of workers per cooperative is higher in labour-deficit areas, a 'paradox' according to the State Planning Committee [47]. Estonia and Latvia have twice as much membership than Azerbaidzhan and Turkmenia. Even if the different proportion of *sovmestitel'stvo* is taken into account, this suggests that cooperatives tend to be a family business in the backward areas and tend to develop towards some form of private enterprise in more developed regions. The annual turnover of Latvian cooperatives on average 3.3 times higher than that of Tadzhikistan cooperatives. These considerations suggest that, while cooperatives are not a recipient of redundant labour in the more advanced republics (where state enterprises remain short of labour), cooperatives in the Central Asian Republics do offer an alternative to state jobs, (but not necessarily a good one compared to 'underground' earnings). Earnings are low and in some cases (Turkmenia) barely reach what is considered a subsistence personal income (80 roubles/month). Nonetheless, if the coöperative is run on a family basis, total cooperative earnings may become competitive compared to the one-wage family income, rather common in backward areas of Muslim culture. Cultural and religious backgrounds may also have an impact on cooperation. In 1989 Armenia had 3 times more cooperatives than Kirghizia and 8 times more than Tadzhikistan, although her labour resources are lower. Armenia, Georgia, Lithuania, Moldavia, Kazakhstan and Latvia have a relatively higher share of cooperatives than their share of effective labour resources (see Table 4.5).

Table 4.5
Labour resources and cooperatives. Distribution by Republics (percentages), 1989.

	1 Effective labour resources	2 Cooperatives	3 = 1 - 2 Difference
URSS	100.0	100.0	0.0
RSFSR	53.7	50.2	3.5
Ukraine	17.8	17.4	0.4
Belorussia	3.6	3.2	0.4
Uzbekistan	5.6	4.2	1.4
Kazakhstan	5.6	5.9	0.3
Georgia	2.0	2.7	- 0.7
Azerbaidzhan	2.5	1.7	0.8
Lithuania	1.3	2.0	- 0.7
Moldavia	1.4	2.1	- 0.7
Latvia	1.0	1.5	- 0.5
Kirghizia	1.2	1.6	0.4
Tadzhikistan	1.4	0.9	0.5
Armenia	1.1	4.7	- 3.6
Turkmenistan	1.0	0.6	0.4
Estonia	0.6	1.2	- 0.6

Sources: Tables 4 and *SSSR v tsifrakh v 1988 godu*, Moskva: Finansy i statistika, 1989, p.179

Different considerations may be made regarding individual activities. One third of workers outside the sphere of state and *kolkhoz* economy are employed as individual workers. Most of them are listed under the category of handicraftsmen (*kustarno-remeslennyi-promysli*). Regional differences are not pronounced. However some republican differences suggest that there is more scope for individual, compared with cooperative activity, in backward republics (in Turkmenia the ratio is 1:1 whilst in Estonia it is 1:1.9). Socio-cultural activities represent 4.7 per cent of individual activities in the Soviet Union and 8.8 per cent in Azerbaidzhan, versus 2.9 per cent in Belorussia. Artistics handicrafts are relatively more diffused in the Ukraina, Georgia, Lithuania and Latvia [48]. Republican traditions are probably the main cause of a different distribution of individual activities. There are no data on individual earnings which could be used to guess future trends. Individual craftmanship and other personal services, however, should not be ruled out as a possible competitors for state services. Intellectual professions are, of course, to the forefront of this possible trend. But other services, such as for instance passengers and commodity transport, offer good opportunities to improve earnings [49].

If we compare republican figures on non working population (which, as mentioned above, according to Soviet criteria, includes voluntary as well as non-voluntary unemployed) with cooperative employment, we see that the higher the number of non employed, the lower the cooperative membership. Table 4.6 presents estimates of republican labour resources, employment in the socialized economy and in the cooperative-individual economy. Participation rates are estimated relative to the socialized economy (state enterprises and cooperative farming) and considering effective labour resources, that is after deduction of students older than 16 from total published data on labour resources. The estimated effective labour resources are slightly below the actual number, considering that part of the students work while completing their studies (see the note under Table 4.6). One also needs stressing that the numbers of non employed represents *maximum estimates*, which include not only people estimated to be employed at home and in their PSE (labour reserves), but also people unable to work in the socialized economy (mothers of many children and invalids) as well as people unwilling to work in state or *kolkhoz* jobs [50].

The table shows that cooperative and individual activities absorb from 2.5 to 5.6 per cent of non employed labour resources in labour-excess republics. In labour-deficit areas, where the rate of non employment (estimated from the above table with respect to effective labour resources) varies from 6 per cent to 13 per cent, they contribute to drain the few labour resources still available. This suggests that in more developed areas, cooperative work becomes competitive with socialized work, because it is more rewarding. In less developed areas, instead, cooperatives and other legal activities may not offer sufficient opportunities for work. It is possible that in those regions,

Table 4.6
Labour resources and employment (million), and participation rates in the USSR, 1988.

Republics	1 Labour resources	2 Effective resources	3 Employment social.eco.	4 Coop. & Ind.Act.	5 Part. rate 3 as % of 2	6 Non-empl mill.	7 4 as % of 6
SSSR	166.3	152.5	129.7	2.00	85.0	22.8	8.8
RSFSR	89.5	81.9	71.3	1.00	87.0	10.6	9.4
Ukraine	29.5	27.1	24.3	0.30	90.0	2.8	10.7
Belorussia	6.0	5.5	5.0	0.06	90.9	0.5	12.0
Uzbekistan	9.7	8.5	6.0	0.10	70.6	2.5	4.0
Kazakhstan	9.1	8.5	6.9	0.09	81.2	1.6	5.6
Georgia	3.2	3.0	2.5	0.05	83.3	0.5	10.0
Azerbaidzhan	4.1	3.8	2.5	0.03	65.8	1.3	2.3
Lithuania	2.2	2.0	1.8	0.07	90.0	0.2	35.0
Moldavia	2.4	2.2	1.9	0.05	86.4	0.3	17.0
Latvia	1.6	1.5	1.4	0.03	93.3	0.1	30.0
Kirghizia	2.1	1.9	1.4	0.02	73.7	0.5	4.0
Tadzhikistan	2.4	2.2	1.4	0.02	63.6	0.8	2.5
Armenia	1.9	1.7	1.4	0.08	82.3	0.3	27.0
Turkmenia	1.7	1.6	1.2	0.01	75.0	0.4	2.5
Estonia	0.9	0.9	0.8	0.02	93.3	0.1	33.3

Sources: *SSSR i soiuznye respubliki v 1988 godu*, Moskva: 1989 and *SSSR v tsifrakh v 1988* godu, p.38. The first source does not publish estimates of the labour resources in RSFSR, Estonia and Turkmenia. These have been estimated, supposing for Turkmenia and Estonia the same labour resources to population ratio as respectively for Uzbekistan and Latvia. Then, the labour resources for the RSFSR have been obtained as the difference between the total for the USSR and the sum of labour resources of all other republics. *Note*: effective labour resources are obtained by deducting all students above 16. In fact, part of these students, (about two million for the USSR) do not attend regular courses.

legal enterprises cannot compete with the illicit earnings of the underground economy which continues to prosper [51].

Detailed information on different types of cooperatives could provide hints on the different availability of skills and other inputs across republics. But from published data it is not easy to understand why Estonia should have the same percentage of cooperatives in everyday services as Uzbekistan (see Table 4.7), nor why cooperatives in restoration should be relatively more developed in backward areas, with lower income per head and Muslim, self-restrained, cultural habits rather than in the Baltic republics which enjoy a higher level of income per head and probably more mundane tastes.

Table 4.7
Republican distribution of cooperatives by branch,
1 January 1989 (percentages)

Republics	Consumer goods	Catering	Everyday services	Purchase and processing of 2nd hand materials	Other	Total
USSR	20.8	9.8	30.6	3.5	35.3	100.0
RSFSR	18.5	8.9	31.2	3.4	38.0	100.0
Ukraine	9.0	6.3	31.4	4.1	39.2	100.0
Belorussia	4.0	3.8	30.0	4.1	40.1	100.0
Uzbekistan	16.0	13.1	34.5	1.4	35.0	100.0
Kazakhstan	18.4	12.8	30.4	5.1	32.3	100.0
Georgia	50.3	19.3	18.0	2.3	10.1	100.0
Azerbaidzhan	23.9	9.7	32.6	3.9	19.9	100.0
Lithuania	33.6	9.1	24.2	6.2	26.9	100.0
Moldavia	19.7	5.2	34.4	2.9	37.8	100.0
Latvia	20.2	6.8	38.1	3.5	31.4	100.0
Kirghizia	19.4	16.2	32.6	3.3	28.5	100.0
Tadzhikistan	13.6	18.0	34.6	6.9	26.9	100.0
Armenia	44.5	18.2	18.9	0.9	27.4	100.0
Turkmenia	25.1	21.2	44.7	6.9	2.1	100.0
Estonia	16.9	9.3	34.2	4.5	35.1	100.0

Source: my estimates from *SSSR v tsifrakh v 1988 godu*, Moskva 1989, pp.179-182

One explanation could be the relatively better availability of inputs in the backward areas, thank to personal plots and household economy. However, an alternative explanation could be that in the backward republics these forms of cooperatives need to emerge as legal trades, due to the registration requirement needed for catering activities while other cooperative activities remain underground [52]. There seems to be also room for a 'demand-pulled' motivation for cooperatives operating in advanced fields. If the number of cooperatives which can be estimated as the difference between the total and the published branch cooperatives include technical-scientific cooperatives (which are unlikely to be included in any of the listed categories), then the data suggest that the main consumers of such services are, indeed, state production enterprises and organizations. Evidence discussed in the economic journals indicates that cooperatives sell 55 per cent of their services and 60 per cent of their consumer goods to enterprises [53]. The Russian Federation, the Ukraine and Belorussia, where most leading enterprises are likely to be situated, are well above the USSR average for 'other' forms of cooperatives. On the other hand, the conspicuous presence of these forms of cooperatives also in backward republics and evidence collected by O.

Shkaratan indicating that in large towns like Moscow the majority of cooperative members have university education [54], suggest that specialists (who can be underutilized in the state economy in general, or unemployed in backward areas) may display a great deal of initiative even within an economic framework which remains much state-dependent.

More information and further research would be necessary to distinguish the positive aspects of the liberation of energy and initiative brought about by the possibility of private enterprise from the short-term profit-making practices which can easily develop in a shortage economy. Legal cooperatives are accused of providing a suitable structure for 'washing' earnings from illegal activities, which still expand [55]. The speculative behaviour of many cooperatives is singled out in their buying at state prices and re-selling at market prices. This evidence is used to disclaim the advantages of cooperative activity. In 1989 an anti-cooperative campaign developed, also in response to social distress produced by increasing shortages and prices [56].

Speculative practices prosper in a situation of shortage. However, what is claimed to be a speculative activity often reflects common trade practice and functions, such as buying in areas of excess supply and selling in deficit areas, storing and contributing to stabilize prices and, in general, responding to demand price signals. These functions are badly needed, but are still considered non-productive in Soviet ideology and planning. The claim by a high Price State Committee official that buying foodstuffs in Moldavia and selling it to customers in Karelia at a price 2-3 times higher is speculation shows not only the lack of appreciation for the geography of transport costs, but mostly how difficult it is to switch from administrative-command rules to economic categories [57]. The transition from a fixed price and shortage economy to some form of market economy is bound to bring about open inflation and affect earning differentials. Fiscal policy is often understood and used as a punitive means, rather than as a means to restore the equilibrium of the budget [58]. Soviet policy-makers manifest still their inclination to use price ceilings, when things get out of their control. In October 1989 method instructions on cooperative goods and service prices prepared by the State Price Committee and designed to bring cooperative prices closer to state prices have been approved by the Supreme Soviet. The number of price inspectors is expected to increase from 300 to 6,000 [59]. These signs indicate that the expansion of private enterprises is under threat. Autonomous republican developments, however, leave room for diversified policies according to national, cultural, economic and social backgrounds [60].

The prospective of a diversified republican policy towards private enterprise is probably the most acceptable solution in the transition to a market economy. This solution allows for a discriminate policy in the field of employment, depending on cultural attitudes, but also on the different distribution of skilled manual and intellectual labour among republics. Skilled workers seem more prepared to work in private enterprise than unskilled labour. A monitoring of people's approach to cooperatives, type and role of membership and performance, conducted by eminent Soviet scholars [61], has found that cooperatives are supported mainly by highly educated specialist and highly skilled workers. Unskilled workers seem to be against this form of organization even when cooperative earnings are higher than state wages for comparable jobs.

However, in the process of modernization state enterprises will increase their demand for highly specialized workers and release less educated workers. This is bound to create competition for labour with private enterprise in a taut labour market. As the results of Soviet research suggests, the very people who should be released from state enterprises are those who resist job changes, whilst more productive, and potentially more dynamic workers, who could contribute to increase the efficiency of state enterprises under the new enterprise statute, are attracted by cooperative work, either as a second job or as a full-time occupation.

Cooperatives do not appear to be recipient of redundant labour. They seem to act as competitors, not so much in the consumer good market, but in the market of production factors, and in the skilled labour market in particular. The fact that many cooperatives employ workers who keep their job with state enterprises appears as a precarious compromise which does not eliminate the antagonism between state and cooperative ownership. Workers are unlikely to put the same efforts in jobs offering different actual and perspective earnings. According to O. Shkaratan the most successful cooperatives are those providing technical-scientific services [62]. This is not surprising, if one considers that most cooperatives depend on inputs supplied by the state sector, whilst the technical-scientific cooperatives use their own know-how. However, even these latter, sometimes, need advanced technology which is not available in the market and can explain the interest in *sovmestitel'stvo*.

The fact that some types of cooperative activities became illegal from 1 January 1989 suggests that this policy is not only meant to curb speculation, but also to release labour for the state economy in the last year of the 12th FYP, when the labour market remains taut. This is evident particularly in female labour intensive branches, where the shortage of workers intensified to the extent that the Supreme Soviet of the RSFSR had to instruct the executive committees in the *oblasti* of Moscow, Ul'ianov, Briansk, Komerov, Tiumen and Chitinski, as well as the Moscow Soviet and the Krasnoiarsk krai, to find the necessary labour [63].

Conclusion

Policy approach towards employment has changed under *perestroika*. The emphasis is falling on the release of labour from the material branches and on its partial redeployment in the service sector in general. Participation rates achieved in the past are considered to be excessive and unhealthy from the social point of view.

Labour redeployment in the state economy, however, does not suggest that under *perestroika* the labour market has become less taut. There are no data on effective unemployment, although in Central Asian republics are, indeed, considered excess-labour areas. Labour released from industry and transport is redeployed in construction. Material branches as a whole do not release labour needed to sustain the growth of consumer goods and services. Large scale redundancies have not been reported.

Cooperative as well as individual activity, embryos of private enterprise, seem to attract ambitious, educated, entrepreneurial people. Neither appears to be recipient of 15 million manual workers expected to be made redundant in the next decade. In the labour-deficit republics, most cooperative members work also in the state economy. In excess-labour areas cooperatives are less developed and have lower membership. Thus, if the state economy succeeds in its programme of modernization and financial resources are not made available to all forms of economic enterprise, the Soviet economy could indeed experience non-voluntary unemployment. Labour laws and social securities schemes have not yet been fully adapted to this eventuality. However, employment data and other estimates do not offer a clear sign that the Soviet economy has, in fact, become less labour dependent. The fact that *sovmestitel'stvo* includes from one third to two thirds of cooperative members means that in the present phase economic growth still needs additional labour.

If cooperative and individual activities succeed in drawing out of the state sphere the best cadres, the inefficiency of the state economy could increase, no matter how advanced new technology will be. This conclusion does not intend to suggest that the experience with cooperatives and individual activity is negative. On the contrary, any effort to restrain their scope militates against a more flexible labour market and increasing earning differentials, which are necessary in a period of rapid technological transformation. Speculative practices stem out of shortage. To fight them, cooperatives should not only compete with state economy, but also among themselves [64]. They should become risk-taking and enlarge their scope of market operations. It is not clear that this solution is widely shared in the Soviet Union.

The decree on taxation of cooperative earnings and recurrent attacks on speculative behaviour by Soviet press and local Soviets suggest that hostility against private initiative is still strong. Some cooperatives do, indeed, benefit from rent positions nested within the state economy. At a meeting with the workers of the Leningrad 'Izhorskii Zavod' in July 1989 Gorbachev stressed the the local Soviets will have the final say on cooperative activities and that he was personally opposed to private ownership [65]. Ideology, power and quite simply fear of change, as argued by P. Hanson, are still powerful motivations for retreat [66].

However, one remark helps concluding this paper with an optimist nuance. The doubling of the number of cooperatives in six months of 1989, in spite of the unfriendly administrative and political surroundings, shows that 70 years of bureaucratic management have not killed entrepreneurship and desire of personal achievement. There are now quite a few who are ready to engage in economic ventures. Scholarly findings suggest that these people are young, healthy and educated. Thus, they represent the future, however long it may take.

Notes

[*] This research has been financed in part by the Italian Ministry of Public Education. The author is grateful for valuable comments on the draft version by A. Chilosi and E. Gasparini. The present version has also benefited from additional insights into different

aspects of labour redeployment offered by Eastern and Western participants at the Conference on 'The socialist enterprise between autonomy and constraints', Padua, 11-12 September 1989. The author only is responsible for any mistake or omission.

[1] See 'Pravo na poluchenie raboty', *Voprosy ekonomiki*, 1989, n.2, p.27

[2] Cf. the guidelines of the Central Committee of the Soviet Communist Party on this issue in *Izvestiia TsK KPSS*, 1989, n.5, pp.29-30, pp.32-9, pp.41-3.

[3] Gosplan foresees that in 1990 200,000 workers - matching the estimated number of additional cooperative jobs - will be made redundant from construction-assembling works, following the decision to cut investment by 4 per cent, see *Ekonomicheskaia gazeta*, 1989, n.40, p.5 and n.42, p.4.

[4] That 'extensive versus intensive growth' has political rather than theoretical implications has been correctly pointed out by A. Chilosi, 'La distribuzione nelle economie socialiste,' *Rivista Internazionale di Scienze Sociali*, 1974, Fasc.5, p.435. Nevertheless, these attributes of growth can still be used as a conventional shortnames which help separating economies in which available resources represent the effective constraint to growth, from alternative models, in which, for instance, demand represents the effective constraint. See J. Kornai, *Contradictions and Dilemmas*, Corvina, Budapest,1985, pp.8-27.

[5] The meaning of labour-release in Soviet planning, as well as other policy tools mentioned in this paper, such as labour balances and productivity indicators, are discussed in detail in S. Malle, *Employment Planning in the Soviet Union. Continuity and Change*, Macmillan, London, 1990.

[6] It is dubious, instead, that, under the present planning mechanism, underutilized labour within state enterprises represents a reserve which can be used for growth. This resource is necessary for the adjustment of short-term imbalances caused by known planning and supply shortcomings at the micro level. On the perception and utilization of slack by Soviet managers, see P. Gregory, 'Productivity, slack and time theft in the Soviet economy', pp.241-78, in J. Millar (ed.), *Politics, work and daily life in the USSR. A Survey of former Soviet citizens,* Cambridge University Press, Cambridge, 1987.

[7] This approach to state employment dates back in the thirties. Strumilin, who may be considered the father of Soviet planning, believed that agricultural labour was underutilized and could be used as labour reserve for the state economy with no harm for personal consumption standard. Kondratev's arguments pointing out low land productivity in agriculture were not only disregarded, but contributed, sadly, to Kondratev's fate, see the reproduction of some Kondratev's and Strumilin's statements on those issues in *EKO,* ' Zadachi sotsialisticheskogo rekonstruktsii' 1989, n.5, pp.26-36.

[8] On the local zeal in implementing this law, see M.Belkindas, 'Privatization of the Soviet economy under Gorbachev', *Berkeley-Duke Occasional Papers*, n.14, April 1989, pp.4-6.

[9] See on this concept, J. Kornai, op.cit., pp.11-12.

[10] See S. Malle, 'Planned and Unplanned Labour Mobility in the Soviet Union Under the Threat of Labour Shortage', *Soviet Studies*, 1987, n.3, pp.378-80.

[11] See F.L. Altmann, 'Employment Policies in Czechoslovakia', in J. Adam (ed.), *Employment Policies in the Soviet Union and Eastern Europe*, Macmillan, London, 1982, pp.82-6; J. Adam, *Employment and Wage Policies in Poland, Czechoslovakia and Hungary Since 1950*, St Martin's Press, New York, 1984, pp.180-3 and L.S. Degtiiar, *Trudovoi potentsial' obshchestva i sotsial'naia politika*, Moskva: Nauka, 1984, pp.90-6.

[12] This approach is discussed in S. Malle, *Soviet Labour-Saving Policies in the Eighties, The Soviet Economy: A New Course?*, NATO Economic Colloquium 1987,Bruxelles: NATO, 1988, pp.74-83. For the resolution on multi-shift regimes, see *Ekonomicheskaia gazeta*, 1987, n.10, p.12.

[13] These regulations affected the period of notice for quit, the duration of admitted interruption between jobs, the possibility of transfer to a lower paid jobs, regardless of function and specialization, etc., see S. Malle, Planned and Unplanned Mobility in the Soviet Union under the Threat of labour Shortage, *Soviet Studies*, 1987, n.3, pp.378-80.

[14] D. Granick, *Job Rights in the Soviet Union. Their Consequences*, Cambridge: Cambridge University Press, 1987.

[15] J. Kornai, *The Economics of Shortage*, 2 vols, North Holland, vol.A, 1980 and P. Hanson, 'The Serendipitous Soviet Achievement of Full Employment: Labour Shortage and Labour

Hoarding in the Soviet Economy', in D. Lane (ed.), *Labour and Employment in the Soviet Union*, Wheatsheaf Books, Brighton, 1986, pp.83-111.

[16] Strumilin's account of the first Five-Year plan is instructive on this point, see S.T. Strumilin, *Problemy planirovaniia v SSSR*, Leningrad: AN SSSR, 1932, pp.142-54.

[17] See the round table on demography (*Ekonomicheskaia gazeta*, 1989, n.30, p.17) discussing the shortage of skilled workers and wrong investment policies in Central Asia.

[18] Pensions remain very low. In 1989 minimum pensions have been raised to 70 roubles a month, below the necessary standard which the state budget was unable to finance, see *Nouvelles de Moscou*, 1989, n.33, p.10 and *Ekonomicheskaia gazeta*, 1989, n.32, p.1.

[19] The new policy approach is clearly presented in V. Kostakov, 'Zaniatost': Defitsit ili izbytok', *Kommunist*, 1987, n.2, pp.78-89.

[20] Interview with O. Shkaratan, Moscow : August 1989.

[21] Since 1930, the word *unemployment* (*bezrabotitsa*) has disappeared from Soviet planning lexicon. Non-employment (*nezaniatost'*) is used to indicate the difference between the estimated labour resources, based on institutional definition of working age and working capability, and the estimated number of employed in the socialized (state and *kolkhoz*) economy. The average annual number of employed in the national economy is the result of the transformation of total worktime used in the state economy in man/days. The difference between the employment of individual workers (whether full-time, part-time, seasonal or temporary) and the estimated annual worktime employed in the economy may be appreciable and becomes evident only when the census (carried out each ten years) provides figures on *individual* employment. Leap years, extraordinary rest days due to celebrations, the holding of more than one job, etc., affect the volume of reported average annual employment. The crucial difference between *nezaniatost'* and unemployment in the Western meaning, however, is one of principle: *nezaniatost'* is an objective estimate based on 'objective' (that is, political) definitions of labour resources and labour planned demand, whilst the concept of unemployment in the West implies 'subjective' work preferences which the demand for labour does

not match. This has become only lately a matter of discussion among Soviet experts, see for instance the round table on employment in *Sotsialisticheskii trud*, 1989, n. 6, pp.48-60 and I. Zaslavskii, 'Problemy zaniatosti: uroki istorii', *Sotsialisticheskii trud*, 1989, n.3, pp.56-63. Unemployment benefits approved in 1987 - equal to two or three months average wage in the case of redundancies or shut-down of enterprises - are low by Western standards. However, any possible extension of unemployment benefits to non-employed people needs a redefinition of unemployment taking into account their *voluntary* supply of labour.

[22] *SSSR i soiuznye respubliki v 1988*, Moskva: Finansy i statistika, 1989, p.142 for the first time ascribes to bad working conditions for women high child mortality in some Central Asian republics. See also 'Pravo na poluchenie raboty', op.cit., pp.16-20.

[23] See T. Zaslavskaia, 'Chelovecheskii faktor: balans tendentsii', *Sel'skoe khoziaistvo Rossii*, 1987, n.2.

[24] See the theses for discussion at the All Union conference on the radical economic reform, *Ekonomicheskaia gazeta*, 1989, n.43, pp.4-5.

[25] See law on cooperatives in *Ekonomicheskaia gazeta*, 1987, n.28, pp.10-15, law on individual activity in *Vedomosti V.S. SSSR*, 1986, n.47 and the project of law on property, *Ekonomicheskaia gazeta*, 1989, n.48, pp.9-11.

[26] See *Trud v SSSR. Statisticheskii sbornik,* Moskva: Finansy i statistika, 1988, p.41. Given the autarchical organization of the Soviet enterprise and the plurality of services (from foodstuffs to repair shops and everyday services, such as hairdressing in some cases) provided to factory workers it is not difficult to reclassify some workers of the non-productive sections to production sections and vice versa, adapting the workforce structure to planners' preferences. Non-production workers are statistically reported in their relative branches (trade, material supply, etc.) although their wages are paid from the enterprise budgets.

[27] The difference between total release and total addition (calculated from branch figures) is, in fact, of 278,000 workers, i.e. twenty thousand units less than the total reported for the state economy. Non-reported branches (the army?) could perhaps explain this difference.

[28] The employment of scientific workers is still under limits in the

main scientific areas (Leningrad and Moscow, towns and *oblasti*), see *Ekonomicheskaia gazeta*, 1988, n.31, p.24.

[29] Industrial employment, as a matter of fact, has diminished also in the excess-labour Republics of the Northern Caucasus and Central Asia (except Uzbekistan), as one can estimate from output and productivity figures published in *Ekonomicheskaia gazeta*, 1989, n.32, p.13.

[30] To prevent labour outflows in 1988, *Minaviaprom* (a branch of the defence industry) has authorized wage increases against central guidelines on wage-productivity relations, see *Ekonomicheskaia gazeta*, 1989, n.30, p.9. The nominal wage outburst of 1988-89 also suggests that adjustment of military priority branches to civilian production, given the present price structure, is more difficult than expected and is becoming an autonomous factor of open inflation.

[31] See *Sotsialisticheskii trud*, 1989, n.7, p.92. Indirect evidence of the failure to stimulate labour release with present policies is also offered by the fact that administrative measures against enterprises which do not adopt advanced technology have been planned by the Moscow Soviet to take place in 1991 and that some enterprises on leasing terms have to pay charges on labour resources, although they are exonerated from paying charges on fixed capital, see *Nouvelles de Moscou*, 1989, n.31, p.14 and *Ekonomicheskaia gazeta*, 1989, n.38, p.11.

[32] I. Zaslavskii, 'Problemy zaniatosti', cit., presents an instructive outline of the steps which characterized the authoritarian shaping of Soviet industrial relations.

[33] In the case of production necessity (a recurrent event in Soviet practice) any worker may be transferred to other jobs. A worker may be punished for violating labour discipline, by being transferred for some time to a lower ranking job. Many forms of intra-factory redeployment do not need workers' consent. When the consent is required by law, it may be tacit, see S. Malle, 'Planned and Unplanned Labour mobility', cit., pp.373-4, 379.

[34] The refusal to accept these changes expose workers to the effects of the law on labour discipline, see *Biulleten' Verkhovnogo Suda SSSR*, 1988, n.3, p.11 and M. Pankin, 'Novoe v zakonodatel'stve o trude', *Sotsialisticheskii trud*, 1988, n.4, p.66.

[35] See *Sovetskoe trudovoe zakonodatel'stvo*, Moskva: Iuridiche-

skaia literatura, 1987, p.72.

[36] 54 per cent of workers' collectives are not even informed about hiring and firing decisions, see N.V. Andreenkova and P.P. Krotov, *Soviet trudovogo kollektiva i demokratizatsiia upravleniia*, Moskva: AN SSSR, ISI-SSA, 1989, p.39.

[37] One needs to remark that strikes in these branches have been motivated by the worsening shift regimes for which no sufficient compensation was offered. In coal mining, for instance, the official 40 per cent night shift wage supplement was not even awarded in many cases (A. Kotliar, personal interview, August 1989)

[38] See A.K.Koshanov (ed.), *Vysvobozhdenie rabochey sily v usloviiakh intensifikatsii proizvodstva (na materiali Kazakskoi SSSR)*, pp.147-8.

[39] See *Ekonomicheskaia gazeta*, 1989, n.40, pp.8-9.

[40] See *Literaturnaia gazeta*, 1988, June 29, p.11.

[41] See *Nouvelles de Moscou*, 1989, n.33, (13 August), p.10.

[42] See *Ekonomicheskaia gazeta*, 1989, n.35, p.6 and n.42, p.4.

[43] See I. Adirim, ' A Note on the Current Level, Pattern and Trends of Unemployment in the USSR', *Soviet Studies*, 1989, n.3, p.460.

[44] In some towns of Central Asia one hour work in loading and unloading is worth 80 roubles. A good construction worker earns 150 roubles a day, i.e. about half a monthly state wage, see *Nouvelles de Moscou*, 1989, n.36, pp.8-9. On the other hand, in Uzbekistan, where most unemployment is alleged to be concentrated, each year the students of the 8-10 classes are mobilized to pick cotton, see V.V. Popov and N.P. Shmelov, 'Plan i ekonomika,' *Znanie: Ekonomika*, 1988, n.11, pp.13-14.

[45] This is still true, according to A. Kotliar, (interview, 15.8.1989). According to V. Buynovskyi, deputy director of the State Committee for Labour, the service sphere is short of 13 million people, SWB, 22.1.1988.

[46] The estimated number for 1990 was 1.2 million full time workers. This figure was overtaken already by July 1989. *Ekonomicheskaia gazeta*, 1989, n.37, p.15.

[47] See S. Sitarian's comment in *Ekonomicheskaia gazeta*, 1989, n.42, p.16.

[48] See *SSSR v tsifrakh v 1988*, Moskva: Finansy i statistika, 1989, p.183.

[49] A private truck transport service in a rural area can yield up to 1,200 roubles a month, about six times the average state wage for the USSR! (interview with N. Andreyenkova, 8 August,1989).

[50] More precise estimates need taking into account the number of working-age women with more than 3 young children, invalids and army servicemen. However, employment figures include also old-age pensioners (more than ten million for the country as a whole) and overtime which should be deducted from total employment in working out meaningful estimates of able-bodied people participation rates.

[51] See T. Koriagina, a senior official of Gosplan, reporting on the underground economy, *Nouvelles de Moscou*, 1989, n.34 (20 August), p.10. For the 'Aslund law' by which private enterprises grow together with the growing underground economy, see P. Hanson, 'Von Mises' Revenge', paper presented at the Conference on 'The Socialist Enterprise between Autonomy and Constraints', Padua, 11-12 September 1989.

[52] For which I am indebted to Dr. S.A. Vasiliev (Leningrad university).

[53] See *Pravda*, 10 August, 1989 and *Ekonomicheskaia gazeta*, 1989, n.19, p.5.

[54] Interview with O. Shkaratan, Moscow, August 1989.

[55] As argued by G. Grossman at the 1989 NATO Economic Colloquium in Bruxelles. See also the Report for the 1990 Plan presented by L.A. Voronin, vice-president of the Council of Ministries of the USSR, *Ekonomicheskaia gazeta*, 1989, n.4, p.5.

[56] At the June 7th 1989 Peoples' Deputies Congress, M. Ryzhkov, the president of the USSR Council of Ministers, stressed that many people wished cooperatives in trade and services to be shut-down, see *Ekonomicheskaia gazeta*, 1989, n.24, p.4.

[57] According to this source, 25 per cent of the total number of cooperatives and 33 per cent of the total number of cooperative members perform speculative activity, see *Ekonomicheskaia gazeta*, 1989, n.31, p.9.

[58] Tax liabilities approved by an Ukas in March 1989 were decisively of punitive nature. Tax rates were highly progressive and fell on gross revenue. In 1989 after some corrections to a new Ukas of February 1989 approved by the Supreme Soviet of the USSR some limits to fiscal policy vis à vis the cooperatives have

been established, which leave, however, much scope for arbitrary tax policy. The approved amendments authorize deduction of fixed capital expenditure, training costs and other fees paid to the state from revenue before tax. Tax rates are approved by republican laws, but cannot exceed 35 per cent of the taxable cooperative revenue, *except in the case of trade, purchasing, catering, intermediation, and entertainments* (my italics), see M. Belkindas, op.cit., pp.46-8, Ekonomicheskaia gazeta, 1989, n.37, p.15.

[59] See *Ekonomicheskaia gazeta*, 1989, n.26, p.16 and *La Stampa*, 18 October 1989, p.7.

[60] The federal congress of cooperatives in Moscow suggested that cooperatives harassed by local soviets become *filialy* of other cooperatives located in more friendly Republics.

[61] O. Shkaratan is the promoter of this research (interview in Moscow, 18 August 1989).

[62] One example is the medical cooperative in Moscow central Arbat, offering a wide range of specialized diagnostics and treatment, highly rated by Muscovites. Nonetheless, other medical cooperatives have been closed down by the Ministry of Health, see *Nouvelles de Moscou*, n.15 (9 April), p.12.

[63] *Sovetskaia Rossiia*, 8 August 1989.

[64] A sign of this development may be the starting of exhibitions of consumer goods in Estonia, see *Ekonomicheskaia gazeta*, 1989, n.28, p.19.

[65] See *Pravda*, 20 August 1989, p.2.

[66] P. Hanson,'Von Mises' Revenge', paper presented at the International Conference on 'The Socialist Enterprise Between Autonomy and Constraints', Padua, 11-12 September 1989.

5 Economic reforms in Poland: a post mortem

ANDRZEJ BRZESKI

Introduction*

History has played a trick on those forever discussing the ways to improve Polish socialism. Their subject may have lost its relevance: a restoration of private market economy is at long last becoming a prospect for the future [1]. This possibility will not be discussed here. My topic lies within the confines of the past. It deals with what some Polish writers label as 'phoney,' 'half-way' and 'crucial' (or 'comprehensive') reforms of the socialist economy, though I admit that I find these distinctions unsatisfactory [2]. In any case, even the last kind is restricted in scope.

As one definition explains, a 'crucial reform' is 'the transition from the "command economy" to an economy with a regulated market, but still within the framework of "real socialism."' [3]. This cautious delimitation serves my purpose. My concern is not with the potentialities of an open-ended future, but with the failures of the past. On this score there can be no equivocation: the 'process of economic reform' in Poland has proven a complete fiasco. In trying to identify some of the causes of this outcome, my remarks are meant as a footnote to that new and elusive field - 'reform economics,' or, as some would have it, 'refonomics' [4]. If the tenor is sceptical, indeed pessimistic about the possibility of improving socialist performance, it is due to a refractory reality: socialism works badly and yet, inherently, resists change.

An overview

Little, if anything, can be added on this occasion to the existing accounts of Polish reforms. Just a brief note on their chronology and nature is intended, a bird's eye view, as it were. Poland's seminal role in the early stage of bloc-wide reform movement merits emphasis: during the mid-1950s, the Poles were in the forefront of the debates, perhaps because of the exceptionally strong theoretic tradition of neoclassicism and liberalism. Ideas, after all, have consequences, at the very least, on ideas. At any rate, before others within the bloc, Polish economists engaged in a thorough critique of the system transplanted from the Soviet Union. They also formulated, prolifically, proposals for change [5]. As I have written elsewhere twenty years ago, 'hardly a notion had been overlooked that has since passed into the stock-in-trade of the diverse schools of reform-mongering. . . (to) list a sample: Pricing: market-determined; selectively controlled according to sector, by levels or limits; based on marginal cost; related to the world market. Profit criteria: absolute; incremental; in relation to cost or assets. Cost accounting: full depreciation; interest charges; rent. Finances: retained profits; discretionary bank loans; money and capital markets. Planning: aggregate through banks and treasury; selective for sectors; limited to few indicators for firms; indicative; long-term only. Enterprise: fully autonomous; self-financing; demand and profit oriented. Nor had this. . . deluge of ideas been restricted to mere technicalities. . . (it dealt) with allocative priorities. . . (and) bureaucracy. Workers' councils and independent trade unions had been advocated. . . (as well as) private role in industry.' [6].

Despite all the clamour, the practical results were inconsequential. Although the proposals of 1956-58 stopped short of advocating the transition to market socialism, they evidently were deemed unacceptable. 'Polish economists, or at least those (. . .) close to the orbit of power,' were said to be, 'aware of the political and economic reasons why decentralization (was) out of the question at the (. . .) time. . . (and) prepared to accept the basic premises of the Soviet model.' [7]. And so they were, but to put the responsibility for continued adherence to the Soviet system on economists is misleading. *Imitatores servum pecus* would be more to the point. To be sure, proposals for improving the system never really ceased, and, of course, there were plenty of reorganizations etc. - the usual bureaucratic response to disappointing performance. With declining growth rates, and mounting difficulties - the sundry 'barriers,' much discussed during the 1960s - ameliorative suggestions abounded. This second phase of reform-mongering coincided with bloc-wide developments. Poland, this time, was in step with others. Not surprisingly, the scope of reform proposals was somewhat more limited than in the earlier Polish debates. Libermanism set the tone. When changes were eventually introduced, in the mid-1960s, they were far from a blueprint for a regulated market, at most qualifying as 'half-way' measures. Their ingredients were perceptibly characterized in a United Nations report applying to all Soviet-bloc reforms at that time: (i) broad directives seeking to improve central planning techniques, requiring, in particular, greater reliance on the medium- and long-term plans which are regarded as devices for achieving greater stability in the conditions under which enterprises operate; (ii) changes and reductions in the centrally planned targets that are mandatory for the enterprise, together with greater emphasis on gross income (i.e., net value added), profit and rate of profitability as criteria for judging the enterprise's success; (iii) the expansion of decentralized investment funds available to enterprises and the larger economic units, and a greater use of bank credits; (iv) the introduction of a capital charge on the fixed assets of enterprises, which will play an increasingly important role in transferring a proportion of profits to the budget; (v) a strengthening of economic incentives (amounting in some cases to changes in the wage system) by establishing closer ties between the remuneration of employees and the enterprise's performance; (vi) the promotion of direct contacts between economic units which, in contrast with the old system, are no longer conceived simply as instruments for the implementation of national plans, but rather as a means of guiding the plan itself; (vii) price reforms, which include changes in the determination of prices and in the price structure; (viii) the concentration of industrial enterprises into larger units (sometimes accounting for a whole branch of industry), . . . [having] administrative responsibilities but being called upon to operate to a greater extent as economically accountable organizations; (ix) the streamlining of the administrative apparatus responsible for the management of industry, and/or various administrative changes having more specific objectives [8].

Even these relatively modest changes were to be soon rolled back, or disregarded in practice. At any rate, they were ineffectual [9]. With hardly a significant modification, the established way of planning and management once again proved its resilience. Various attempts to streamline and revitalize the economy followed, but they do not warrant elaboration; none classifies as genuine reform. According to a view common among Polish economists the 'first four attempts of the reforms in Poland: 1955-58, 1965-67, 1969-70, 1973-75, were . . . phoney (i.e. designed) in such a way as to preserve the command economy.' [10]. I concur in this assessment. It took the dramatic - for the regime also traumatic - challenge of 'Solidarity' to raise the pitch of reformist agitation to new levels. The enormous outpouring of literature is yet to be surveyed, indeed catalogued - something that cannot be done here. Most of the proposals were far-reaching, and even the official Directions of Economic Reform adopted by the IXth Extraordinary Congress of the Polish United Workers Party in July 1981, set ambitious goals. As to the actual measures, formally introduced in 1982, already under the Martial Law, they fell short of a 'crucial reform.' The avowed intent of the reform, epitomized by the 'three S's' - samodzielnosc, samofinansowanie, samorzadnosc - which stand for enterprise autonomy, self-financing and self-management, might have seemed promising enough. There was to be a reliance on profit (or value added) maximization, gradual replacement of plan targets by indirect 'regulators,' and 'steering instruments' (mainly financial), and, in general, a diminished role for the centre - with the effect of decentralization and depolitization of economic decision making. Already at that stage, however, in programmatic proclamations, there was ambivalence and ambiguity. The programme of Directions 'rejects both the idea that the market is the only regulator of the economy or that the enterprises should be dominated by the central authorities.' Instead, it postulates, 'an economy (that) will function on the basis of central planning with the use of the market mechanism.' [11]. I will return to this eclecticism later; right now, suffice it to say that in practice, the original concept of reform was greatly scaled down. Pricing remained for a large part administrative, but disorderly and irrational. Finances were left in a chaos, and allocation in kind, led by the numerous 'operational programmes' of the Martial Law regime and 'government orders,' prevailed throughout. Central administration, though allegedly deemphasizing the sectoral principle, swelled in ranks, and the formally liquidated associations of enterprises (zjednoczenia) - a part of the sectoral hierarchy - reemerged under a different guise (zrzeszenia). To make a long and rather well-known story short: apart from the increasingly painful shortages and deteriorating living conditions, not much changed as a result of the Jaruzelski round of reforms. The critics are fully justified in concluding that:

> The reform has not resulted in the establishment of a self-regulatory economic mechanism. The old centrally planned system has been modified as the result of a mass of legislation, administrative regulations and discretionary decisions by the central authorities. This has not, however, resulted in the change in the direction of an increased use of market instruments that was envisaged in the officially adopted program. Poland's 'new' economic system is not the traditional command system, nor is it a socialist market system. It is a system in which the authorities try to manipulate the decisions of formally autonomous enterprises with the help of financial and direct administrative measures. On their part, enterprises try to manipulate the decisions of the authorities by bargaining for exemptions, favorable treatment, and the allocation of scarce resources. It is doubtful, however, that the outcome of this 'manipulative system' is an improvement in economic efficiency [12].

More recently, the reform, which was admittedly derailed by extraordinary circumstances during the Martial Law, was to be put back on the track. Numerous additional laws and regulations have been adopted in 1988 to implement the so called Second Stage of the Economic Reform. Rather optimistically summarized, the avowed goals were: 'radical changes in the administrative center, abolishing of rationing and broad introduction of a market mechanism in which enterprises are to be given almost total independence in their choice of productive (sic) targets and purchasing of inputs . . . (and, of course, a) wide range of free market pricing.' [13]. For once, perhaps a 'crucial reform' was really about to get underway, but by then, it was too late. By early 1989, more profound and elemental changes were obviously superseding all deliberate programmes. Months before the Party's electoral defeat, a highly placed academic weather vane pronounced 'the existing model of real socialism a "failed attempt at mutation of civilizational process". . . common to European countries.' [14]. Whatever else this could mean, it correctly reflects the circumstance that, despite posturing, the politbureau gang and their hangers-on have in fact given up. For the Poland of 'Solidarity' that soon followed, the Second Stage of Economic Reform has been rendered irrelevant.

Why the treadmill?

Borrowing Gertrud Schroeder's apt simile, the Polish 'reform process' of the last three decades can be likened to a treadmill: a lot of movement, but no advance. The pattern is cyclical consisting of recurrent attempts to solve the same problems. Not that things don't change at all. They do, though most Poles would probably say, for the worse. The objectives of the reforms, however, are never accomplished; consequently, the same measures are being advocated in each successive phase. Again and again, in an implicit admission of the futility of previous efforts, there is more talk of enterprise autonomy, rational pricing, profit incentives, markets and so on. It is usual to explain this curious state of affairs by the resistance of the Party leadership. Such resistance, according to one view, is grounded in four overlapping groups of motives: vested interest, distrust of benefits, Marxist ideology, and most importantly, political considerations [15]. Brus - whose work I am referring to - constructs a model sequence of the 'reform process' which deserves to be presented in extenso:

> Under economic and political pressure, resistance would periodically turn into reluctant acceptance of reform, after which the following sequence would appear: (1) the elimination of directly political aspects of reform; (2) the limitation of the actual scope of changes in the economic mechanism; (3) a gradual implementation, with particular attention to preservation of the institutional set-up in the center of the nomenklatura principle in appointments; and (4) the utilization of all avenues promising to overcome economic difficulties without reform, while preserved institutional structure provided the framework for a return to the old system [16].

This description includes all the elements in the cyclical and ultimately futile 'reform process.' Still, some important facets need amplification. Furthermore, one must probe the deeper logic of the 'treadmill,' which, I believe, is systemic. To put it differently: it is normal for 'real socialism' to desperately need 'reforms,' but it also is normal to routinely abort them. The subject is involved; it calls for an argument, and for empirical support which are beyond my compass. Another Max Weber would probably be necessary, with a sequel to Wirtschaft und Gesellschaft; certainly not however, another Marx: the vicissitudes of reforming 'real socialism' cannot be reduced to historical materialism, however flexibly interpreted. Whatever their complexities - and there are many, cutting across academic compartmentalization - the Polish difficulties had their origin in 'ideas determining existence,' rather than vice versa. Wrong-headed social engineers, in their reckless pursuit of socialist ideals have caused the troubles. Be this as it may, I can no more than outline a few notions which, in my opinion, require further exploration if we are to understand the phenomenon of 'reform treadmill.'

Issues to think about

Of the issues bedevilling the economic reform in 'real socialism,' several strike me as particularly noteworthy.

(a) Socialism and the Party

Clearly the Party, having gained and retained power by brute force needs legitimation. Geopolitics alone is not enough even in Poland, although it may suffice for a while as an argument in keeping the party power supreme. The only possible legitimation can come from the control over the economy - 'planning,' 'steering,' 'regulating,' and what not. Laissez-faire is irreconciliable with the Party's continuing sense of identity, and hence existence. Given the well publicized defects of Soviet type planning and management, the Party turns to schemes purportedly combining central control - inevitably also micro - with enterprise autonomy, etc. However, as long as it is committed to holding power, the Party qua Party does not and cannot opt for a genuine, truly decentralized market economy. It only wants to utilize the market mechanism to reap its putative advantages - efficiency and equilibrium - but without a significant loss of control over allocation. In this connection, there is much talk about 'parametric methods,' 'indirect instruments (mainly monetary and financial), incentives and so on. What exactly this means, and how it would work is far from clear. Party leaders may be quite sincere when they speak of 'marketization' and 'strengthened national planning' in the same breath. But, in the face of the unavoidable conflict between central control and market forces, they predictably choose control. The backsliding in the 'reform process' is not merely a matter of deliberate choice dictated by self-interest. It also is the more fundamental matter of self-definition and political ontology, i.e., of existence. That is why destruction or self-destruction of the classic marxist-leninist Party - vide Poland 1989 - is a precondition to open-ended reform.

(b) The intractability

A 'comprehensive' economic reform, even a 'half-way' one, represents an immensely complicated task, entailing a high degree of uncertainty. Economics does provide useful ideas on effects of *ceteris paribus* changes in prices, tariffs, taxes, etc., but it has little if anything to say about the consequences of a massive overhaul of institutions. The latter belongs conceptually (and computationally) to a category known as 'problems of great complexity.' Attempts at 'parametric' control add to the intractability of the reform measures. Not surprisingly, this acts as a conservative influence against reform. Even limited governments in the West hesitate to destabilize the economic status quo. For Party regimes, programmatically and historically inseparable from the economy, the uncertainties must seem intolerable.

(c) The unknowns of autonomy

This is the intractability issue as it manifests itself at the decisive level of the enterprise. Autonomous managers - free of targets and quotas - may be serving their own interests more eagerly than those of the society. And why shouldn't they? The familiar problem of incentive compatibility arises in all seriousness when constraints of planning are loosened by reform. There are no compelling reasons why cost should be minimized, marginal cost equated to price, etc. etc., except of course, under conditions and arrangements that are functionally indistinguishable from capitalist competition. Oskar Lange assumed the difficulty away, by simply postulating goodwill. The Party leaders know better, and when confronted with the unknowns of managerial behaviour tend to opt for constraints that guarantee minimum performance, i.e. viability. Similar reservations apply *mutatis mutandis* to workers' management, although, because of the latter's populist appeal, it is much more difficult to skirt it openly. In rationalizing the Party's resistance to reform, I have reluctantly assumed the role of devil's advocate. There is, however, the other side too: a vulgar self-interest of the *nomenklatura*. This interest must not be underestimated, especially since, with the passage of time, the ideological fervour tends to die down, while appetites grow. The point hardly needs belabouring. Nor will I dwell on the importance of Marxist-Leninist doctrine, which enters into the picture in every way. It does so by: (1) defining the essential components of 'socialism,' (2) determining the self-image and identity of the Party, (3) providing a pseudo-rationale for the existing system, etc, etc. Alec Nove, still dreaming about 'good socialism,' is right in stressing that 'Marx had little to say about the economics of socialism, and that the little he did say was either irrelevant or directly misleading.' [17]. Unquestionably, there is little if anything useful in Marx when it comes to the economics of a satisfactory social order. But without Marx (and Lenin), there could be no 'real socialism' at all. Nor once established, could a system so beset by shortcomings outlive most of its would-be reformers. Of special importance for the durability of 'real socialism,' and of its economics, has been the harsh social discipline of Marxism-Leninism. When this discipline was relaxed, as a result of the Party's growing self-doubts, the bottom fell out from under the edifice of central planning and management. Inflation, which was both a result and a symptom, has been decisive in eventually destabilizing Poland's 'real socialism.' At the same time, by intensifying the risks of freeing prices, inflation, especially the repressed kind, has acted as a restraining influence against the reform [18]. This was a particularity of Poland, though obviously, the problem exists elsewhere too, notably in the Soviet Union. To clarify, let me add: soft-budgets are paradigmatic of 'real socialism' because of the commitment to production (and employment) at any cost. In some sense, they are a part and parcel of the social compact. The inflationary consequences of soft budgets, however, are greatly magnified when, due to disintegration of the ancien régime, a cost push operates virtually without restraint on the labour side. The resultant market imbalance undermines the existing system, and simultaneously, in a dialectical double-bind, creates an added obstacle to a 'crucial reform.' Stalin might not have been necessary for the system and policies of 'real socialism,' - very likely Trotsky would have done just as well - but the gulag was. It helped to keep inflation in check. Another influence against reform - this too characteristic of, but not limited to Poland - was the seemingly infinite flow of Western credit. Optimism rises high when banks are generous. The illusions that Gierek *et consortes* still harboured about the workability of traditional Soviet-style institutions during the 1970s, were no doubt fortified by Western loans. Whatever the bankers' hopes, in the case of Poland at least, loans were a substitute for systemic change. Unfortunately, they also were largely wasted, thus confirming the familiar saw about socialism's capital mistakes being much worse than capitalism's social mistakes.

I began these remarks about economic reforms in Poland on a 'sceptical, indeed pessimistic' note. In essence, I doubt the reformability of 'real socialism' in which Marxist-Leninist parties preside over economic life of countries. Not surprisingly, from this vantage point, the majority of the avowed reforms - and not in Poland alone - fell into the category of 'phoney' and 'half-way'; they were quickly reversed if not simply forgotten. But even much more ambitious attempts - as the New Economic Mechanism in Hungary - stopped short of decisive changes. A combination of systemic inertia, vested interest, and most importantly, ideological constraints, have prevailed upon the reformers' best intentions. 'The Hungarian experience demonstrates that after twenty years of reforms, real change may finally be in sight...but (not) in the near future,' observed Vaclav Klaus [19]. And if, at last, due to the progressing disintegration of the Marxist-Leninist regime in Budapest, such a change is on the agenda, it will be an escape from not a reform of socialism. The implications for Soviet perestroika are inescapable. Mr. Gorbachev has been trying to strike a compromise between preserving the Party and getting ahead on the economic front. A clearcut choice between the two cannot be postponed for long, it would seem.

Postscript

Upon consideration, I have abandoned the idea of significantly expanding the original version of this paper. Developments throughout the area which used to be known as the Soviet Bloc - from East Germany to Mongolia - have reinforced my view that the time for socialist reforms is pretty much over. With the new, still uncertain perspectives for more fundamental changes having finally opened, other problems arise. The issue nowadays is not how to improve 'real socialism' but how to dismantle it, and how to overcome its baneful heritage [20]. Sovietological economics is therefore on its way out, and ordinary economics is coming into its own. Even so, the need for scholarly work on the (failed) economic reforms of 'real socialism' remains. Centuries hence, the subject, (by then a matter for systemic archeology, akin to our studies of Roman slave economy), will not have lost its intrinsic interest. Probably it will also retain its practical import, of a warning.

Notes

[*] Prepared for the International Conference on 'The Socialist Enterprise Between Autonomy and Constraint: A Comparative Analysis of the Economic Reform Process in the U.S.S.R and East European Countries,' University of Padua (Italy), September 11-12, 1989. A few minor changes have been introduced and a postscript added.

[1] See 'Shock Therapy,' *The Economist*, 2 September, 1989, pp. 47-8.

[2] See, e.g., M. Nasilowski, 'The Reform Experiences in Poland,' in K. Pecsi (ed.), *Alternative Models of Socialist Economic Systems* , Budapest, 1988, p. 113.

[3] T. Kowalik, *On Crucial Reform of Real Socialism*, Vienna, The Vienna Institute for Comparative Economic Studies, 1986, p. 3. Original emphasis.

[4] See the various papers appearing under the auspices of the Vienna Institut fur die Wissenschaften von Menschen esp. M. Tardos and J.M. Kovacs, 'Plan and (or) Market. A Comparative Study of 'Reform Economics' in Soviet-Type Societies' (1987), and J. M. Kovacs, 'Reform Economics: The Classification Gap' (1988) and 'Compassionate Doubts about "Refonomics" in Hungary' (1988).

[5] See J.M. Montias, *Central Planning in Poland*, New Haven, Yale University Press, 1962, esp. chapter 9.

[6] A. Brzeski, 'Poland as a Catalyst of Change in the Communist Economic System,' *Polish Review*,1971, n.2, pp. 9-10.

[7] Montias, op. cit., p. 332.

[8] Quoted after G. Grossman, 'Economic Reforms: A Balance Sheet,' *Problems of Communism*, 1966, n.6, p. 46.

[9] See J. G. Zielinski, *Economic Reforms in Polish Industry*, London, Oxford University Press, 1973, esp. chapter 9.

[10] Nasilowski, loc. cit.

[11] Quoted after Z. Fallenbuchl, 'Present State of the Economic Reform,' in P. Marer and W. Siwinski (eds) *Creditworthiness and Reform in Poland*, Bloomington, Indiana University Press, 1988, p. 116.

[12] Fallenbuchl, op. cit, p. 128.

[13] Nasilowski, loc. cit.

[14] Professor Jozef Pajestka in a session of the Polish Academy of Sciences, as reported by *Zycie Warszawy*, March 1989.

[15] See W. Brus, 'The Political Economy of Reforms' in Marer and Siwinski (eds), op. cit., p. 75-6.

[16] Brus, op. cit., p. 74.

[17] A. Nove, *The Economics of Feasible Socialism*, London, Allen and Unwin, 1983, p. 10.

[18] See J. Lipinski and U. Wojciechowska (eds), *Proces wdrazania reformy gospodarczej*, Warszawa, PWE, 1987, *passim*.

[19] V. Klaus, *Socialist Economies, Economic Reforms and Economists*, Praha, Prognosticky ustav Csav, 1989, p. 41.

[20] See, C. Watrin, 'Transforming the Command Economies,' *The World and I*, November 1989, pp. 93-105; as well as A. Brzeski, 'Unscrambling the (Communist) Omelette,' *Pathfinder*, 1990, n.1.

6 Private sector and economic reforms in the Soviet Union and China

GIANNI SALVINI

Introduction

Before economic reforms began, in the People's Republic of China - PRC (1979) and the Soviet Union (1985), the system of ownership of the means of production, in both countries, basically consisted of two forms of public ownership existing side by side: ownership by the state and collective ownership.

This system was, for the most part, formed in the 1930s in the Soviet Union, when the socialist transformation of the system of ownership was basically completed according to a model which was later transferred to all socialist countries. In terms of managerial methods, units under each type of system of ownership all tended to become similar to the state-run economy. This trend toward a unified system of economic form and economic management prevented the development of economic forms outside the state-owned economy and led to increasing rigidity in the mechanism of economic activity. This was a major factor in the set-backs suffered in the economic development of China and the Soviet Union.

In this respect one can understand why the reforms of the economic system under way in both countries include two related aspects: the reform of the mechanism of economic activity and the reform of ownership relations. Reforms of the mechanism of economic activity are aimed at transforming past mechanisms which had excessive concentration of decision-making power and inhibited the role of the market. These reforms affect the existing ownership relations. As the experience with economic reforms in Eastern Europe has demonstrated, changes in the mechanism of economic activity, including changes in the decision-making structure and strengthening of the market mechanism, invariably involved not only changes in the forms of management but also changes in asset relationship. In fact, the adjustment and improvement of ownership relations is a necessary condition for the reform of the mechanism of economic activity. Only if the two are undertaken together can the reform be successful.

Consider, for instance, the motivation. The problem of how to motivate producers to behave competitively under state resource ownership has not been solved: how to induce them to to economize on resources, to seek new markets, and to develop new products and processes. Private and cooperative businesses, however, do provide that motivation. In other words, the question is whether the economic reforms are compatible with the existing structure of ownership.

The latter element cannot be neglected, even if the danger of oversimplifications is always present in the making of major generalizations. Some traditional elements of the Chinese character, in fact, promoted conditions favourable to radical reforms: entrepreneurship, pragmatism, a strong work ethic, cultural adaptability and self-confidence. On the contrary, the Russian tradition always emphasized the political factor and neglected the value of individual initiative and entrepreneurship. Consequently the Russian and Soviet tradition has developed an aversion to risk-taking, to the spontaneity necessary for economic ventures, to devolution of economic power and to a pragmatic approach. In this respect pressures for economic change from below are minimal.

This article will examine, consecutively, the role of the private sector in the Soviet Union and PRC, and in the conclusions will consider some implications of the related changes on the economic reforms under way in these two countries.

The reappraisal of private economic activity in the USSR

In the Soviet Union the dogma of the superiority and the ultimate exclusive role of state property has been stated in party pronouncements for decades. The only exceptions to this occurred in agriculture, where more than one quarter of total production in value terms has long been attributable to sideline activities carried out by farmers in agricultural cooperatives (kolkhozy) or on state-managed estates (sovkhozy), but has been tolerated politically.

This attitude has changed during the course of Gorbachev's economic reforms. In his speech to the party plenum in January 1987, he said:

> Special mention should be made of socialist property. It became nobody's property, having no real owner. There was an incorrect attitude towards cooperative property, which was viewed as something second-rate and having no future. All this had grievous consequences for agrarian and social policies, bred management by decree in relations with collective farms, and led to the abolition of producer cooperatives. There were also grave misconceptions about personal subsidiary holdings and individual labour activity, which did much economic and social harm as well (Kommunist, 3, 1987).

Since then, many Soviet economists have underlined some positive effects expected by an expansion of private economic activity, namely: 1) an increase in the quantity and variety of consumer goods and services available to the population; 2) more effective control over the large amount of activity in the black market and 3) an increase in government income from taxation of private individuals. Consequently various measures have been taken to reinforce private, i.e. non state-controlled economic activity.

The 'Law on Individual Enterprise' was enacted on November 1986 and came into force on May 1987. The law considerably extended the list of permissible individual activities compared with previous regulations, and it actually distinguished between those activities which are allowed and those which are not: nevertheless, there remain a large number of activities whose legal position is uncertain. There is also the added difficulty that an official license needs to be obtained before any private economic activity can be carried out.

The 'Law on Cooperation' was adopted on 26 May 1988. This law in a sense marked the emancipation of private enterprise in the USSR. It defined the two primary purposes of the cooperatives as producing goods and services for the population and improving the standard of living of cooperative members. In a remarkable departure from the past, the law specifically guaranteed that cooperatives could own private productive property. Moreover, it instructed government authorities not to interfere with the cooperatives and explicitly stated that local authorities had no power to 'approve' (i.e. prohibit) registration of a cooperative.

Initially the 'Law of Cooperation' stated that cooperatives had the right to be engaged in any kind of activity. However, the decision of the USSR Council of Ministers of 29 December 1988 specified certain kinds of activities which the cooperatives are not authorized to carry out. For instance, manufacturing of any kinds of weapons; rendering of certain kinds of medical services; distilling spirits and making wines; manufacturing, purchase and sale of articles made of precious metal and stones; carrying out any operations with foreign currency; organization of general education schools. The above mentioned decision specified also certain activities which cooperatives may carry out only on the basis of an agreement concluded with state enterprise and organizations for which these kinds of activity are the main ones.

The law placed no restriction on the number of workers a cooperative might employ or the amount of its assets; and it granted cooperatives the right to issue shares to members in proportion to their contribution, and to grant members income in proportion to both their financial investment and the amount of their work, and to employ part-time workers on a contractual basis. The law imposed also restrictions on cooperatives. All cooperative members actually had to work in the business. Bonds could be sold only to cooperative members, to employees, to state enterprises, or to other cooperatives.

New types of economy and accordingly new types of organization were regulated by the decree 'Basis of Lease Relations in the USSR' and by the 'Regulations of Economic and Organization Grounds of Lease Relations in the USSR'. According to the amendment to the 'Law of State Enterprises', transfer to the lease could be carried out by the enterprise independently, without permission of a superior organization. A collective of the leased enterprise would independently decide the directions of its activity and control its production and its own income in accordance with existing legislation and the lease agreement. The supreme organ of control of a leased enterprise would become a General Meeting of Leaseholders. The term of the lease might be from 5 to 50 years.

The organization of leaseholders would realize its production at the prices established for state enterprises. Out of the receipts from the realization of production, first of all the rent would be paid and material expenses compensated. Out of the remaining amount taxes and other payments would be effected to the budget and interest on credit paid. The residual revenue would be used for payment of labour, for social activities of the enterprise and for strengthening the production potential. As practice has shown, leaseholders achieved their aims by raising the rationalization of production and eliminating the 'leading tutelage' on the part of Ministries.

The number of leased enterprises has increased rather quickly. In October 1988 there were 60 of them in industry, 15 in construction, 14 in trade and catering, 4 in health services. At the end of June 1989 there were 1,120 leased enterprises in industry, 449 in construction, 434 in retail trade, 139 in public catering. The above mentioned amendment to the 'Law of State Enterprises', which eliminated the necessity of superior organization permission for taking a lease, has caused a further increase in the number of leased enterprises.

The reservation expressed by opponents of this scheme is that it amounts to a re-privatization by stealth of substantial area of economic activity, especially in the agriculture sphere. Its proponents point out that such an arrangement would increase production where bottlenecks have existed and could lower production costs.

Moreover, academician Leonid Abalkin, at that time Deputy Prime Minister chairing a commission on economic reform, began in earnest to draft (Fall 1989) a new reform programme whose centrepiece were property rights. The draft of this radical reform made provision for de-nationalization (*nazgosudarstvlenie*) of the bulk of state property either 'de jure', by selling factories to workers or co-operatives, or 'de facto', through leasing factories to workers or co-operatives and leasing land to peasants. According to the programme, by 1995 at least 40 per cent of state enterprises (by value of capital stock) were to be converted to joint-stock companies; another third or more were to be operating on leases.

A final significant factor is that the 'Law on Cooperation' included special provisions granting collective farms, which previously were closely tied into state production and distribution plans, the right to govern their own production and to market it as they would see fit, either to state trading organizations or to other wholesale or retail buyers, or indeed to final consumers. Given that kolkhozy generate more than one third of the country's agricultural production, these stipulations represented a revolutionary innovation, even more significant than the introduction of NEP in the 1920s.

Spurred by the new legislation and surmounting many difficulties, Soviet entrepreneurs have wrought a phenomenal growth in the number of cooperatives. From 8,000 in autumn 1987, the number of operating cooperatives soared to 133,000 in July 1989 (see Table 6.1), while another 100,000 had been registered as for the latter date but were not yet operating. The value of goods and services produced by cooperatives has risen dramatically. Output, estimated at 350 million roubles for 1987, rose to more than 6 billion roubles in 1988, and in 1989 registered 4.3 billion roubles in the first quarter alone and a staggering 12.9 billion by the end of June.

The 1987 figure represented 0.1 per cent of Soviet national product, while the mid-1989 estimate put cooperative production at 2-3 per cent of all goods and services. What is striking here is that this increasing level of output is produced by only 1.5 per cent (without considering the 200-300,000 working individual enterprises) of the 130 million people in the Soviet labour force.

Table 6.1
Growth in the number of Soviet Cooperatives

Date	Number of operating cooperatives	Total employed in cooperatives
October 1, 1987	8,000	88,000
January 1, 1988	14,000	n.a.
January 1, 1989	77,500	1,392,000
July 1, 1989	133,000	2,900,000

Sources: *Moscow News*, n.28, 1989; *Ekonomicheskaya gazeta*, n. 37, 1989.

What is also important is the large number of people working in the black economy - approximately 20 million people - and the many agricultural sidelines. The sideline operations by the members and workers of collective farms account for a remarkably high proportion of overall production (26 per cent). The statistics are more significant still if one considers that the land area used for the sideline businesses is only a very small percentage of the total cultivated area. This suggests that the sidelines are highly productive or at least that a large proportion of further processing takes place in this sphere.

The assessment of the various measures designed to encourage initiative outside the socialist sector needs to underline that the effectiveness of the 'Law on Individual Enterprise' is limited by some restrictive provisions (a large number of activities are still prohibited; application must be made to responsible authorities for a license and self-employed businesses are only permitted to employ members of the proprietor's own family who live in the same household).

Compared with the above, the 'Law on Cooperation' is less restrictive. In spite of that, Soviet cooperatives face a number of serious obstacles. First of all, they do not receive sufficient financing from the state banking system. Cooperatives complain that loans are usually for small amounts and granted only on a short-term basis, thereby making it difficult for cooperatives to buy needed equipment. Cooperatives have also found it extremely difficult to obtain reliable access to supply: a problem aggravated by a dual pricing system, which often forces cooperatives to pay much higher prices than do state enterprises purchasing the same goods. This results in considerable insecurity in maintaining the desired level of output.

Secondly, as a market environment is introduced in a situation of severe disequilibrium, the sharpest among the entrepreneurs will indeed focus on trade and arbitrage rather than production. Quick fortunes are likely to be made in speculative activities, and those who earn them are not likely to have a great popularity.

If the results achieved by the new economic policies for the private sector are compared with the official expectations, the conclusion is a sobering one. There has hardly been any improvement in the supply of consumer goods and services; the black economy continues to flourish; hardly any labour has been transferred from state to private or cooperative sector; finally, no adequate reduction in distrust has been achieved.

In 1991 however, above all after the August aborted putsch, the private sector situation has enter a dynamic phase, along the following lines:

a) The most evident new phenomenon has been the creation of Trade Exchanges which, after the formal dissolution of GOSSNAB, try to organize a wholesale market. There are more than 400 exchanges, 50 of which have been established in Moscow. While an increasing part of inter-enterprise transactions takes place within these exchanges, they still exhibit a rather fragile structure. There are no laws regulating their activities and the transactions, often in dollars, are sometimes adventurous, as stable contractual modalities have yet to emerge.

b) The banking sector, following the lead of the commercial and the industrial sectors, has acquired a definite importance within private activities. At the end of 1991 in the USSR there were already more than 1,500 banks, while even greater is the number of joint-ventures that associate local and foreign capital, mainly in providing banking services to foreign residents.

c) A third phenomenon is that of "spontaneous" privatisation, arranged from below. Russian enterprises, for instance, can now be transformed into join stock companies, with ownership divided among the employees. In some cases the State retains a minority stake, but in others it hands over the complete control of the enterprise. The relevant laws, however, remain highly inadequate and contradictory.

Due to the lack of official statistics, it is difficult to evaluate the real importance of all these new phenomena. According to some estimates, about 20 million people are working in the private and semi-private sector (with respect to a total working population of 160 million). Their contribution to the GDP has been estimated at about 20 per cent in 1991, compared to 7 per cent in 1990.

These changes, however, have had a great diffusion mainly in trading activities, without affecting too much the industrial sector. The transition from a system dominated by state-ownership and central planning can be considered, so far, rather limited.

Reforms and the private economy in China

The Chinese communists seem to have been more successful than their Soviet counterparts in eradicating private business after consolidating their power, especially in the urban areas. The State began actual socialist transformation in 1953, the same year that the First Five Year Plan got underway. The process was expected to end in 1962. Through a process of joint ownership and then buying out of private shares the state took over large and medium private industrial firms. The state declared the victory of peaceful socialist transformation in 1956 when even the complete collectivization of agriculture was accomplished. China had thus gone very far in eliminating the legal private sector and much of the second economy, urban and rural.

The ten years of the Cultural Revolution (1966-1976) saw the apogee of politicization of the economy, including the denigration of experts, efficiency, consumption and markets. The post-Mao leadership under Deng Xiaoping formally shifted the focus of the party's work from class struggle to economic development: the achievement of the Four Modernizations. The aim of the programme is to forge ahead with the development of agriculture, industry, science and technology, and defence; the intention is to increase production and output several times over in each of these fields in order to catch up with developments elsewhere in the world. In order to achieve this aim by the year 2000, the party's intent is to mobilize all forces and groups within society by giving them a material interest in the success of this programme.

As the People's Republic of China also has the problem that its state enterprises and regulated production cooperatives do not generally work very productively, private economic initiative is intended to give a new impetus. First the leadership hoped to fill the gaps in food production by decollectivizing agriculture. To that end, in 1979 it introduced the Agricultural Responsibility System, in which individuals, families or groups sign contracts with the state to sell a certain amount of a crop at a state-determined price. Everything above that can be sold to the state at a negotiated price, or on the newly opened free markets. Farmers are also encouraged to develop sideline business.

In the cities, collective enterprises, mostly based in neighbourhoods, were seen as having the flexibility and appropriate scale to rapidly supply consumers. Individuals working for themselves could also perform this role.

In 1982, the National People's Congress published a new state constitution. Of central importance to private business is Article 11: 'The individual economy of urban and rural working people, operated within the limits prescribed by law, is a complement to the socialist public economy. The state protects the lawful rights and interests of the individual economy by exercising administrative control'. In April 1988, the National People's Congress voted to allow private businessmen to hire more than the previously permitted seven non-family employees, creating a new category of private business. In July 1988, it published a new set of regulations for these enterprises and also decreed that they could sign contracts with foreign business concerns.

By 1988, China had 12.6 million enterprises termed as 'individual business', which are 'family ventures', and 225,000 larger operations known as 'private businesses' taking urban and rural areas together but not including the millions of small farmers who produce on a private basis.

Table 6.2 reveals that the private sector grew very slowly in the first years after 1978. People were still quite sceptical about the government's sincerity. Their fears were confirmed in 1983 with the campaign to eliminate 'spiritual pollution'. This was supposed to be limited to pornography and other 'unhealthy tendencies', but party cadres used it as a pretext to harass private businessmen whose wealth they resented. The campaign, however, suffered a humiliating defeat and, in 1984, the party decided to press ahead with urban reforms. As the figures demonstrate, that year witnessed a tremendous explosion in the size of the private sector.

Table 6.2
Individual enterprises and employees in China

Year	Number of enterprises (millions)	Number of employees (millions)
1949-50	4.14	8.26
1956	0.43	0.51
1957	n.a.	1.04
1978	0.30	0.33
1979	0.56	0.68
1980	0.89	1.56
1981	1.50	2.57
1982	2.64	3.19
1983	5.86	7.55
1984	9.30	13.00
1985	11.69	17.57
1986	12.11	18.46
1987	13.72	20.16
1988	14.13	26.14

Source: *Beijing Review* (various issues).

In 1988, the National People's Congress officially recognized a new category, 'private business', for those companies with eight or more employees. Some businesses have as many as several hundred people on pay-roll. At the end of 1988 there were officially 225,000 'privately-managed enterprises' with 3.68 million employees. This figure included 115,000 privately-owned firms (with 1.85 million employees) and 100,000 collective and cooperatively-owned ventures (with a total of 1.83 million employees).

In contrast to the Soviet Union, China now has private businesses operating in almost all branches of both the productive economy and the service sector. The range goes from raw material extraction (e.g. small mines operated by farmers) via processing industries (e.g. fertilizer manufacture), hotels and restaurants, cinemas, theatres and other entertainment business, medical practices, private clinics and pharmacies, private school and kindergartens (42,000 in 1985 with 500,00 children in all) and banks through to the main areas of wholesale and retail trade and transport. An estimated 20-25 per cent of the country's total sales of goods are now attributable to private retailers (not including direct sales from farms), and this proportion can be expected to increase still further. According to Chinese accounts, private transport services are now responsible for carrying 40 per cent of all passengers or freight movements; however, this figure presumably only applies to local or intraregional traffics. In the industrial sector, private businesses' share of total output is much smaller at just 1 per cent, though the figure of 3 per cent is occasionally mentioned. It is interesting to note that 80 per cent of the private businesses are located in the countryside and a large proportion of these are connected to the building trade. This is due, among other factors, to the intense building activity among farmers, to the widespread tile-manufacturing business in rural areas and to a large pool of cheap labour available in the villages.

It is clear that the initiatives of private enterprises are indispensable for overcoming the bottlenecks and shortages which increasingly arise as the economy grows. Such initiatives are needed to ensure that enough raw materials and other inputs are made available, to put up the funding for new businesses or expansions of existing ones, to improve the nation's financial position and to generate jobs. Creating a sufficient number of jobs, in particular, may well only be possible in the future with the private sector's help, for the Chinese economy is faced with the task of finding work for at least 300 million farmers and farm workers by about the year 2000, as technical progress in agriculture makes them redundant. On top of that, about another 20 million employees in state enterprises could be made redundant by measures to improve productivity. Finally, there will be an especially large number of school-leavers coming on to the labour market in the years immediately ahead. The Party hopes that some of the newly available labour will be taken up by the establishment of new businesses in the individual sector and the creation of more jobs by private businesses. The hope has been expressed that the current number of 225,000 private businesses might be increased ten times, raising the numbers employed in them from 3.6 to 36 million. Another indication that the number of private-sector employees really would increase by many times is provided by estimates, or at least wishful thinking, from planners in Peking which assume 50 million employees in that sector in the early 1990s.

For several years, the reformists made strenuous efforts to develop the private sector, and even experimented with privatization and share flotation in selected state enterprises. However, since the conservatives gained political predominance (June 1989) they have criticized the privatization policy and have stressed the predominant position and leading role of large and medium-sized state enterprises. They have also introduced more stringent measures to control and rectify the private sector for the purpose of resolving such problems as unfair distribution of income and serious tax evasion. This, of course, will contribute to the sound development of the private sector. However, the samples about further policy changes and deviations in policy implementation by cadres may dampen the enthusiasm for production on the part of entrepreneurs in the private sector.

In a meeting in October 1989 Ren Zhonghin, director of the State Industry and Commerce Administration, declared that China's private and individual businesses should still be protected while supervision work in this area must be strengthened. There must be a balanced policy that does not overstress private ownership to the detriment of state-ownership, Ren said. Similarly, private ownership must not be neglected.

However, statistics presented at the meeting show that the number of Chinese engaged in private businesses dropped from 23 million by the end of 1988 to 19.43 million by the first half of 1989. The main reason behind the decrease, according to the State Industry and Commerce Administration, was that with the State's rectification of private businesses, many illegal businessmen and those who registered with local authorities but actually were not engaged in business were suspended. Many private enterprises and individuals had to close their business because they could not afford expensive and limited raw materials and fuels, and because of the restraints on loans and credit decided by the State. More individual firms, moreover, were gradually eliminated from market competition because of bad management, poor information, backward technology and low-quality of production.

Conclusions

From the above analysis the following general observations can be drawn.

a) In the Soviet Union and China reformers have tried to introduce market processes in order to improve the efficiency of their economies. In so doing they found out that they had to face the issue of ownership of land and capital assets. In other words property rights and the sequence of reform are closely linked.

The question of whether or not markets can function efficiently in the absence of divisible and transferable private property ownership of capital assets is an old one. It is the 'socialist controversy', held in the 1930s, over the possibility of achieving efficient resource allocation under socialism in practice. Ludwig von Mises argued that efficient outcomes were impossible under socialism. The absence of capital markets in public ownership meant that prices of products could not reflect the opportunity cost of the capital used in their production. He argued, in effect, that efficient evaluations can be revealed only through rivalrous behaviour of owners seeking to put capital to its highest valued use. Rising to that fundamental challenge, Oscar Lange devised a model of 'competitive market socialism' that implicitly denied that property ownership mattered. Efficient markets could be held under state ownership with trail and error pricing by a central planning board and instructions to managers to follow the behavioural rules enforced in an environment of pure competition. Although Friedrick Hayek and Abram Bergson denied the efficiency of the Lange proposal, they did not address the matter of property rights 'per se'. Don Lavoie defends and elaborates the position taken by Mises. Lavoie points out that under private property, decision makers risk their own capital, competing for its use in various uncertain outcomes, whereas 'When property is common, all decision makers are part of a joint project and they cannot contend with one another in their manner'. In that case, society's capital has to be administratively allocated or reallocated to 'better' uses. But these better uses cannot be ascertained without correct (efficient) prices and profit signals, which are lacking.

In fact, reformers in the Soviet Union and China argue that property rights matter greatly and that markets of capital assets are essential. Decades of experience with a production system based on socially owned property have revealed that the basic problems are inefficient allocation of resources, wasteful use of resources, poor quality of products and sluggish growth. So far, social ownership and central allocation of resources have prevented a capital market.

On the other hand market socialism (prevailing state property plus market coordination) experimented in Yugoslavia and Hungary did not yield the desired outcomes. This decentralized approach presents two fundamental defects. The first is the question of property relations. The decentralized enterprise lacking an owner with an interest in the value of the firm, would still have been grossly inefficient in investment, wage-setting and recruitment. The second is, according to Janos Kornai, the financial environment of the socialist enterprises which permits the existence of a 'soft budget constraint': enterprises' spending is not limited to their own resources plus borrowing on commercial terms, because prices play virtually no role and the socialist manager generates continuous excess demand for inputs, a level of demand that can never be met. Thus, without widespread private ownership of the means of production and freedom of enterprise, the market system will be an ineffective sham. Consequently in both countries many economists suggested to political leaders that they had to introduce more private property rights to improve those markets. Similar developments were occurring in China, before June 1989.

b) Great importance is attached to expanding the private sector in both the USSR and the People's Republic of China. Nevertheless, the conditions under which private economic activity is required to take place differ greatly between the two countries.

In the first place theoretical discussion of the private sector in China is conducted for the most part with an undogmatic approach. In the Soviet Union, on the other hand, the exploitation line of argument still plays a considerable part, and this is one of the factors contributing to the fact that paid workers may not be employed by private businesses and that access to a large number of economic activities is prohibited to private individuals.

Then there are substantial differences in the quantitative importance of the private sector economy. Agriculture in China has now already been largely privatized. More than 90 per cent of agricultural production now comes from the large number of small family farms and the compulsory purchase by the state was transformed, up to 1985, into a purchase by contract. Not surprisingly the 1985-86 Chinese agricultural crisis has revealed the system of purchase by contract to be just another instrument of state power on the production and distribution decisions. Similarly the Soviet recommendations on the leasing system in agriculture can in principle be put on a par with the Chinese responsibility system. But, in fact, the peasant farmer is still not a private owner either in China or in the USSR. In the Soviet Union, however, the individual sideline enterprises in the agricultural sector have only been tolerated so far. Even today their legal position does not have a firm foundation. In the other sectors also autonomous private enterprises or cooperatives play a far lesser part in the Soviet Union than they do in China, where 15 per cent of all industrial production is attributable to cooperatives, 3 per cent to the 'individual sector' and 80 per cent to state enterprises.

c) If we accept the economic implications of points a) and b) we have to conclude that the situation in the USSR is tending to change suddenly.

In the Soviet Union, although some economists have made radical proposals on the issue of property rights, so far formal ownership rights, either in industrial or agricultural sectors, remain unchanged. Although enterprises are given more freedom of action about the use of socially-owned property and the disposition of profits, there is no competitive market either for capital or for products. As Gertrude E. Schroeder has argued, and her point is still valid after the August 1991 coup,

> the effort to produce ownership mentality and behaviour in firms will be frustrated, because managers and workers do not have divisible and transferable rights to the firm's property, because the firm remains formally subordinated to a government agency and because its activities and the use of its profits are regulated by numerous government set rules, proscriptions and prescriptions. Thus the firm is likely to remain basically risk-averse and centre-oriented, as is now the case. (Schroeder, 1988)

Actually the transition from 'real Soviet socialism' to the market system will involve enormous political and economic problems. In fact to have any hope of implementing their privatization programme the Soviet and the Chinese governments must not only liberate all forms of private economic activity, including those now denounced as speculation, but even guarantee by law the enforcement of private contracts, secure private property rights, create a credit system favouring the private sector rather then the government-owned monopolies, and finally command 'social respect' for private economic activity. There is no precedent for these structural changes, and it would be an understatement to say that it would be difficult to attain.

References

Bergson, A. (1967), 'Market Socialism Revisited', *Journal of Political Economy*, n.4, December.

Bohnet, A., and Jaehne, G. (1989), 'The Private Sector in the Soviet Union and China', *Intereconomics*, n. 2, March-April.

Brus, W., and Laski, K. (1989), *From Marx to the Market: Socialism in Search of an Economic System*, Clarendon Press, Oxford.

Golo, T.B. (1989), 'Urban Private Business in China', *Studies in Comparative Communism*, n.2.

Kornai, J. (1986), 'The Hungarian Economic Reform Process: Visions, Hopes and Reality', *Journal of Economic Literature*, December.

Lavoie, D. (1985), *Rivalry and Central Planning: The Socialist Calculation Debate Reconsidered*, Cambridge University Press, New York.

Lockett, M. (1986), 'Small Business and Socialism in Urban China', *Development and Change*, n. 1.

MaJisen, (1988), 'A General Survey of the Resurgence of Private Sector of China's Economy', *Social Science in China*, n. 3.

Pomorski, P. (1988), 'Privatization of the Soviet Economy under Gorbachev', Berkeley-Duke Occasional Papers on the Second Economy, n. 13, October.

Roucek, L. (1988), 'Private Enterprise in Soviet Political Debates', *Soviet Studies*, n.1, January.

Schroeder, G. E. (1988), 'Property Rights Issues in Economic Reforms in Socialist Countries', *Studies in Comparatives Communism*, n.2.

7 The reform of industrial enterprises in East European economies and the incentives to export

MARIE LAVIGNE

Foreword

This article refers to a 'pretransition' stage in the East European reforms. Since the time of writing, the Central European countries (Czechoslovakia, Hungary, Poland) have engaged in the transition to the market, Bulgaria and Romania have initiated a similar shift, the Soviet reform of foreign trade has been engulfed in the general disintegration of the country.

What has changed in the field of foreign trade? All these countries have taken steps to dismantle the foreign trade state monopoly which existed under central planning. There were many good reasons for suppressing the foreign trade organizations: (i) as a necessary component of a policy of privatization and liberalization; (ii) as a requirement from international organizations (EEC, World Bank, EBRD etc.) whose help is needed for the transition; (iii) as an instrument for opening up the economy.

In actual fact, in 1990 and 1991 there was a correlation between the progress of reforms and the surge in exports to the West. The growth of exports was strongest in Poland, Hungary and to a lesser extent Czechoslovakia. Such results may be explained by a successful decentralization of decision-making to enterprises in the field of foreign trade, and by the beginning of privatization in the foreign trade sector. In particular, small-scale private import-export activities have been booming, often on a semi-legal basis. Macroeconomic policies have also their share in these achievements, such as the devaluation of the domestic currency linked with a shift towards internal convertibility (virtually achieved in Poland and Hungary), and a foreign trade policy geared towards the West and away from the traditional CMEA partners. However large-scale restructuring has yet to occur in the industrial sector and consequently in the organization of foreign trade, as a result of the mass privatization of big enterprises. In none of the countries under review is there a clear concept of what should replace the former foreign trade organizations: should they be disbanded, replaced by foreign trade commercial companies, incorporated into the industrial enterprises? No significant pattern is yet emerging.

Introduction

In Eastern Europe and the USSR, the changes which occurred since the early eighties in the traditional state trading system stem from two major ideas, to be found also in the domestic economic reforms. First, foreign trade is now considered as an economic activity of the firm, and not as a set of administrative procedures. Therefore, production firms have to be involved directly in the foreign trade process, either through a closer cooperation with the foreign trade organizations (FTOs) or by trading on their own account. The degree of flexibility of state monopoly depends on the extent to which the domestic reform itself has liberalized the economic activity in each country. Second, the production units have to be interested in the outcome of their foreign trade activity just as they are in the outcome of their domestic activity, through material incentives. Foreign trade will not be successful if conducted through plan commands. We find here the twin ideas of autonomy and incentives which lay at the bottom of the domestic reforms.

This obvious link between domestic management of enterprise and foreign economic activity has to be supplemented with a reverse link. The constraints in foreign economic relations, in the framework of a growing openness which mainly applies to the USSR, Hungary and Poland, and also partly to Bulgaria and Czechoslovakia, react on the enterprise reform. The most significant case is that of joint ventures. In need of foreign capital, these countries have tended to relax the rules on direct foreign investment so as to make it more attractive. New regulations have been adopted end-1988. In parallel, the domestic legal framework for business activities has been liberalized. 'Company' laws are meant to expand the private sector (Hungary, Poland) and to revamp the state-owned sector through the creation of stock ownership (Poland, Hungary, and in a preliminary form the USSR, in 1988). In the case of Poland and Hungary, it is not just a new step toward a market economy, but also a way of solving the problem of foreign debt. While Hungary offers its enterprises for sale (the buy-out of Tungsram by an Austrian consortium in April 1989 is a striking case), the Polish debt rescheduling scheme (tentative, June 1989) suggests that debt-for-equity swaps might become a major instrument of repayment.

In this presentation, I shall elaborate mainly on the first line. It is clear, however, that the emergence of domestic capital markets, due to external constraints probably even more than to internal political developments, may in the future strongly affect the management of foreign trade and economic relations.

The changes in the state trading system

The very reference to state trading is now discarded in several countries, to begin with Hungary where the leadership wants to ban the concept in the country's relations with the West. Even in the least reforming countries, the traditional state trading system is gradually evolving. But despite the official statements, the actual rights of the enterprises remain constrained for economic reasons, the state of the balance of payments remaining the most compelling.

In Hungary, beginning in 1988, all enterprises, whatever their activity, may export and import under the condition that they register at the Ministry of Foreign Trade for the goods or services which they want to export or import. In 1989, the number of enterprises engaged in foreign trade had already soared to 600, including private firms, and this number should reach one thousand in 1990. However, not all the goods or services may be traded that way. In trade with socialist countries, the enterprises have still assigned tasks from above, due to the necessity of implementing the agreements concluded with the other Comecon countries. In trade with capitalist countries, about 58 per cent of Hungarian exports and 48 per cent of imports are covered by restrictions, meaning that the non-specialized (in foreign trade) agencies cannot obtain rights for exporting or importing the relevant goods. Not only bureaucratic structures impede the liberalization of foreign trade. Firm managers especially appreciate the newly acquired rights in certain fields, for example in the import of spare parts of specific semi-products. However, it has been noticed that firms prefer to trade though the FTOs for traditional foreign trade deals, e.g. for raw materials and basic semi-finished goods imports and for the export of traditional goods.

In Poland, reforms tending towards an increase in the firms' rights to carry out foreign trade have not yet proved fruitful. Poland had begun earlier than other countries, but experiments with 'pilot firms' which got underway in 1973, were shelved almost immediately due to the world crisis and the growing indebtedness of the country. In the framework of the Polish economic reform of 1982, enterprises in the manufacturing industry were granted the right to export directly if they held a trade permit delivered by the Ministry of Foreign Trade. The granting of the permit was subject to certain criteria: the enterprise had to export at least 5 per cent of its production (since 1988; originally, 25 per cent), or for a minimum amount which was initially fixed at 1 billion zlotys (since 1988: 4 billion). Other firms were supposed to be able to chose between FTOs in order to make the FTOs compete with each other. In 1988 this right to export or import on their own account without any prior permit was granted to firms supplying or buying specific goods according to a list drawn by the ministry of Foreign trade (78 export goods, 20 import goods). Finally, beginning in 1989, no permit is necessary except for importing or exporting specific goods. On the import side the list mainly includes food items, medicines, and some strategic raw materials. On the export side it includes all raw materials and all goods which are subject to quotas and restrictions on Western markets. The FTOs themselves have been reorganized. The traditional FTOs have been retained only for coal and strategic raw materials. For other goods, the FTOs have been transformed into FTC (foreign trade companies) in which the Polish state has the majority of shares.

As a result of these measures, already by 1987, 250 state enterprises, 45 cooperatives and 200 small firms had the right to trade with foreign partners. By the end of 1988, the overall number of such units exceeded 1,700. One can hardly say, however, that these measures helped to reduce the scope of the state monopoly. In the light of Poland's financial constraints, the enterprises have better access to foreign trade and especially to import if they use the FTOs or

FTCs. They do not really compete with the FTOs in the field of foreign trade. In fact, even with the liberalization process, export or import transactions remain subject to licensing. Up to 1988, a licence had to be issued by the Ministry of Foreign Trade for each transaction, since then general licences may be issued for transactions similar in kind.

Bulgaria has several times reformed its foreign trade organization, in 1978, 1979, 1982 and 1986, along with the rather disorderly pace of its economic reform. Since 1982, different types of foreign trade organizations have come into existence. Several FTOs specialising in engineering have been set up, particularly for the export of complete sets of equipment to developing or to socialist countries. There seems thus to be a decentralization of foreign trade management. One must remember that the industrial structure is very concentrated in Bulgaria, with about 140 'economic associations' only. The devolution of foreign trade rights is by no means the end of the foreign trade monopoly. True, the decision adopted in December 1988 by the Bulgarian Communist Party plenum suggests a deep restructuring of industry with the 'firm' to become the new unit of management. The outcome of the following legislation adopted in January 1989 is yet far from clear, especially after the new course taken in the end of 1989.

When Czechoslovakia cautiously decided to follow the Soviet path of prestavba (the Czech word for perestroika), the foreign trade sector also benefited from some decentralization. According to measures taken end-1986, about a quarter of the Czechoslovak export of machinery has been transferred to the competence of the production enterprises and is no longer controlled by the Ministry of Foreign Trade. The Czechoslovak law on the socialist enterprise adopted in 1988, following the Soviet model of 1987, embodies increased rights for the enterprises in the field of foreign trade. However, knowing the reluctance of the Czechoslovak leadership to abandon the traditional principles of central planning, one could doubt that radical changes would soon affect the foreign trade sector. Here again, the shift toward a market-type economy announced end-1989 leaves the door open for radical changes.

In Romania, the December 1980 law 'on the strengthening of self-management and financial autonomy in foreign trade' amended the 1971 law on foreign trade activities and economic, scientific and technical cooperation. According to the 1980 law, most of the 55 FTOs were directly subordinated to branch industrial ministries, or incorporated in the large enterprises, and only 9 remained directly subordinated to the Ministry of Foreign Trade and Economic Cooperation. A further 'reform' re-centralized the system and re-attached the FTOs to the Ministry of Foreign Trade (Lhomel, 1987). The restructuring of the Romanian industry and trade following the end of Ceaucescu's rule should bring about decentralization in due course.

In the GDR, the restructuring of industry into 'combines' (148 since 1979) has brought about the reorganization of foreign trade. In 1984, of the 53 FTOs, these combines have absorbed 22 (these are major industrial units such as Carl Zeiss Iena, Robotron, the Magdeburg engineering works, etc.), 20 come under an industrial ministry and cater for the enterprises subordinated to that ministry, while another 5 are still attached to the Ministry of Foreign Trade, mainly in the field of service trade. In 1981 the FTOs subordinated to ministries were subdivided into narrowly specialized so-called 'firms' (in the chemical, electrotechnical and electronic industries), each one working for a combine. 64 combines benefited from this last measure, mainly in the chemical and machine-tools industry. In 1990 all combines are to be allowed to export and import, and should be granted the right of borrowing in hard currency.

In all the various reforms carried out by the Eastern European countries, there is above all the desire to integrate production and marketing activities. The Ministries of Foreign Trade have had their functions considerably reduced on the microeconomic level, while basically retaining their controlling and coordinating role at the macro level.

Up to 1986, the USSR appeared as far behind these reforms. All this was dramatically changed in 1986. The restructuring of foreign trade was launched by a joint decree issued by the Central Committee of the Communist Party and the Council of Ministers on August 19, 1986, followed by various regulations and decisions in 1987, 1988 and 1989. Among these regulations, the most substantial is the Decree of the Council of Ministers published on December 2, 1988, 'On the further development of the foreign economic activities conducted by state, cooperative and other social enterprises, associations and organizations'. This decree was followed by technical implementation measures in March 1989, which however marked a step backwards from the devised liberalization.

The Soviet approach is specific in the way it has integrated foreign trade and domestic economic reforms. Unlike in the case of the other countries, the foreign trade reform was not a by-product of the domestic reform but came first, under the pressure of the external constraint. In 1986, following the fall of world oil prices, it became obvious that the standard Soviet export model, oriented toward the export of oil and gas as hard-currency earners, could no longer be continued. Thus it was decided to prepare a restructuring of Soviet exports, and to create the conditions allowing the Soviet industry to develop the export of manufactured goods. However it made little sense to give the Soviet enterprises increased rights in the field of foreign trade while in the management of their domestic activity they had hardly any autonomy. Thus the measures adopted in the field of foreign trade largely pulled the developments occurring in the internal perestroika process.

Since 1986, foreign trade activities are controlled and coordinated through a new body, the State Commission on Foreign Economic Relations (the acronym in Russian is GVK). The new body is a sort of super-ministry which chairman has the rank of Deputy Prime Minister. The current management of foreign trade is conducted by a Ministry of Foreign Economic Relations which since January 1988 replaced the former Ministry of Foreign Trade and the State Committee for Foreign Economic Relations (GKES) which used to deal with cooperation agreements with developing and socialist countries. The aim of such a merger is to integrate trade stricto sensu and cooperation activities. Again to symbolize this widening of perspective, the Foreign Trade Bank has changed it name and became the Bank for Foreign Economic Activities (Russian acronym *Vneshnekonombank* or VEB). Finally, still in the framework of the state monopoly on foreign trade, foreign trade rights were given to 21 ministries and central agencies and to individual enterprises which were 68 in 1987 and amounted to over 90 end-1988. In addition the federated Soviet Republics also got foreign trade rights on their own, allowing them to set their FTOs. The distribution of competences between the revamped traditional actors (the Ministry of Foreign Economic Relations and its FTOs) and the new actors (industrial ministries and enterprises) had a rationale. The traditional procedures still applied to trade in raw materials, fuels, food products, to imports of turnkey plants and large sets of machinery, to cooperation based upon inter-governmental agreements. The new setting mainly concerned trade in manufactured goods (and primarily machinery and chemicals). In 1987, approximately 25 per cent of the Soviet foreign trade was affected by these changes.

As from April 1, 1989, all interested enterprises and organizations (state, cooperative or belonging to 'social organizations' such as trade unions, associations, etc.) 'which are competitive on foreign markets' (text of the December 1988 decree) were given the right of access to foreign markets. This right is only subject to registration. Import has to be financed by exports. The GVK is entitled to deprive from this right any enterprise in cases of 'unfair competition' (a way of preventing the enterprises from fixing dumping prices) or of 'activities damageable to the interests of state'. To conduct foreign trade activities, the enterprises may set up any type of foreign trade organizations ('unions, consortia, various associations, joint stock companies, merchant houses and others, with the participation of the producers (of goods and services), the foreign trade organizations, and if needed with the participation of banks, supply organizations and other').

These opportunities are however not easy to finalize. By a decree of March 7, 1989 'on measures ensuring state regulation of foreign economic activities', a general ban was placed on any barter or trading (middleman) activity, meaning that in principle economic entities should only buy what they will use, or sell what they have produced. Barter is also forbidden to joint ventures unless they are specifically authorized by the Ministry of foreign economic relations. Cooperatives are totally excluded from such activities. State enterprises may engage into trading only on the basis of case by case licences. Complaints have been numerous. Many enterprises stress that to limit trade to buying or selling one's own production may create severe constraints. The alternative is to use the state FTOs which are considered as quite ineffective. In fact, the reason for such regulations may be found in the early moves of some enterprising cooperatives which engaged in trading activities, especially buying abroad and re-selling in the Soviet Union video equipment, computers, with huge returns as the domestic prices for such goods are very high.

The right to export or import is not extended to producers or users of goods the trade of which is to be regulated centrally. As before, the FTOs of the Ministry of foreign economic relations are to manage the export of fuels and raw materials, the import of agricultural goods, raw materials, a large share of the intermediate goods (for instance, tubes for pipelines), equipment for new projects. This already excludes from free trade over 80 per cent of the Soviet exports to OECD countries, and probably more than 50 per cent of Soviet imports to begin with. In addition, export and import rights are to be limited by restrictions, in cases when a licence is needed in addition to the registration [1].

Finally, for all the goods produced under the procedure of a 'state order' (*goszakaz*), that is, earmarked for the domestic market, the enterprises will not be free to divert a part of their production to the foreign markets. All this taken into account, there might be cases when a Soviet enterprise will contract with a foreign partner, then be unable to fulfill its obligations.

All this set of complex rules shows how difficult it is to combine openness to world trade and domestic policy requirements, when the authorities wish at the same time to retain the planning principle and to implement the market rationale but not to allow too easy gains.

The reforms implemented in the Eastern European countries and the USSR assume that the enterprises will be willing to engage in foreign trade, first and foremost to get new markets in developed market economies. What are the incentives provided ?

The incentives to export

In the traditional foreign trade management the enterprises were paid by the FTOs at domestic prices and in domestic currency for their exports, though this could include the particular expenses incurred for a specific order (better quality packaging, different paintwork, additional devices for a machine, etc.). Apart from this, there was no distinction between working for export of for the domestic market.

This traditional pattern was altered much earlier in Eastern Europe than in the USSR, along different ways. Incentive procedures have been introduced to encourage firms to export, especially to countries with convertible currencies. These procedures went hand in hand with an overall reduction of compulsory planning indices for foreign trade. The incentive system was designed to support the centralized policy decisions as to the directions of exports and their composition. It did not mean *per se* a departure from the monopoly of foreign trade and just appeared as a change in the instruments of central regulation.

But so as to make Eastern exports competitive on foreign markets, it was soon acknowledged that exporters should be more deeply involved in gaining revenue from their foreign currency earnings. So as to achieve this, their proceeds had be converted into domestic currency at a realistic rate of exchange. In addition, it was suggested that the enterprise should have the right to directly retain a share in the total amount of hard currency earned, or should be given other means to earn foreign currency.

The nature of the incentive is thus linked with the degree of autonomy allowed to the enterprise in the field of foreign trade. When autonomy is limited, granting an export incentive is a way of rewarding the enterprise for an adequate implementation of the foreign trade plan. When the enterprise is allowed to operate on foreign markets directly, it has to be able to import as well as to export, so as to buy abroad the investment goods required for a successful export strategy. This may be achieved through a retention right of part of the foreign currency earnings. The ultimate stage of the process is logically internal convertibility, allowing resident enterprises to buy and sell foreign currency.

All these solutions are now applied or tested in various ways. Most often, the exporting firm receives the equivalent in domestic currency of its foreign currency earnings converted by means of a coefficient. The coefficient is usually determined as the average cost (in domestic currency) required to obtain one unit of foreign currency from export for a weighted basked of exports. It may therefore be that earnings in domestic currency, once calculated in this way, turn out to be below the price which would be obtained on the domestic market. In this case a subsidy may be used as a bonus over the average conversion coefficient. A set of differentiated coefficients thus emerge, by currency areas and often by products or groups of products, so as to stimulate exports.

Western experts and also economists from socialist countries have often argued that such coefficients ought to be calculated as the marginal cost of earning a unit of foreign currency. This would avoid the need for subsidies; some enterprises would earn very high profits, but those might then be taxed if necessary.

The GDR is the only country which by 1989 had not significantly integrated the foreign trade results of the enterprises (combines) in the overall results of the enterprise activity. However conversion coefficients are applied to calculate the amount of export earnings. These coefficients are only differentiated by currency areas (convertible currencies, clearing, transferable rouble), but subsidies over the coefficient do apply if the calculated price is inferior to the usual domestic one.

For the countries which have introduced a 'realistic' exchange rate deriving from the conversion coefficients (Hungary since 1976, Romania - quite cosmetically, with reservations as to the 'realism' of the rate - since 1981, Poland since 1982 and Czechoslovakia since 1989) this new commercial rate replaced both the former 'official' overvalued rate and the multiple conversion coefficients. However subsidies did not altogether disappear. The case of Hungary is significant. When it was decided, in 1980, that Hungary's domestic wholesale prices (for around 60 per cent of output from the processing industry) would be fixed as so-called 'competitive prices' based on world prices, firms which could only make a loss if they respected these prices obtained subsidies which were 10-16 per cent of the total price plus an 'exchange rate subsidy' equal to up to 20 per cent of the current rate. In principle, export subsidies are gradually to be phased out in Hungary. However the fulfilment of this policy aim could be uneasy as at the same time exports are being encouraged as much as possible. Poland has equally committed itself to phase out subsidies except for agricultural goods and shipbuilding. But it is very difficult to assess the actual operation of the complicated Polish system of 'Price Equalization Account' which has the aim of insulating domestic producers from the adverse effect of world prices.

The USSR is heading toward the introduction of a 'realistic exchange rate' as from January 1, 1991. Already since 1987, the export proceeds are recalculated in domestic currency by using special differentiated currency coefficients applied to the official foreign exchange rate for converting values expressed in foreign prices. Here the Soviet Union follows what was already for a time the practise of other Eastern European countries. But it does so in a much greater confusion. There is a great number of coefficients, up to 3,000, and perhaps even more. The rates vary from 0.2 to 6.6 (a coefficient of 1 means that the rate applied is the official rate of exchange, for instance, end-1988, $ 1 = 0.6 rouble. A coefficient of 2 means that the amount of roubles allotted for 1 dollar is doubled, i.e. equal to 1.2 rouble for $ 1). The reason for it is that the domestic prices in the USSR are still more irrational than in other countries, with relative prices widely diverging from the 'world' relative prices. The coefficients are supposed to be reduced in number when the price reform is implemented, but this will not be the case before 1991 at best. The price reform itself is supposed to 'bring nearer' the Soviet and the world relative prices, but the very concept of 'world prices' is highly controversial, especially for manufactured goods. The wording mainly suggests that the domestic prices for raw materials (food included) should be raised, and the prices for manufactured goods decreased. But apart from this principle, there is no precise concept for this reform, which in turn should command the revision of the currency coefficients and ultimately the introduction of a rational exchange rate of the rouble. For the time being, the wide dispersion of the coefficients distorts the measure of the efficiency of exports and may create perverse effects (encouraging costly exports or dissuading from efficient imports).

According to the December 1988 decree quoted above, this system is to be replaced by another one, based upon an exchange rate reform. Beginning from January 1, 1990, there will be a 100 per cent bonus to the rate of exchange of the free convertible currencies against the rouble. This means in principle that the multiple coefficients (vis-à-vis the 'dollar' area) are to be replaced by a single one, through the introduction of a 100 per cent bonus over the present official exchange rate of the rouble. This new rate (amounting to a coefficient of 2 according to the above definitions) will be used for converting the export gains of the state Soviet enterprises into roubles for their accountancy. As for many enterprises the new rate will not ensure export profitability, there will probably again be a set of additional subsidies. In fact, already by the end of 1989, the Soviet authorities seemed to be contemplating a two-tier commercial exchange rate already for 1990, close to the present official rate for raw materials and fuels, and 5 times that official rate, in roubles per dollar, for manufactured goods. This would clearly act as an export subsidy to the producers of manufactured goods, and also delay the implementation of a single rate perhaps well after 1991.

In most countries, enterprises may now retain a part of their hard currency earnings, with which they may purchase from abroad the intermediate goods they require to expand their exports, finance such expenses as participation in trade fairs, etc. In most cases this is a right on a certain amount of hard currency, not the immediate availability of the currency itself. The distinction is far from trivial. The rate of retention is usually small, and the right to use the retained currency is subject to dire restrictions.

All the previous incentives are just substitutes to internal convertibility allowing any domestic enterprise to buy foreign currency so as to engage in foreign trade activities, or to sell it at a good rate. In Hungary, the enterprises allowed to engage in foreign trade activities may buy the currency they need for their imports, from the National Bank, but only for buying the goods for which they are authorized. This excludes the bulk of equipment goods. The foreign exchange monopoly is strictly maintained although the banking system itself has been decentralized. It is expected to introduce in 1989 a small foreign currency market between commercial banks and the National Bank; this market should be fully operational by 1990. By 1990 also, most of the restrictions on hard-currency imports are to be lifted. This will bring about an increase in imports and a worsening of the trade balance, which might then require some kind of restrictive regulation.

A proxy to internal convertibility is a currency auction market. This has been introduced first in Poland, in 1983. Such auctions take place twice a month since 1987 (before then, they were irregular). The tenderers put forward those projects for which they require imports. A selection committee grants the hard currency at the current official rate, to the highest bidder. The criteria followed by the committee include the value of the exports resulting from the imports to be made, the value and the type of the good to be exported. All the enterprises of the socialized sector (state and cooperative) may take part in the auctions. The hard currency is provided by the enterprises wishing to sell their hard currency rights. The total price paid by a given buyer is the contract price in zlotys paid to the seller of hard currency rights, the price paid to the Export Development Bank for the purchase of the corresponding amount of currency, at the official rate, and the fee paid to the Bank. The $/zloty rates derived from these auction prices are very near the black market rates, i.e. 4-5 times the official commercial rate. In fact the mechanism is described here in a very simplified way, and one can identify several channels through which enterprises can actually have access to hard currency, thus creating a segmented 'market' for hard currency. The legalization of the private hard currency black market in March 1989 may add to these opportunities. These measures are supposed to help the introduction of a convertibility of the zloty in 1990. The nineteen devaluations of the zloty in 1989 have almost brought the official rate to the level of the free market rate.

Bulgaria has introduced a somewhat comparable procedure to Polish hard currency auctions in 1988. Following the Polish and Bulgarian practice, the Soviet reform of December 1988 provides for auctions of hard currency to be organized under the auspices of the Bank for foreign trade activities. These auctions would offer hard currency sold by enterprises or cooperatives, as well as 'from centralized funds'. As foreign experiences show, such auctions, especially if they are conducted on a rather narrow basis and if the demand largely exceeds the supply, lead to an exchange rate sometimes higher than the black market one, and the first auction held in November 1989 confirmed that point. Even so it may be advantageous in cases when the enterprise may hope to legally 'recover' only 10 per cent of the hard currency it is entitled to as in the procedure described above.

Thus the desire to provide enterprises with incentives to export has already led several socialist countries to contemplate the full implications of internal convertibility. But here the balance of payments constraints act as a powerful brake to substantial moves towards convertibility. Such constraints may be alleviated by Western help, as might be the case for Poland and Hungary, and maybe also several other countries, in 1990.

Joint ventures: export generating entities or debt relief schemes ?

Let us first review the latest regulations. End-1988, the Hungarian Parliament passed two laws, a Company Act and a Foreign Investment Act, which entered in force beginning 1989. Both acts combined should as well facilitate the setting of joint ventures by Hungarian individuals. The Foreign Investment Act provides tax incentives for joint ventures operating in fields of high priority, or in the case when the annual profit is small, which should encourage the setting up of such ventures by small enterprises.

Poland has altered its legislation several times since 1976, making it more restrictive in 1979, and then providing more favourable terms for foreign capital since 1982. The 1986 law was meant to attract other partners to different sectors, and namely high-technology engineering industries. The lack of enthusiasm of the investors prompted the authorities to relax the rules, especially the taxation ones, and to ease the conditions on the resale of the hard currency earnings, as of January 1, 1989. The new law ('On Economic Activity with the participation of foreign parties') of December 23, 1988 is in fact a mix of the previous legislation, both favouring small joint ventures wholly foreign-owned (however, with a minimum amount of investment), and larger companies (joint stock or limited liability) in priority sectors.

The main feature of the Czechoslovak approach is its cautiousness. The joint ventures were admitted in 1986 only and for three years the rules applied to joint ventures were in fact a compendium of various texts providing a legal framework. As from January 1, 1989, there is a single legal framework, the Act 'On Enterprises with foreign property participation'. The new Act does not limit foreign equity to a share of 49 per cent as previously, but it is to be expected that the authorities will dissuade the partners from giving too high a share to the capitalist party. The Western partners are not particularly attracted by favourable fiscal rules: the Czechoslovak regulations are the most dissuasive. A few sectors are to be developed through joint ventures, including electronics, machine-tools, special chemicals, and tourism. The new course taken by Czechoslovakia since the end of 1989 may increase the openness to foreign direct investment. In the GDR a similar evolution might induce the setting up of a joint venture regulation, though probably more strict than in other countries as to the share of foreign equity allowed.

The case of the Soviet Union is certainly the most fascinating. The legislation on the joint ventures developed in several stages. The decree setting the framework of the foreign trade reform, of August 19, 1986, barely mentioned the possibility of creating co-enterprises with Western (as well as with socialist) participation. Later on a decree of January 13, 1987, provided the first comprehensive set of rules, along with it a great number of contradictions and obscurities which were only partly lifted in September 1987 by a new set of regulations. Finally the December 2, 1988 decree relaxed several constraints without totally satisfying the Western partners. It also created new uncertainties in launching a reform of the foreign exchange regulations, the impact of which on the operation of joint ventures remains unclear. It had however an immediate impact on the creation of joint ventures. Already in January-June 1989, almost 400 new ventures were finalized.

Although acquiring technology was claimed in the USSR, as in most East European countries, as one of the first motives for creating co-enterprises, most of the ventures do not belong to high technology industries. On a total of almost 200 (end-1988) the 'social' complex comes first with 25 enterprises (hotels, restaurants, medical and cultural services), then comes the food processing industry (21 ventures), the chemical and wood processing industry (19), engineering (15). As for the other aim of the joint venture creation, namely strengthening the export base, it does not seem to be reached either as most of the existing ventures seem to be geared to the domestic market. Is this good news for the Western investors ? Not quite so as one of the basic principles of the joint venture is that any transfer of hard currency abroad must be generated by an export gain. True, it is also said that the joint ventures must create import substitutes and help to eliminate 'irrational imports'. But in actual practice this did not seem to have allowed the foreign partner more easy hard currency transfers abroad.

The Soviet case thus exemplifies that joint ventures are not the easiest way to increase exports and obtain hard currency, whatever the incentives given to Western investors. They may be a good school of management for domestic entrepreneurs, though on a still very limited scale. They may assist the general marketization of the economy, but only if their share in domestic economic activity is significant, which is not yet the case in any country.

Thus it may be tempting to force Western capital involvement in a more straightforward fashion and on a macro-economic level. This policy is now apparently initiated both by Hungary and Poland. As I said in the beginning of my presentation, I shall not elaborate, both because these developments are still in their very early stage, and also because my purpose is more limited.

My general conclusion, offered for discussion, would be the following. The reforms which occurred in the field of foreign trade have up to now been at large unable to spur exports or to induce a structural modernization of the export pattern. Whatever has been achieved largely remains due to the traditional instruments of state trading, which is however much more efficient in restraining imports than in promoting exports. I agree that this should be evidenced through a detailed statistical analysis not provided here. On the other hand, the foreign trade reforms played their part in the general trend toward marketization and monetization of the domestic economies, and in this systemic sense they appear as more significant than as instruments of structural changes in foreign trade.

Table 7.1
The foreign trade reforms in the Eastern countries (main provisions)
(as by mid-1989)

	BUL	CZ	GDR	HUN	POL	ROM	USSR
Organisation of foreign trade							
FTOs subordinated to the Ministry of Foreign Trade	x	x	x	x	x	x	x
FTOs subordinated to industrial ministries and other state agencies	x	x		x		x	x
FTOs attached to a combine or enterprise	x	x	x	x			x
Enterprises granted rights to trade on their own	x	x		x	x		x
Incentives to export							
Special export prices	x	x	x	x	x	x	x
Use of conversion coefficients	x	x	x				x
Rights to retain a part of hard currency gains	x	x			x	x	x
Export credits in domestic currency		x (1)		x	x		x
Bonus funds	x	x			x	x	x
Credits in hard currency	x	x (1)		x			x (2)

Source: Author's elaboration from various sources on the foreign trade reforms.
Notes: (1) Only on an experimental basis.
(2) Only for joint ventures.

Notes

[1] The list of the relevant goods includes eight commodity and services groups on the import side and 28 groups on the export side. On the restricted import list, we find medicines, pesticides; virtually all cultural, artistic and intellectual goods (printed material; video material, movies, cassettes; services linked with the organization of all types of shows, concerts, etc.); the hiring of foreign labour; all financial services. The export list includes as expected all raw materials, most of the chemicals, virtually all food products, medicines and medical equipment, intellectual property (patents and licences), art and cultural services, financial services. Some imports and exports are totally forbidden to enterprises, such as military equipment, drugs, precious metals. (Regulations of March 1989).

References

Bubnov, B. (1987), *Foreign Trade with the USSR: A Manager's Guide to Recent Reforms*, Pergamon Press, Oxford.

Clement, H. (1988-89), "Changes in the Soviet Foreign Trade System", *Soviet and Eastern European Foreign Trade*, vol. 24 n. 4, Winter 1988-89, special issue.

ECE-UN (1988), *East-West Joint Ventures*, United Nations, Geneva. This is the most comprehensive survey on joint ventures to date, with detailed analyses of the legislation and of the practice of Western firms involved in this activity. A permanent review is provided by ECE-UN, East-West Joint Ventures, a Quarterly Newsletter, as from the beginning of 1989.

Haendcke-Hoppe, M. (1988) (ed.), *Aussenwirtschaftssysteme und Aussenwirtschaftsreformen sozialistischer Lander, ein intrasystemarer Vergleich*, Duncker und Humblot, Berlin.

Ivanov, I.D. (1987), "Restructuring the mechanism of foreign economic relations in the USSR", *Soviet Economy*, vol. 3, n. 3, p. 192-218.

Lhomel, E. (1987), "Les aménagements de l'organisation du commerce extérieur roumain", *Le Courrier des pays de l'Est*, n. 314, janvier, p. 64-71.

NATO, (1987) (ed.), *The Soviet Economy: A New Course? (L'économie soviétique á un tournant ?)*, Nato Colloquium, 1-3 April 1987, NATO, Brussels.

NATO, (1988) (ed.), *The Economies of Eastern Europe Under Gorbachev's Influence (Les Economies d'Europe de l'Est sous l'influence de M. Gorbatchev)*, Nato Colloquium, 23-25 March 1988, NATO, Brussels.

Salgo, I. (1986), 'Economic mechanism and foreign trade organization in Hungary', *Acta Oeconomica*, vol.36 (3-4), p. 271-87.

Wienert, H. - Slater, J. (1986), *East-West Technology Transfer, The Trade and Economic Aspects*, OECD, Paris.

Wolf, T.A. (1988), *Foreign Trade in the Centrally Planned Economy*, International Monetary Fund, Chur, Harwood Academic Publishers.

8 Manufactures export performance and perestroika

GIOVANNI GRAZIANI

The crisis of the export model based on raw materials and fuels

For some time now Soviet policy-makers have been affirming the need to modify substantially USSR's export structure, namely toward the West. They stress in particular the will to 'industrialize' these commercial flows, i.e. to make more room for the manufactured goods vis à vis primary products.

The Soviet export model towards the West, based on raw materials - namely oil, gas and their products - was, in the 1970s, the source of 75-80 per cent of convertible currency export receipts on Western markets. The two oil shocks in 1973-74 and 1979-80 multiplied these receipts. Together with Soviet gold sales and the recourse to international lending, they meant an inflow of real resources from the West and an absorption largely superior to the income produced. The entire process is synthesized by the ascending trend of Soviet terms-of-trade with the West during that period.

The beneficial effects derived by the Soviet economy from such a situation led to the erroneous idea that the USSR might be free from an external constraint, which was recognized as existing for the other East European economies (Andreff, Graziani, 1985). As from 1982, however, both the oil world price and the Soviet terms-of-trade started exhibiting an opposite, downward trend, which accelerated further in 1986. Starting from 1985, the devastating effects on Soviet receipts due to the decline in the oil price cumulated with the depreciation of the dollar. Although the latter does not affect directly Soviet export receipts from fuels, which are paid in dollars, it nevertheless decreases its purchasing power, since it increases the price in dollars of Soviet imports from Western Europe, labelled in other currencies than the dollar. As a general consequence, Soviet terms-of-trade with the West have been declining, with a loss of more than 50 per cent over the last four years.

These events also brought with them the necessity for the Soviet Union to adjust to the external constraint. The main strategy of Soviet policy was to contract its imports from the West, when the terms-of-trade deterioration was conspicuous, and to increase the volume of oil sales, even through massive imports of OPEC crude for re-export (Graziani, 1987 d). Yet the global result has meant a new period of net transfer of resources from the USSR to the West.

Present options for Soviet policy-makers are rather limited (Graziani, 1987 b). Increasing extraction costs in inhospitable regions run counter to an acceleration of oil production. The USSR could: 1) further cut oil supplies to its former CMEA partners, which she has done, aggravating their external constraint; and/or 2) raise the volume of crude imported from OPEC, mostly in exchange for weapons. The cost of such transactions is however on the increase, since military equipment often incorporate sophisticated materials with a high import-content from the West. Let us finally recall that waste limitations in the use of petrol and its substitution by other fuels in electrical production proceed very slowly. An obvious alternative would be to sell higher quantities of natural gas. However the estimated growth of West European demand seems to be moderate.

On the other hand, massive gold sales in the world market have tended to deplete Soviet reserves. Finally international indebtedness has rapidly increased from US $ 26 billion (net) in 1988 to 43.4 billion (net) in 1990 (89 per cent of Soviet exports). The negative experience of other East European countries might be a stimulus to a cautious behaviour.

Summing up, increasing the sale of Soviet manufactured goods in the Western markets would be crucial for guaranteeing a steady growth of convertible currency export receipts. But this is also the real Achille's heel of Soviet exports.

The structure of Soviet trade

The commodity composition of Soviet trade with the West reveals at first glance the difficulty of such restructuration. Fuels and raw materials represent the majority of Soviet exports: more than 4/5 in 1980 and more the 3/4 in 1986, in current prices. Measured at constant prices, the share has even grown, fuels by themselves representing in 1986 72 per cent of Soviet export (Table 8.1).

Table 8.1
Commodity composition of Soviet trade with the West, in %, at current and constant prices, 1980 and 1986

	Soviet Exports				Soviet Imports			
Commodity groups	1980	1986 at current prices	1986 at 1980 prices	Volume change	1980	1986 at current prices	1986 at 1980 prices	Volume change
All food items (SITC 0+1+22+4)	0.6	1.8	1.3	+ 114.8	22.3	18.8	23.8	+ 32.2
Agricultural raw materials (SITC 2-22-27-28)	8.0	8.2	7.5	- 2.7	3.0	2.8	3.6	+ 8.8
Ores,metals,crude fertilizer (SITC 27+28+68)	1.0	0.5	0.6	-35.6	1.9	1.3	2.1	- 5.3
Fuels (SITC 3)	71.1	66.3	71.8	+ 5.5	0.6	1.0	1.2	+ 90.4
Chemicals (SITC 5)	2.3	3.8	2.4	+ 8.3	12.3	11.0	9.9	- 28.4
Machinery and transport equipment (SITC 7)	2.8	3.3	2.0	- 25.4	25.6	30.9	28.2	- 1.8
Other manufactured goods (SITC 6 and 8-68)	1.7	1.9	1.1	- 31.4	33.5	32.7	29.6	- 21.1
Residual	12.5	14.2	13.3	+12.3	0.8	1.5	1.6	+77.3
Total	100.0	100.0	100:0	100.0	100.0	100.0	100.0	100.0

Source: Authors's estimates on the basis of U.N. Monthly Bulletin of Statistics, May 1988. Data in current dollars were adjusted taking into account price changes for the different groups of products.

Among the other major commodity groups, only the share of chemicals shows an increase, both at current and constant prices. 'Machinery and transport equipment' and 'other manufactured goods' account for very small shares, showing, moreover, a regression in volume.

The structure of Soviet imports from the West is to a certain extent a mirror image of the export side. Here manufactures prevail, although their share is shrinking in volume. Food products are important, and increasingly so in real terms.

Three relevant features emerge from an analysis of Table 8.1.

First of all, the expansion in volume of Soviet exports (+4.5 per cent) and the reduction of imports (-10.9 per cent), which seems to confirm the process of adjustment indicated above.

Second, the growing trade in primary products - Soviet fuels for Western foodstuffs - which partially modifies traditional ideas about an international division of labour based only on the exchange of Soviet raw materials for Western finished products. However, mutual trade remains highly complementary. The Soviet Union tends to have a 'vent for surplus' approach to trade, based on primary products. Such a structure strengthens the greater relative importance of the West for the USSR, which imports goods that cannot be bought elsewhere (high technology products), while it exports to the West goods such as oil, which have alternative suppliers (OPEC). It follows for the USSR a certain role of marginal supplier and a higher dependence on mutual trade (Graziani, 1987 c).

Thirdly, quantitative data leave few doubts about the poor performance of Soviet manufactures on Western markets: 'machinery and transport equipment' and 'other manufactures goods' decline in volume by 25 and 31 per cent, respectively. 'Chemicals' is the only commodity group which increases in volume slightly above the average, although such a 'success' is largely due to compensation agreements. The latter covered two thirds of total convertible currency exports of chemicals to the West in the first quinquennium of the 1980s (Borin, 1988, p. 31).

Finally, one should not forget that the USSR is encountering similar difficulties in the less demanding Third World markets as well. Calculations at constant prices show that the most dynamic groups in Soviet export are represented by military equipment, fuels and intermediates like iron and steel, while civilian machinery and equipment are particularly stagnant (Graziani 1987 a, 1987 d, 1989, 1990a).

An analysis of manufactures trade by resource dependence and factor intensity

A better insight into the comparative advantages revealed by trade in manufactures can be gained by broadening the statistical definition of manufactures so as to include primary products at a first stage of processing and other industries with relatively little value-added content. Such a procedure seems justified by the fact that these products represent important component parts both of Soviet world exports and of its imports from Third World countries. Following a similar approach adopted in a UNIDO study- limited to the analysis of developing countries' overall world exports (UNIDO, 1981)-, Soviet trade in manufactures with the West and the Third World was then divided into 'resource-based' and 'non-resource-based' manufactures, the latter category being further characterized by capital-intensive or labour-intensive productive processes (Table 8.2).

Table 8.2
Soviet trade by resource dependence and factor intensity, in %
1974-1976 and 1982-1984

	With the West				With the developing countries			
	Exports		Imports		Exports		Imports	
	1974-76	1982-84	1974-76	1982-84	1974-76	1982-84	1974-76	1982-84
Resource-based manufactures	83.1	92.5	14.6	21.8	43.4	47.7	52.3	70.5
Non-resource-based manufactures	16.9	7.5	85.4	78.2	56.6	52.3	47.7	29.5
of which:								
capital intensive	3.6	2.4	31.2	27.2	19.3	18.8	5.8	5.2
labour-intensive	7.0	2.6	46.8	39.7	23.2	19.2	41.9	23.8
others	6.3	2.5	7.4	11.3	14.1	14.3	-	0.5

Source: Calculated from U.N. COMTRADE and Graziani, 1989.

Notes: Developing countries: 40 developing countries for which data were available.

Resource-based manufactures: all industries from sections 0-4 (including the food processing industries and petroleum products), SITC division 51 (organic and inorganic chemicals), 52 (mineral tar), 63 (wood and cork manufactures), 64 (paper), 68 (non-ferrous metals) and SITC group 561 (manufactured fertilizers)

Others:industries for which the classification 'capital-intensive' or 'labour-intensive' was not applicable. It comprises ten 3-digit SITC products, among which the most important are manufactures of metal, power generating machines, non-electric, road-motor vehicles, other road vehicles and aircraft.

The periods chosen for comparison were the middle 1970s and the most recent years (1982-1984) for which available data existed in the U.N. CONTRADE Data Bank for at least 40 developing countries, while all the Western countries are represented in the sample. Three-year averages were calculated to correct for year-to-year fluctuation in trade performance.

Table 8.2 shows the main results for the two periods under consideration. Resource-based products are predominant in Soviet exports to the West. Their share rises further from 83 to 92 per cent at the end of the period. Non-resource-based manufactures then represent only 8 per cent of total exports of manufactured goods, equally divided into capital-intensive, labour-intensive and other products.

A great part of resource-intensive manufactures - iron and steel, low value-added basic chemicals, metalliferous ores, non ferrous metals, petroleum products - are characterized by highly capital-intensive techniques. The ratio fixed capital/manpower is three times as high as the average for industry at large in the Soviet fuel sector, and twice as large in the metal working and the chemical sectors. Since the share of capital-intensive products is on the increase also for non-resource-based manufactures, one can conclude that Soviet manufactures to the West are particularly and increasingly capital-intensive.

There seems to be a similar trend for Soviet imports of manufactures. Although still dominant, the share of non-resource-based products has declined - from 85 to 78 per cent - and among them, the portion of labour-intensive products has also diminished. If we aggregate all capital-intensive manufactures (partly identical to resource-based products), the result is a loss of dominance by labour-intensive products in Soviet imports from the West too.

An analysis of Soviet trade balances by commodity groups would corroborate the above results. The USSR is a net importer in its overall manufactures trade, but a net exporter in resource-based products.

It is interesting to note that the share of the resource-based products has gained importance also in Soviet exports of manufactures to the Third World. In 1982-1984 it had almost reached the share of non-resource-based manufactures - 48 against 52 per cent. Soviet exports are becoming more capital-intensive too as far as the non-resource-based products are concerned. A similar tendency can be seen in Soviet imports from the developing countries: a substantial rise of resource-based products up to 70 per cent of the total, and a decline of the share of labour-intensive products in non-resource-based manufactures.

Two general trends seem then to result from our analysis of Soviet trade flows: a) the increase of the share of resource-based and capital-intensive manufactures; b) a contraction of the share of labour-intensive products in non-resource-based manufactures.

The rationality of a model based on the relative endowment of productive factors would therefore seem to be supported for the USSR, rich as it is in resources and capital compared to labour. But this would be a partial and static approach.

First of all, such a model is strongly at odds with Western historical experience, where countries have become less dependent in their trade on natural resources and more competitive in other types of exports, as their level of development was improving.

To further clarify the reality of Soviet patterns of trade, a more detailed statistical analysis would be necessary in order to identify research and skill-intensive products, as well as a more precise position in the product life-cycle (new, mature and so on).

As an indication, we shall only recall that the majority of Soviet exports of manufactures are iron and steel, basic chemicals and other intermediate or final products requiring unskilled manpower and/or low levels of research. Research and skill-intensive manufactures like electrical and non-electrical engineering products, computers, telecommunications, control and scientific instruments, refined chemicals, pharmaceutical products, are only minor elements. The raw materials export model is then probably a consequence of the peculiar evolution of technological structures inside the USSR. We shall return to this later on.

Market shares and international competition

Soviet manufactures were clearly a failure on Western markets, especially in the 1980s. This can be seen in Table 8.3, where market shares and trade intensity coefficients are calculated for five groups of manufactures. Also called 'delta' coefficients in economic literature (Theil, 1967; Nagy, 1979), trade intensity coefficients express the relative propensity to trade with different partners. A coefficient higher (lower) than 1 reveals a higher (lower) trade propensity than expected on the basis of the exporter's place in the world market.

Table 8.3
Exports of manufactures to the Western markets:market shares in % (a) and trade intensity coefficients (b), 1980 and 1986

Commodity groups and regions		1980	1986	1980	1986
		Chemicals (SITC 5)		Other manufactured goods (SITC 6 and 8-68)	
USSR	a	0.7	0.6	0.2	0.1
	b	0.57	0.38	0.14	0.07
West	a	92.9	92.4	83.3	76.5
	b	1.06	1.09	1.07	1.09
East. Europe	a	2.0	1.8	2.0	1.8
	b	0.46	0.36	0.46	0.39
CPE Asia	a	0.7	0.7	1.0	1.5
	b	0.87	0.70	0.53	0.55
Developing	a	3.8	4.5	13.5	20.1
countries	b	0.64	0.56	0.93	0.96
of which:					
* Latin America					
	a	1.5	1.5	1.4	2.0
	b	0.75	0.65	0.75	0.91
* Asia	a	1.0	1.8	11.0	16.3
	b	0.43	0.53	0.98	1.01
		Machinery and transport equipment (SITC 7)		Iron and steel (SITC 67)	
USSR	a	0.2	0.1	0.6	0.4
	b	0.10	0.06	0.13	0.06
West	a	94.2	91.4	90.6	86.8
	b	1.10	1.09	1.07	1.15
East.Europe	a	1.0	0.4	3.6	3.2
	b	0.15	0.07	0.76	0.50
Developing	a	4.6	8.0	5.1	9.5
countries	b	0.85	0.94	0.86	0.84
of which:					
*Latin America	a	0.6	1.4	1.9	3.6
	b	0.60	1.08	1.03	0.86
*Asia	a	3.8	6.2	2.3	4.3
	b	0.97	0.98	0.71	0.90
		Passenger road vehicles and parts (SITC 781.0, 784.1, 785.1, 785.2, and 785.31)			
USSR	a	0.3	0.2		
	b	0.27	0.28		
West	a	98.2	97.5		
	b	1.03	1.02		
Developing	a	0.6	2.2		
countries	b	0.30	0.78		
East. Europe	a	1.2	0.1		
	b	0.75	0.14		

Source: Calculated from U.N. Monthly Bulletin of Statistics, May 1986-88.

In Western markets, still dominated by the West itself (from 76 to 97 per cent, according to the various product groups), Soviet export performance has been really disappointing. Soviet shares of the Western market for all product groups are: a) lower than one per cent; b) lower in 1986 then in 1980; and c) decreasing, as from 1981-1984. Trade intensity coefficients don't fare much better. Their value is well under one and they all decline over time, except the coefficient concerning 'passenger road vehicles'.

Comparison with developing countries is often painful. As a whole, these countries improve their position in the Western market for all product groups. Their market share is more than tripled for 'passenger road vehicles' (but from a very modest base), almost doubled in iron and steel and in 'machinery and transport equipment', finally increased by two thirds and one quarter in the 'other manufactured goods' and in 'chemicals'. For all those products Third World market shares are largely superior to the shares of the USSR and Eastern Europe taken together. As expected, the best performance comes from the Asian developing countries, which account for three quarters of Third World overall shares in machinery and other manufactured goods, almost half of iron and steel, more than one third of chemicals. All their trade intensity coefficients move in the same ascending direction, exceeding the value of one in the case of the 'other manufactured goods'.

Finally the evolution of export specialization on Western markets may be derived from a further statistical indicator, the so-called 'revealed comparative advantage' (RCA) index. A figure higher than one indicates a revealed comparative advantage in exporting that product. Table 8.4 compares the performance of the USSR, the West and the Third World over time, for five commodity groups of manufactures.

Very briefly the results are the following. The West still has a comparative advantage in all products, but its RCA indices have declined. As from 1984, it even lost its lead in the 'other manufactured goods', and was overtaken by the Third World by the end of the period. All developing countries' RCA indices are rising considerably. Finally, all Soviet RCA indices are much lower than one, that is to say the USSR is substantially despecialized in these exports.

Failures of Soviet manufactures in Western markets have gone hand in hand with similar increasing difficulties in Third World markets. A previous study of ours conducted for the first half of the 1980s in terms of the 'constant market share' analysis sheds some light on the matter (Graziani, 1987 e). Here the Soviet overall share in manufactures is stagnant in comparison with substantial improvements of the Third World, especially from Asia. The USSR's competitiveness compared to developing countries has declined both in the 'machinery and transport equipment' (civilian) and in the 'other manufactured goods' group. Considering that the Soviet access to Third World market is not discriminated against and that the majority of the (few) 'positive' results for the USSR are due to arms sales or to export concerning countries which have bilateral privileged relations with the Soviet Union, we may conclude that its results are far from brilliant.

Table 8.4
Specialization indices in the export of manufactures towards the West, by commodity groups and regions, 1980-1986

Years	1980	1981	1982	1983	1984	1985	1986
Chemicals							
USSR	0.337	0.419	0.343	0.358	0.464	0.516	0.470
West	1.390	1.367	1.319	1.298	1.279	1.242	1.188
Developing countries	0.130	0.159	0.199	0.199	0.217	0.226	0.240
Machinery and transport equipment							
USSR	0.123	0.113	0.103	0.092	0.081	0.063	0.098
West	1.410	1.394	1.347	1.300	1.278	1.243	1.174
Developing countries	0.158	0.186	0.228	0.318	0.357	0.369	0.427
Passenger road vehicles and parts							
USSR	0.169	0.216	0.177	0.147	0.125	0.104	0.181
West	1.470	1.461	1.425	1.410	1.391	1.340	1.252
Developing countries	0.020	0.032	0.033	0.030	0.040	0.070	0.120
Other manufactured goods							
USSR	0.070	0.070	0.073	0.065	0.047	0.037	0.068
West	1.092	1.088	1.060	1.005	0.980	0.961	0.913
Developing countries	0.408	0.502	0.568	0.661	0.761	0.822	1.001
Iron and steel							
USSR	0.280	0.205	0.274	0.250	0.207	0.090	0.285
West	1.356	1.335	1.280	1.224	1.201	1.180	1.115
Developing countries	0.177	0.213	0.265	0.387	0.430	0.787	0.511

Source: Calculated from U.N. Monthly Bulletin of Statistics, May 1986-88.
Note: The index has sometimes been called 'revealed comparative advantage index'. A figure higher than one would show a revealed comparative advantage in the exports of the commodity group.

As with the West, in its relations with the Third World one can notice a growing contrast between the Soviet internal economic structure, which is highly industrialized, and the commodity composition of its trade.

Systemic obstacles to the expansion of Soviet manufactures exports

Soviet economists recognize that these failures are not due to protectionism, Western biased attitudes or even price characteristics. The majority of Soviet products cannot compete on technical standards, quality and other 'non-price' characteristics. A well placed specialist gives an interesting example of such inadequacy.

> Our industry - he writes - has been turning out planes, motor vehicles, tractors, farm and road construction machinery having practically no differences from earlier models in terms of their specifications and exterior design. In particular, the main truck models are hopelessly outdated and do not meet the world market specifications as regards engine life. They are 25 and even more per cent heavier than foreign analogues, often fail to meet the requirements regarding vibration and safety, and consume more fuel and lubricants (Seltsovsky 1988, p. 11).

The failure to observe international technical standards has become a real obsession among Soviet authorities. There is good reason to worry. The figures that circulate mostly in the scientific community in Moscow are the following: less than 30 per cent of the products of the machine production industry, 14 per cent of machine tools and 17 per cent of the products of the machine tool construction industry are regarded as on a par with world standards.

The technological gap between the USSR and the West is reckoned to be very large still even in the Soviet Union. The best Western studies on the subject indicate that defence, including the space sector, is the only sector in which the USSR can compare well with the West (Amann, Cooper, 1986). Generally speaking, the Soviet lag seems to be smaller during the first two phases of the 'research-production' cycle (research and experimental development) than in the third (production) and especially in the fourth phase (diffusion). According to Soviet specialists, the time span between the development of a new technology and series production ranges between 8-10 years in the USSR, compared to one and a half years in the West ('Kogda bolesn ...', 1988). In the machine-building sector, only 20 per cent of the products are produced in the same year as the prototype, 30 per cent in the following year, 18 per cent in the third year. The rest are produced later (Zavyalov, 1987, p. 11). Moreover, Soviet industries tend to produce few variants compared to a vast assortment offered by Western firms. A typical and extreme example is represented by compressors, produced in only one standard measure by the USSR, as compared to 10 by a West Germany firm and 25 and 30 variants by Swiss and US firms (Usachev, 1987, p. 38).

Even if they were competitive as far as technical standards and prices are concerned, Soviet products can still fail in Western markets. Foreign trade organizations have been very weak in developing marketing techniques, from market research to after-sales technical assistance and spare parts supply. Besides, this is all the more true of Soviet domestic economy, characterized by a chronic shortage of spare parts. This leads to the well known situation in which every factory tried, as far as possible, to produce all the pieces it needed. Lack of specialization naturally causes a lowering of quality, which in turn affects the functioning of the machinery (Gladkii, 1986. p. 16).

The technological gap, quality and marketing inadequacies, all point to systemic obstacles in the Soviet economy. We shall recall them very briefly before evaluating the extent to which present reforms may be liable to relaunch Soviet manufactures export.

The first set of factors belongs to the planned system as it stood before recent change. Administrative directives from above, physical quantities or global value targets, absence of competition, pushed factory directors to reach planned targets, without paying due attention to the quality and the novelty of products, often considered as factors of uncertainty and risk to be accurately avoided (Shastitko, 1986, p. 20). The system of price fixing for new products did not encourage any initiative. Industrial innovation was further obstructed by the all-embracing bureaucratic phenomenon. Every innovation required a complex network of administrative and institutional relations, generating chaos and rivalry among the various departments and ministries. Research was separated from production and the latter from diffusion. Finally, directors preferred to increase the capital stock than to innovate and improve the existing one.

Neither was traditional foreign trade system more conducive to manufactures exports expansion. Exports were considered a residual element, to pay the imports necessary to reach the planned growth rates (Graziani, 1982). Producing firms were separated from international markets by the filter of the foreign trade organizations which depended on the Ministry of Foreign Trade. No sure way exists of calculating exactly the efficiency of foreign trade operations (Potapov, 1985; Shagalov, 1987). Neither can the official exchange rate, artificially and centrally fixed, help in calculating the efficiency of commercial transactions, as it is used only ex-post and for accounting purposes. The domestic price level has no connection with world prices, neither does it reflect relative factor or good scarcities. In particular it underestimates the interest rate on investment and the cost of production of raw materials and low value-added products, while it overestimates the cost of production of higher value-added products. The latter are thus penalized, since the foreign trade organizations, which reasoned in terms of domestic wholesale prices, found it more convenient to promote resource-based and capital-intensive exports, apparently less costly to them. Finally, excess demand characterizing the whole system meant the planners tended to ignore export promotion.

Perestroika and manufactures: what kind of prospects?

The restructuring of industry, namely the engineering industry, is one of the priorities of Soviet perestroika. We shall here list briefly the measures which are most liable to have an impact on Soviet manufactures exports.

A first group is aimed at improving the quality and the technical standard of products. Such are: a) the reduction of planned targets and the introduction of quality indicators (productivity, efficiency, technical progress); b) the creation of horizontal links among enterprises; c) financial autonomy and self-financing; d) the system of state acceptance, and quality control.

Truly enough, the first impact on industrial production has been negative. The quality control, for instance, has provoked (in 1987) the elimination of a considerable amount of faulty products, so that the control level had to be lifted after a few months. More recently, a system of 'product certification' was introduced, under which testing centres evaluate the quality of industrial manufactures vis à vis international standards. Furthermore, the new autonomy allowed, on paper, to enterprises is bound to create some confusion, without the reform both of the price system and of the supply system of raw materials and intermediate products. Finally, material incentives may not have the hoped for result, while the 'internal' rouble inconvertibility remains.

The same principles of autonomy have been extended to the foreign trade sector. All enterprises and organizations now have the right in principle to trade freely abroad, provided they produce competitive goods. The majority of the manufacturing sector is covered by these measures, while the export of fuels, raw materials and some strategic goods remain under the aegis of State monopoly. A later decree, however, established that the export operations allowed are strictly limited to the goods produced by the same enterprise. Quantitative restrictions have also been applied to the export of many chemicals and medical equipment, besides other non-manufactured goods. A further limitation to this right is that the enterprises are not allowed to redirect abroad the goods produced under state orders for the domestic market.

Particularly important as an incentive to export would seem the right of the enterprises to retain part of their hard currency earnings, the rate of retention varying from two per cent for low value-added products to 85 per cent for high value-added products. The principle of self-financing in convertible currencies may paradoxically have a boomerang effects on the improvement of competitiveness. It implies, in fact, that the enterprise cannot apply any more for state funds in hard currencies in order to pay for the necessary imports. It is likely, as a consequence, that Soviet enterprises may press Western partners to accept growing quantities of their products under compensation agreements, a form of exchange which does not push exporters to improve competitiveness.

The introduction of so-called 'differentiated currency coefficients' for the conversion of foreign trade prices in domestic rubles has met many difficulties and growing criticism. Their excessive number - more than 3000 - and their reference to domestic costs of production has even led to paradoxical situations where an export product costs more than a similar imported good. As from the beginning of 1990, Soviet enterprises saw the unification of the many coefficients through the application of a 100 per cent devaluation rate to the rouble in their export transactions in hard currencies. However, this measure, like the introduction of a new exchange rate in early 1991, will probably be accompanied by a whole set of subsidies, as was the experience of other East European countries.

Finally, joint-ventures with Western countries or NICs and the creation of 'free economic zones' should bring a competitive incentive and a 'demonstration effect' for local enterprises. But, for the time being most of the joint-ventures have not been established in the high-tech sectors and are producing for the Soviet market (Graziani, 1990 b).

By way of conclusion, I must stress that the reforms undertaken up to now do not seem capable of inducing an export promotion of Soviet manufactures. Administrative decisions from above and decentralization are not sufficient by themselves to stimulate an expansion of manufactures exports to the extent that the systemic obstacles, indicated above, are not removed: irrational price structure, inadequate technological base, chronic shortages which frustrate any incentive system. Until then, we should not be surprised by the survival of the Soviet export model prevailing at present, a model dominated, with few exceptions, by fuels, raw materials and resource-based, capital-intensive, low skill- and low research-intensive manufactures.

References

Amann, R., Cooper, J. (1986) (eds), *Technical Progress and Soviet Economic Development*, Basil Blackwell, Oxford.

Andreff, W., Graziani, G. (1985), 'Contrainte exterieure et politiques d'adaptation dans les economies planifiees du centre', in Lavigne M., Andreff W., (eds), *La realite socialiste. Crise, adaptation, progres*, Editions Economica, Paris.

Borin, V. (1988), 'USSR Compensation-Based Cooperation with Developed Capitalist Countries', *Foreign Trade*, n. 2 pp. 30-4.

Economic Bulletin for Europe, (1988), vol. 40, United Nations, New York.

Gladkii, V. (1986), 'Garantiya', *Ekonomicheskaya Gazeta*, n. 45, November, p. 16.

Graziani, G. (1982), *Comecon, domination et dependances*, Maspero, Paris.

Graziani, G. (1987a), 'The Non-European Members of Comecon: A Model for Developing Countries?', in Kanet, R.E., (ed.), *The Soviet Union. Eastern Europe and the Third World*, Cambridge University Press, Cambridge, pp. 163-79.

Graziani, G. (1987b), 'Energy in Soviet-West European Relations'

in Ayoub, A., Percebois, J., (eds), *Petrole: Marches et Strategies*, Economica, Paris, pp. 302-20.
Graziani, G. (1987c), 'La CEE e il Comecon: Concorrenza e Complementarità' in Parboni, R., Wallerstein, I., (eds), *L'Europa e l'economia politica del Sistema-Mondo*, Franco Angeli, Milano, pp. 80-101.
Graziani, G. (1987d), 'Soviet Strategy in Restructuring Trade with the Third World' , in Weichhardt, R. (ed.), *The Soviet Economy: A New Course?*, NATO Economics Directorate, Brussels, pp. 289-314.
Graziani, G. (1987e), 'Concorrenza tra PVS e Paesi dell'Est sui mercati del Terzo Mondo', 4th Annual Meeting of AISSEC, Sorrento.
Graziani, G. (1989), 'Influence and policy implications of the major factors in intersystems trade, especially the East-South trade', study prepared for the UNCTAD Secretariat, United Nations, Geneva.
Graziani, G. (1990a), *Gorbachev's economic strategy in the Third World*, Center for Strategic and International Studies, Praeger Special Studies, Praeger, New York.
Graziani, G. (1990b), 'Le joint ventures in Unione Sovietica', *Note Economiche*, n. 2, pp. 461-89)
'Kogda bolesn obgoniaet lekarstva', 1988, Literaturnaya Gazeta, February 3.
Nagy, A. (1979), *Methods of Structural Analysis and Projection of International Trade*, Studies No.13, Institute of Economics, Hungarian Academy of Sciences, Budapest.
Potapov, V.I. (1985), *Organizatsia i tekhnika vneshnetorgovykh operatsii v SSSR*, Academy of Foreign Trade, Moscow.
Seltsovski, V. (1988), 'The Structure of the USSR's Foreign Trade and Ways to Improve it', *Foreign Trade*, n. 11, pp. 10-13.
Shagalov, G.L. (1987), 'Kriterii i metody opredeleniya ekonomicheskoi effektivnosti vneshneekonomicheskikh sviazei sotsialisticheskikh gosudarstv so stranami zapada', in *Problemy effektivnosti ekonomicheskikh sviazei mezhdu sotsialisticheskimi i kapitalisticheskimi stranami*, Moscow University, Moscow.
Shastitko, V. (1986), 'Rasshirenie funktsii khozrascheta', *Ekonomicheskya Gazeta*, n. 6, February, p. 20.
Theil, H. (1967), *Information and Economic Theory*, North Holland, Amsterdam.
UNIDO (1981), *World Industry in 1980*, United Nations, New York.

Usachev, A. (1987), 'Relationship Between the Quality of Exported Machines and Their Prices', *Foreign Trade*, n. 12, pp. 37-40.
Zavyalov, P. (1987), 'An Integrated Approach to Soviet Export Problems', *Foreign Trade*, n. 8, pp. 10-13.

9 Economic reforms and foreign trade policies: reflections on the East European experience

CARLO FRATESCHI

The foreign trade debate in Eastern Europe

In centrally planned economies (CPEs) the mere existence of foreign trade flows, insofar as it enlarges the range of possible choices of planners and other economic agents, tends to increase, *ceteris paribus*, the need for decision-making methods based on a certain degree of economic rationality as opposed to administrative procedures.

In the historical development of the CPEs of Eastern Europe this fact, together with the progressively increasing role of external trade, has generated strong pressures for change in the economic system and policies: these pressures, however, have in fact been pushing in two opposing directions. Indeed, since external trade depends, among other things, on prices and on demand and supply conditions in foreign markets, which are subject to frequent and rapid changes, the decentralization of decision-making in the field of foreign trade can be regarded as an almost unavoidable ingredient of an increasing openness of a CPE. On the other hand, however, the parallel and equally strong necessity of maintaining the equilibrium in the balance of payments can also become the main reason for a strengthening in the degree of centralization in the external sector (Levine 1968, pp. 274-6). From a slightly different perspective, it is possible to speak of a permanent contradiction, under central planning, between the macro- and the microsphere of the economy in the field of external relations: a contradiction, that is to say, between the 'compulsion to export' felt by the centre (motivated by the hard constraint represented, for central organs, by the balance of payments equilibrium), and the 'damped export interest' of the enterprises, that can be traced back mainly to the shortage conditions existing in the domestic economy and to the characteristics and consequences of the foreign trade monopoly (Mérey, pp. 181-3).

The debate on all the issues related to foreign trade has been alive in the centrally planned economies of Eastern Europe for more than three decades. If one tries to trace the evolution of both analyses and policies in these years one can identify, along a general tendency towards an increasing urgency of the matter and an enlargement in the number of countries involved in reform experiments, three main phases during which the debates were very intense and the changes in foreign trade planning and management took place at an accelerated pace.

In an early period, the beginning of which dates back to the mid-fifties, in some East European economies (mainly Czechoslovakia, Eastern Germany and Hungary), new attitudes started to emerge towards foreign trade (U.N.-E.C.E. 1955, pp.125-31). Increased attention began to be devoted to the benefits of international specialization and, at the same time, theoretical studies on the criteria and methods for assessing domestic and foreign comparative costs, mainly as a guide in planning, were published [1].

In that phase the emphasis was mainly in devising and utilizing appropriate criteria for evaluating the degree of 'financial effectiveness of exports', based on a comparison between the internal costs for producing exportable goods (valued at internal wholesale prices) and the amount of foreign exchange earned through the exportation of the same goods. This apparently simple calculation becomes very complicated when, as in 'classic' CPEs, domestic costs cannot be easily evaluated, because the price system does not reflect in any significant way the relative scarcities of factors (neglecting the role of interest, rent, and realistic depreciation of assets), and at the same time the foreign exchange obtained (or to be expended) in the external transactions cannot be converted in national currency [2].

The aim of these coefficients, whose reliability as indicators of economic efficiency is rather limited, was in fact a quite narrow one: they were calculated by central planners mainly in order to obtain some operative parameters that could be utilized to determine, in a rational way, which goods could be more conveniently exported in order to cover the costs of the planned necessary imports. In a period where the external trade flows were still fixed mainly in physical quantities and on the basis of material balances, any economic calculation could intervene only after the drawing up of the plan, with the limited objective of evaluating the profitability of planned external flows, in the sense of the gains in foreign exchange deriving from them (Szymkiewicz 1977, pp. 101-3).

The second phase began around the mid-sixties, when the serious difficulties encountered in the first half of the decade by many small CPEs (mainly Czechoslovakia, Hungary, East Germany and Bulgaria), in terms of both external disequilibrium and declining growth rates of net material product, exercised strong economic pressures for reforms in the domestic economy and in the external sector. The attention of the reformers was directed mainly towards the observed inefficiencies in foreign trade: in coincidence with the launching of a number of more or less ambitious reform projects, various programmes were developed and implemented in order to enlarge the role of external trade and to attain an increased degree of 'foreign trade effectiveness'.

In those years the reform measures were mainly of three types: reforms of the foreign trade monopoly; reforms of the foreign trade planning and management system; reforms of prices and exchange rates.

In the first case, the purpose was to somewhat loosen the traditional monopoly of foreign trade, a process that was carried out at unequal speed in the different countries. The general tendency was towards a reinforcement of organizational links between foreign traders and internal producers (and users). The more common change was the introduction of a differentiation in the institutional setup of Foreign Trade Organizations (FTOs): some of them remained under the traditional subordination to the Foreign Trade Ministry, others were 'attached' to ministries, or amalgamated with industrial associations or big enterprises, or even given the status of autonomous entities (not hierarchically depending on superior bodies). At the same time, some producing enterprises, as a rule very big ones, were granted the right to engage autonomously in foreign trade activities for a strictly specified range of products. Moreover, the character of the relationships between the FTOs and the internal producers was also diversified. The traditional arrangement, typical of the Soviet version of foreign trade monopoly, where FTOs acted on their own account, buying (and selling) the products from (to) internal producers at internal wholesale prices, was in some instances replaced by partnerships arrangements (with profit and risk sharing) or commercial agency arrangements (involving the payment of commissions) with producing enterprises (U.N.-E.C.E. 1973; Tosi 1984).

As to the second kind of reforms, the changes were of a more limited nature: again the general tendency was an evolution from very detailed plans, containing strictly binding targets expressed in physical quantities, towards a reduction in the number of centralized targets and the establishment of plans in value terms (but maintaining as a rule the quantitative planning for trade in fuels, basic raw-materials and semifabricates). At the same time, new forms of incentives were devised and utilized, mainly in order to encourage producing enterprises in fulfilling, in an efficient way, their foreign trade plans. These programmes contained provisions such as: 1) the possibility for both exporting and producing enterprises of obtaining bonuses linked to the degree of 'financial effectiveness of exports'; 2) the right, given in some cases to producers, to retain part of their foreign exchange receipts, and to use them for the acquisition of additional quantities of raw materials, semifinished goods or machinery from abroad; 3) the possibility, for producing enterprises, of converting their foreign exchange receipts into national currency at a favourable exchange rate, that is to say a rate more or less strongly undervalued with respect to the official one (U.N.-E.C.E. 1973; Szymkiewicz 1977, pp. 139-51). In some instances, moreover, enterprises producing for exports were granted various other privileges: special treatment in the delivery of supplies, investment credits and foreign currency allotments, reduced restrictions in wage fund and employment growth, etc. (U.N.-E.C.E. 1968, pp. 102-15).

As to the reforms of prices and exchange rates, their main objective was the creation of meaningful links between foreign and domestic prices. In the second half of the sixties all East European countries, except Romania, carried out changes in the structure and level of wholesale prices, with the intention of bringing them in line with factor costs and, to a lesser degree, with external prices. In the same countries, with the exception again of Romania and of the USSR, that period saw an expansion of the role of profitability coefficients, that were linked to the calculation and utilization of various 'adjustment coefficients' which, while differently denominated (conversion factors, foreign trade coefficients, trade multipliers), amounted all to shadow or 'surrogate' exchange rates (Brown-Marer 1973, p.164; Brabant 1985a, p.131).

These coefficients were based on the so-called 'average reproduction costs of earning a unit of foreign exchange', resulting as a rule from the ex-post calculation of the ratio between the value of exports at domestic wholesale prices (or at production costs) in domestic currency and the value of exports in actual prices (i.e. in foreign currency) [3]. On the basis of such calculations, often disaggregated by different trade partners, currencies, trade directions or commodity groups, 'parametric' or 'internal' exchange rates (IERs) were derived (Vanous 1986, p. 85-7).

The research and debate over the calculation and application of internal exchange rates and foreign trade multipliers were most intense during the heydays of economic reforms in the mid-sixties. The main novelty with respect to the preceding phase, at least at the level of intentions, was that the purpose of these calculations was not only to create the possibilities for rational macroeconomic choices by the planners, but also to use these coefficients as microeconomic allocatory guides, in order to stimulate the efficiency and the growth of exports through a direct involvement of enterprises. The utilization of these surrogate exchange rates, however, varied greatly from country to country, depending both on the differences in the original design of the overall reform packages and, more importantly, on the differing degrees in which the reforms were subsequently scaled down, stopped or put into reverse gear (Brabant, 1985b, pp.14-5).

It should be noted, in this regard, that the modifications adopted at that time in the field of foreign trade, and in particular in the use of shadow exchange rates, were the most resilient ones: while in many East European countries the beginning of the seventies witnessed a retreat from the previously enacted reforms and a return to centralization of economic control, in most cases 'the role of these coefficients as guides to macroeconomic resource allocation and, in the case of the IERs, also in support of enterprise decision-making and price formation was strengthened' (Brabant 1985a, p.132). At the same time, exactly because of the slowdown or the reversal in the evolution of overall economic reforms, it became highly unlikely that the persistence of partially isolated instruments, aiming at a greater efficiency in the external sector, could produce the desired results.

In fact, as the subsequent experience of both 'traditional' and 'modified CPEs' (MCPEs) [4] has shown, the efficacy of any kind of 'parametric' indicator (prices, taxes, exchange rates, etc.) in influencing the decision-making process at the micro level is strictly contingent upon the degree of autonomy and responsibility that the system of economic control leaves, formally or informally, to the enterprises: in Kornai-style terminology, on the 'hardness' of their budget constraint. In a situation were the domestic economy of all these countries was still characterized by widespread shortages and excess demand, and by the consequent existence of a sellers' market, financial, fiscal and other incentives to exports were bound to yield very scarce results: the stimulations provided were not sufficient to get the enterprises really concerned with the competitiveness and/or the expansion of exports (Szymkiewicz 1977, pp.145-51).

It must be added, at this point, that in the second half of the seventies all East European countries entered a period of very high 'external trade concern', which however did not lead towards an expansion of reforms but, instead, to the widespread reimposition of central controls and directives (Tyson 1984 and 1986; Winiecki 1988). It is well known that in that period the increasing size of external disequilibria and indebtedness towards the West, common to most of these countries, determined a serious foreign exchange crisis in almost all CPEs.

> The reaction to the emerging crisis was in several instances postponed, until the proportions became simply unmanageable; it then took the form of the ruthless slashing of imports, the fast promotion of exports even at the cost of deteriorating terms of trade and aggravating domestic imbalances, the indiscriminate pruning of investments, and the compression of final consumption. Only in some instances, and then usually in muted form, were these maneuvers anchored to shifts in enterprise guidelines of a more indirect nature. The imposition of trade controls through explicit or implicit quantitative import restrictions proved to work much faster and more widely than changing the IER(s). (Brabant 1985b, p. 23).

It is worthwhile stressing, in this regard, that while MCPEs, having at their disposal a wider range of direct and indirect instruments, were generally thought to be capable of reacting in a better way to external disturbances, the recent experience of external adjustment casts many doubts on this assumption (Winiecki 1988, p.3 and 9-15). Indeed, even if there may be a dispute over the direction of causality, it must be underlined that the countries which at the beginning of the eighties had more troubles in terms of external disequilibria and convertible currencies indebtedness (i.e. Poland, Hungary and Romania) were indeed the countries that during the seventies had more drastically modified their foreign trade systems, especially in terms of exchange rates mechanisms and policies. It should also be added, moreover, that it was probably in this difficult period that the already mentioned contradiction between the micro- and the macrosphere was most strongly felt, leading in many instances to a definite clash of interests between the central organs and the producing enterprises (Merėy 1983).

We can now turn briefly to the third and last phase of intensified discussion and more profound changes relating to the external sector in Eastern Europe. In the second half of the eighties we have witnessed a deepening and widening of the economic debate, abounding in criticisms of the past experiences and centred on the necessity of 'opening up' these economies in order to achieve a stronger integration in the international economy. It can be said, in fact, that the almost totality of reform-minded economists and a vast majority of decision-makers in these countries accepted the necessity of moving towards a pattern of growth firmly based on economic efficiency, rejecting at the same time the possibility of obtaining these results on the basis of limited changes, confined to the foreign trade field, and stressing the necessity to view any particular measure in the broader framework of a radical 'rethinking' of the whole economic system.

As to the specificities of the reforms more connected to the external sector, it is sufficient at this point to say, without entering into details [5], that they involved initiatives whose purpose was the expansion of enterprise autonomy and incentives in foreign trade, the breaking up of the institutional monopoly of foreign trade, the modification of the exchange rate system, and the reform of the domestic price structure and price system (Wolf 1989, p.3).

In a certain sense, this listing shows how the third wave of foreign trade reforms followed the same directions of the reform packages of the sixties: there were, however, two big differences. First of all, practically in all cases and in all countries, even if at different speed and starting from different positions, the limits of the previous experiments were clearly surpassed in the direction of a much stronger presence of market-type solutions. Secondly, and probably more importantly, the small East European countries were joined in the reform 'race' by the Soviet Union, a country which after having neglected the foreign trade sector in the previously enacted economic reforms (1965, 1979), decided in 1986 to make up for lost time by passing, in about three/four years, through all the stages which the leading Eastern European reformers had gone through in more than twenty years.

The attempted switch from import-substitution to export-promotion

In addition to the above cited similarities in many aspects of foreign trade reforms, it is important to stress that what emerged in the eighties as a common theme of discussion in many of these countries [6] was the intention, or the desire, to switch to a completely new strategy of development, based on outward-oriented and strong export-promoting policies, somehow trying to follow the example of the most successful newly industrializing countries (NICs) [7]. In order to assess the reasons and the feasibility of this change of strategy, however, it is necessary first of all to compare the development strategies and foreign economic policies of CPEs and developing countries in the last decades.

According to recent contributions in the fields of comparative economic systems and of development economics, the foreign economic strategies of various countries can be compared and classified along a continuum going from extremely outward-oriented economies, adopting extreme versions of export-promotion (EP) strategies with little or no import protection, to very closed and inward-oriented ones, characterized by a very tight protectionism and by development strategies based on import-substitution (IS), or even by policies of self-reliance and autarky (Marer 1988; Edwards 1989a).

A strategy of industrialization based on replacing the imports of manufactured goods with domestic production was forcefully expounded in the work of the Argentinian economist Raúl Prebisch (Prebisch, 1950 and 1959), and advocated as the decisive solution for the economic problems of underdeveloped countries. This strategy was based on four main arguments: 1) 'infant industry' considerations, which in most developing countries meant that the entire industrial sector was considered as an 'infant'; 2) 'export pessimism', motivated by the persuasion that trade could not be accounted as the 'engine of growth' for developing countries, because their export earnings could grow only slowly, if at all, while economic growth would entail a rapidly increasing import demand; 3) 'terms of trade pessimism', based on the persuasion that the terms of trade would turn inevitably against exporters of primary commodities if their supply was expanded; 4) a strong scepticism on the possibility to rely upon the international market, because of its presumedly high instability (as far as prices, quantities demanded, and earnings were concerned).

The most important feature of all IS trade policies, as adopted by most developing countries in the fifties and early sixties, was the extremely high level of protection granted to domestic producers, achieved with a combination of various elements such as: high or even prohibitive tariffs; severe quantitative restrictions; pervasive and time-consuming systems of import licensing (with imports allocated by category of commodity, by type of domestic user, by source of foreign exchange, and by type of use - capital, intermediate good, or raw material); domestic content requirements for domestic assemblers; and, at times, prohibition for certain imports (considered inessential because 'luxurious' or locally available). At the same time, these policies were characterized by strong disincentives to export, deriving mainly from an overvaluation of the exchange rate. (Donges 1976, pp. 630-6; Krueger 1983).

Industrialization policies based on IS came under severe criticism in the second half of the sixties [8], when many economists started to question their alleged benefits: it was then increasingly realized that these policies, even if evaluated only in terms of their own goals, were indeed unsuccessful. In fact, as the disappointing experience of many developing countries has shown, the pursuing for long periods of time of these strategies of development tends to create more problems than it solves, and from many points of view produces results that are exactly the opposite of the original intentions.

These perverse effects could be most clearly seen in the repercussions of IS policies on the external equilibrium: a striking majority of the countries that adopted strongly inward-looking policies started very soon to suffer from severe and chronic balance of payments deficits at the current exchange rate. Since IS regimes were generally expected to determine important savings of foreign exchange, this result could seem rather puzzling: such a negative phenomenon, however, is not difficult to explain.

An important aspect of these strategies, almost totally neglected by their proponents, is indeed the degree of 'import intensity of import substitution' (Diaz-Alejandro, 1965): the domestic production of many final goods (previously imported) requires very often substantial amounts of imported raw materials, semifabricates and capital goods, especially in the first phases of industrialization, through the operation of a kind of acceleration principle on both investment and imports. In fact, with the structure of industrial production evolving, in developing countries, from very simple to more sophisticated goods, the demand for intermediate and complementary products that could not, or not yet, be produced internally tended to rise more than proportionally: at the same time, severe difficulties were experienced in the expansion of exports of manufactured and primary products. As a result, recurrent balance of payments crises forced the authorities, unwilling to allow a devaluation of the currency, to repeatedly use monetary and fiscal policies tools to restrain or stop altogether the growth of the economy (contradicting, by so doing, the very aim of their development policies, namely the acceleration of economic growth).

At the same time, the changes in the structure of imports induced, directly or indirectly, by the strategy pursued (with a decrease of imports of consumer and other manufactured goods and a corresponding increase in imported semifabricates, equipment and machinery), raised in a serious manner the vulnerability of the economy to possible interruptions in the flow of imports. In fact, since a successful IS implies a gradual decrease of the value of imports with respect to national income, this process does not necessarily entails a reduction of the vulnerability of the economy to external factors and shocks, since the remaining imports tend to have such an important role in the structure of production that they cannot be easily curtailed without hampering severely the growth prospects and the capacity utilization levels of the economy. (Donges 1974, p. 342; Diaz-Alejandro 1965, p. 495).

One cannot avoid being struck by the similarities between these negative and perverse phenomena and the problems encountered, already from the end of the fifties and more clearly in the following decades, by the small East European economies, where the creation of many new branches in the manufacturing sector meant in a first phase a jump in imports of machinery and equipment and, subsequently, a steady increase in the flows of imported raw materials, semi-manufacures, parts, and components whose internal production was either missing or quantitatively/qualitatively insufficient:

> Sooner or later it has come to light that *industrialization based on import substitution does not reduce imports, it only transforms the composition of imports*. If previously the country was importing commodities that have been replaced with new do-

mestic capacity, then afterwards the import requirements will consist of goods made necessary by the process of import substitution itself. (Csikós-Nagy, 1968)

Indeed, exactly because of the perverse effects resulting from the application of inward-looking development strategies, with the intentions of central planners so clearly contradicted by results, the foreign trade policy of small East European countries has been labelled 'attempted import substitution' (Brown-Marer 1973, p.153).

Such similar outcomes have arisen, in fact, by substantially similar policies. The analogies between the development strategies of East European CPEs and of inward-looking developing countries have been stressed in recent years by many authors (Tyson 1984 and 1986; Marer 1988; Fishlow 1986; Comisso 1986; Poznanski 1986; Winiecki 1989). An extraordinary high level of protection is indeed one of the most remarkable characteristics of both 'classical' and 'modified' CPEs, where the separation of internal and external transactions and prices, realized mainly through the state monopoly of foreign trade and with the help of complex schemes of highly diversified taxes and subsidies, gives rise to the fact that no domestic producer really faces the actual or potential competition of foreign enterprises. This hyper-protectionist policy is not supported, as in many LDCs, by tariffs or quantitative restrictions on imports (at least as understood and applied in market economies), but is more directly achieved through an almost absolute control by the central bureaucracy over the evolution of trade flows, particularly of imports, in physical terms: a practice which could be equated, to a certain extent, to a complete and pervasive system of quotas.

The adoption by East European CPEs of strategies of development that relied heavily on protection and IS can be explained by various factors. Some authors have stressed, for example, certain elements of historical continuity with the interwar experience of these countries, when after the dissolution of the Austro-Hungarian monarchy all the successor states imposed very high trade barriers, choosing IS industrialization strategies (Berend-Ranki 1977, p. 80-91): in other words, 'import substitution was not invented in Latin America after World War II; it had emerged much earlier, and naturally, among East European states as a response to their industrial backwardness relative to Western neighbors' (Fishlow 1986, p. 567). Moreover, historical precedents could also be important, in orienting the choice between different development strategies in favour of protectionism and IS, in the cases where existed a long tradition of strong intervention in economic affairs by the state, as in Russia or China (Marer 1988, p. 205).

Other elements that can be thought of as favouring the choice of IS strategies can be recalled, even if it must be stressed that not all of them seem to be equally relevant for East European economies. First, a very low level of development, implying the lack of an industrial base, of infrastructures, and of skilled workers, is not a good starting point for open and outward-oriented policies: the classical case of infant industry protection could then be, and has been, used for explaining the initial choice of most East European countries (excluding, however, both the GDR and Czechoslovakia, and possibly Hungary). Secondly, the size of the country and the natural resources endowment, which are generally considered as more conducive to the adoption of inward-looking policies, could be regarded as relevant only in the case of the USSR or, to a lesser degree, Poland. Thirdly, the existence of antagonistic political relations with prospective partners, as was obviously the case in Europe during the Cold War, creates a strong inducement to the adoption of inward-looking or semi-autarkic policies.

Another factor, important for both East European CPEs and market-oriented developing countries, is the political doctrine supporting the development strategies based on IS: rapid industrialization, aimed at building a broadly based industrial structure, was seen in both groups of countries as a means to escape from a situation of dependency and exploitation by developed capitalist countries. From this point of view, the political elites in all these states regarded the choice of inward-looking industrialization strategies as a highly significant manifestation of political autonomy, self-respect and national sovereignty (Winiecki 1989, pp. 64-5).

However important all these aspects might be, it is quite clear that in Eastern Europe, as convincingly argued by many authors (Holzman 1974; Okólski-Winiecki 1983; Winiecki 1985; Marer 1988; Mérey 1983; Salgó 1986), the most direct and strong influence in favour of inward-oriented, hyper-protectionist strategies has been exercised by systemic and institutional factors, among which the very existence of central planning is the dominant one.

Strategies of IS are extremely attractive for central planners. On the one hand, for a central bureaucratic decision-making body, lacking almost necessarily the detailed knowledge of the situation and evolution of external markets requested by a successful export drive in manufactured goods, they are much simpler to devise and manage than export-promotion policies, since the hitherto existing import flows provide already the necessary information for identifying internal lines of production suitable for expansion. From this point of view, the practice of 'reverse-engineering', a typical ingredient of the early Soviet approach to technology transfer, may be seen as the most extreme version of IS policy as applied by central planners. On the other hand, while IS per se does not imply necessarily a tendency towards trade-aversion, it fits perfectly in the 'functionally autarkic' [9] setup of all traditional CPEs, where foreign trade is treated as a residual, imports are determined on the basis of material balances (in physical quantities), and exports are seen as an unfortunate drain on the resources of the country that has to be accepted only in order to pay for the necessary imports.

Both in CPEs and in developing market economies, the inadequacy of IS policies, apart from the afore-mentioned negative effects on the balance of payments equilibrium, is revealed by a common pattern of negative phenomena arising from the serious misallocation of resources inherent in the policies pursued: intense distortions in cost structures, generalized inefficiencies in business, waste of scarce resources, lack of specialization, low degree of exploitation of economies of scale. Owing to these and other related problems, many developing countries that had previously chosen more or less extreme versions of inward-looking strategies started to move (in some cases already from the late fifties [10]) towards more open and outward-looking policies. While this policy switch took place with different speed and intensity in different countries, its main elements were very similar:

1) in most countries the exchange rate was substantially devalued and, were existing, the system of multiple exchange rates abandoned in favour of a unified and realistic rate: in a few cases, floating rates, crawling pegs or sliding parity adjustment were adopted in order to prevent the possibility of a future overvaluation of the currency (due to the differences between internal and world inflation rates);

2) in a first move towards import liberalization, all countries eased their system of import licensing, replacing quotas by tariffs: the level of overall protection granted to internal producers, and its variability among industrial sectors, declined substantially;

3) export-oriented manufacturing activities were additionally helped (in general just in order to offset their cost disadvantages due to the remaining import protection) with schemes for remittances of custom duties (or direct duty-free imports) for imported materials

and components used for manufacturing export goods, combined in many countries with income-tax exemptions for the earnings deriving from exports.

The results of the policy change were remarkably favourable for the countries concerned, as indicated by the general increase, compared to their past standards, in the rates of growth of real GDP, manufacturing production and, especially, manufactured exports (Donges 1976, p. 653-4; Krueger 1983, p. 7; Edwards 1989a). In the 1987 issue of the 'World development report', prepared by the World Bank, one can find an assessment of the relative success of IS and EP strategies. The general conclusion, pointing to the superiority of EP policies, is supported by the data presented in Table 9.1.

Table 9.1
Comparison of the growth performance of inward oriented and outward oriented countries
1963-1985

		Inward oriented countries	Outward oriented countries
Average growth rate of employment in manufacturing	1963-73	3.3	6.1
	1973-85	4.2	4.9
Marginal capital/output ratio (investment/growth of GDP)	1963-73	3.3 - 5.2	2.5
	1973-85	6.2 - 8.7	4.5 - 5.0
Average growth rate of real value added in manufacturing	1963-73	6.8	10.3
	1973-85	4.3	5.2

Source: World Bank, *World Development Report 1987*.

On all the three indicators chosen, and in both sub-periods, outward oriented countries outperform inward oriented ones, even if in the post-oil-shock period (1973-1985) the superiority in terms of growth performance is not as dramatic as in the previous one. In this second period, however, the experience of developing countries in coping with the serious external disturbances originating in the real, monetary and financial spheres of the world economy has shown one additional and positive aspects of outward-oriented policies, namely the superior capacity to adjust to external shocks that they seem to assure.

From this point of view, however, it is necessary to distinguish, among the developing market economies, the case of the East Asian NICs from that of the Latin American countries.

In spite of the fact that the small, poorly resource-endowed, strongly outward-oriented economies of East Asia are much more dependent on trade, and therefore much more directly exposed to external shocks, the speed and relative unbiasedness with which market signals were transmitted inside their economic system, combined with the existence of enterprises already accustomed to the rules of international trade and competitiveness, gave them ample opportunity to adapt much more rapidly their microeconomic structure and trade flows to the changed international conditions, without incurring in excessive indebtedness, in the whole decade following the first oil-shock. These positive results can be obviously associated with the fact that the development strategies of the East Asian NICs, even in their first phase of import-substitution (and much more powerfully after their switch to export-promotion), have been strongly shaped by a sense of dependence on world markets, whose opportunities and constraints have always been a crucial factor in orienting the choices regarding the domestic industrial structure [11].

On the other hand, the generally bigger, better endowed and richer Latin American countries, which moved away more slowly, if at all, from their traditional inward-looking policies, showed much less flexibility in their adjustment processes: the sensitivity to price and profitability signals was lowered, in the private sector, by the recurring overvaluation of the exchange rate and by tax-subsidy schemes; public enterprises, on the other hand, were even less sensitive to market signals, because of their relatively soft budget constraint (Tyson 1986, p. 266). This sluggishness in response to external disturbances entailed a necessarily greater resort to external aid and finance, with the ensuing much worse evolution of external indebtedness: these countries integrated into the world economy in a very asymmetric way, 'much more on capital account than on trade account. They accumulated debt on a scale that was incompatible with their internally oriented production structures and that would not have automatically led to sustained growth of exports which was the only way to serve it' (Fishlow 1986, p.573). Again, the much lower flexibility of Latin American countries is at least partially attributable to their IS-based development policies and to their primary concern for the domestic market as opposed to the foreign market (a choice only partially justified by the size of the market and the abundant natural resources endowment) [12].

From this point of view, the experience of Latin American countries has strong analogies with that of East European economies, with differences more of degree than of quality: 'the East European countries and the Latin American countries were saddled with a structural dependence on imports, a domestic industrial base that was largely noncompetitive on world markets, and a lack of expertise in world marketing' (Tyson 1986, p. 250). The development strategies of Eastern Europe, obviously, have been even more strongly inward-oriented than in Latin America, with industrialization processes driven mostly by domestic considerations or, in a lesser degree, intra-CMEA relationships. (Tyson 1986, p. 248-9). In CPEs, moreover, the microeconomic incentives to adjust the structure of both inputs and outputs to the changed conditions have been almost nonexistent, mainly because of the rigidities and distortions of the price system and the indifference of enterprises, because of their soft budget constraint, to prices and profit signals.

It should be noted, at this regard, that in most cases the adoption of IS development strategies is justified by the consideration that they are a first unavoidable phase in the industrialization of an underdeveloped country, and thus a necessary precondition for export-oriented policies. As rightly pointed out by Diaz-Alejandro, this thesis has in fact two versions. The first one, somehow recalling 'product life cycle' arguments, stresses the fact that the more typical way of developing a particular industrial sector or product is by counting first on the domestic market and then, only after a certain period of time, trying to expand towards foreign markets. The second, more radical and less defensible one, assumes that a country, in order to become a net exporter of manufactured goods, has first to develop its domestic industrial base across the board, in a broad and highly integrated way: the whole industrial sector of the country, in this case, is treated as an 'infant sector' [13]. In both cases, then, the strategies of import substitution and export promotion are seen not as opposite but as complementary ones: the main concept is that, after a certain period of IS, there should be a 'spillover' leading to the expansion of manufactured exports, based upon the experience obtained in the production for the protected domestic market.

The possibility, timing, and success of such a spillover depend heavily, however, on the type of approach chosen during the first IS phase and also on the length of the phase itself: here, again, while the experience of East Asian countries, in their more intense relation with export markets, diverges, as previously said, from that of Latin American ones, it is undeniable that East European CPEs stand on their own, because their first semi-autarkic approach to industrialization does not even contain the idea of a spillover towards the expansion of exports. Only for some of these countries, namely Poland, Hungary and Romania, one could identify a form of a belated (and ineffectual) adoption of this 'spillover approach' in their decision, taken between the late sixties and the early seventies, to embark on a strategy of 'import-led growth': a rapid increase in the import of Western machinery, technology and know-how, paid for with an intense borrowing in the world capital markets, was conceived as conducive to an important improvement in productivity and in the technological level of the domestic industrial base, and hence, in due time, to a powerful boost to the capabilities for exporting manufactured goods in Western markets (Hanson 1982, pp. 130-1).

Summarizing the above considerations, three main conclusions can be drawn:

1) the three groups of countries examined (East Asian and Latin American developing market economies and East European centrally planned economies), on the basis of an appraisal of their 'external stance' combining their development strategies, foreign trade policies, and foreign trade outcomes, appear distributed along a continuum going from extremely open to almost autarkic economies;

2) along this continuum the Latin American countries seem to be much closer to the East European ones, with which they share quite a number of common features, policies and (mostly negative) outcomes, than to their East Asian counterpart. To put it in a different way, the differences (or analogies) in the policies pursued, from this point of view, seem to prevail over the differences (or analogies) in the economic system (market-based or centrally planned);

3) on the other hand, while in the first two groups of countries the selection of certain development strategies has arisen as a result of a policy choice, East European countries were characterized by a 'built-in' and invariable inward-orientation stemming from their centrally planned economic system, which caused their trade policies to be highly protectionist and made their economies extremely inflexible in responding to external economic signals.

The foreign trade sector in the first phase of the transition

In the eighties, quite different evaluations were given of the foreign economic policy options open to the Eastern European economies, and in particular of the possibility of a switch from IS to EP policies. Some authors, by emphasizing the relative prevalence of policies over systems (as in point 2 of the preceding conclusions) inferred a fairly favourable assessment [14]. Stressing the specificities of centrally planned systems (point 3), on the contrary, provided the basis for a much more pessimistic outlook: as in the following quotation by Marer, the crucial point was seen in the severe constraint imposed by the economic system on the ability of these countries to successfully implement a change from and inward- to an outward-oriented economic strategy:

> ...such a transformation is much easier for economies that are predominantly market based than for CPEs, whose protectionist trade policies are determined more by their economic *system* than by feasible policy choices. Whatever the ownership arrangements, in the absence of a real market mechanism (as distinct from central planners using market-type instruments to implement the central plan), including substantial domestic and import competition, no real transformation is likely even if imports from the West increase rapidly, if attitudes and laws towards F[oreign] D[irect] I[nvestment] are liberalized, and if large and foreign loans are taken. (Marer 1988, p. 213)

Given the rather limited results obtained during the 1980s by all East European countries in their export-promotion efforts, such a pessimistic outlook has to be judged as the more realistic one, insofar as we refer to the situation in the second part of the decade. The revolutionary events of end-1989, however, caused a complete redefinition of the whole economic and political framework determining the role of the foreign sector and of foreign trade policies. In all East European countries, engaged in a more or less rapid and complete transition towards a market-based economic system, from 1990 onwards the debate on these issues has entered a totally new phase. In particular, after the abolition of the main systemic constituents of these economies, like central planning and the foreign trade monopoly, the experiences of Latin American and East Asian countries acquired for them a much higher relevance.

Various important lessons may be learnt from such experiences, as far as the trade policy switch is concerned. First of all, it must be stressed that while in many instances IS policies have been a preliminary step towards EP policies, this does not imply that the change is either necessary or automatic. Almost all developing countries have gone through a phase of import-substitution, of varying length and intensity, in the very first stages of their industrialization (mainly during the 1950s and 1960s), and in the following decades some of these countries have in fact moved away from those policies, in the direction of outward-orientation. This process, however, has taken place with very different speed and determination in the countries concerned: indeed, between 1973 and 1985, inward-orientation was still the preferred option in almost three quarters of the countries studied by the World Bank [15].

Secondly, activating an export-oriented policy is much more difficult than starting an inward-oriented one, because it requires a combination of different policy measures that modify many important aspects of the economic policy and have a powerful impact on the economic structure of the country, therefore necessitating a strong determination on the part of the government.

In particular, to achieve and maintain for a relatively long period of time an array of economic and political conditions favourable for a policy switch towards EP is quite a demanding task, for the following reasons:

a) In countries whose industrial structure has been shaped by IS policies, market forces are generally not strong enough to make the enterprises 'export conscious'. This is because export activities involve very high and different risks, with respect to those prevailing in domestic markets: enterprises, in order to export, have to confront new and serious challenges with a substantial lack of information (about the world market; about the wishes of potential buyers as to the quality, design and price of products; about the prevalent laws in the importing countries). Moreover, there are the problems associated with the rather costly development of distributive networks abroad and also, quite often, with the relatively high import barriers in developed countries (Donges 1974, p. 350).

b) A second important point is that in order to fully reap both the static and dynamic gains of a switch toward EP policies it is not sufficient to realize a more favourable treatment for exportables (in the form of a combination of a devalued exchange rate, tax rebates, special subsidies, etc.): the other cornerstone of a successful outward oriented development policy is a strong commitment to import liberalization. The trade reforms undertaken in the past decades in LDCs show that this necessity is a crucial element of a successful 'policy switch': indeed, if domestic producers are expected to become competitive in the world market for manufactured goods, they must be given a real freedom of sourcing, which implies an ideally unrestricted access to foreign raw materials, semifabricates, machinery and equipment [16]. The many cases of unsuccessful EP efforts, both in LDCs and, more recently, in some East European CPEs, can be mostly explained by the fact that in those instances the necessity of a liberalization of the import regime has been either totally overlooked or strongly underestimated [17].

c) A third problem is that the shift toward outward orientation has inevitably a high price. Reforms that liberalize the trade regime are accompanied by unavoidable transitional costs associated with the shifts in resources and structural adjustment caused by the changes in prices. If the initial situation of the economy is characterized by strong distortions, both the changes that are likely to be necessary and their associated costs are very large. Moreover, generally 'trade liberalization comes in the wake of economic crises, usually associated with budget and balance of payments deficits and inflation. Such crises may help create the political will for change - an important ingredient for undertaking trade reforms - but reforms undertaken in a crisis atmosphere may not be sustainable.' (Rajapatirana 1987, p.3) [18].

d) A fourth aspect, strictly connected to the third one, is the lack or weakness of 'internal constituencies' that favour export-promotion. It can been argued, indeed, that the most important obstacle to a policy reform liberalizing the foreign trade regime is the political resistance that it causes: while it is easy for economic agents to recognize the immediate adjustment costs of such reforms, their advantages have a long-term character and are much more diffused to be readily identified. On the contrary, the policies of import substitution are not just based on theoretical arguments, but are vigorously supported by strong groups whose main interest is in the perpetuation of monopoly positions in the domestic market, combined with preferential treatment, subsidies, etc. [19].

e) Lastly, the lessons of the last decades in most LDCs show that reforms of the trade regime are not sufficient to move the economy toward a new, outward-oriented pattern of development, and cannot be launched in an isolated way. If, as most of the times happens, the policy switch comes as a result of serious difficulties in the external equilibrium, the adoption of sound macroeconomic policies that prevent currency appreciation and reduce inflation is a crucial element of the 'reform package': the level and stability of the exchange rate being the most important condition allowing domestic producers to perceive the new set of incentives as a permanent one, and therefore to incorporate them in their expectations and decision-making process (Rajapatirana 1987, pp.4-5).

In the first phase of the transition process in Central and East European countries, many of these lessons have indeed been taken into account by their new representative governments. The strongest impulse in this direction came undoubtedly from the IMF and the World Bank: in providing these countries with technical and financial assistance, and in designing their adjustment programmes, both these institutions drew heavily on their previous experiences with stabilization and liberalization policies in developing countries and NICs (Corbo 1991). As a result, the foreign economic policy debate showed a certain change of emphasis, being centered not so much on a shift from import substitution to export promotion, but more on the efforts towards full liberalization: ideally, a non-interventionist policy, involving the removal of all major economic distortions deriving from governments activity not only in foreign trade and payments but also in the domestic economic system and policies.

As a first consequence of the new political and economic setting, the trade policy switch, instead of being treated as a collection of measures to be implemented in a sort of 'self-contained' process, came to be seen, more correctly, as just one element of an integrated and global strategy of systemic transformation. In 1990 and 1991 all Eastern European countries adopted strict stabilization measures, implemented major price reforms for traded goods, devalued their currencies (attaining varying degrees of internal convertibility), significantly opened their economies to international trade, and revised their legal frameworks to allow most forms of private ownership.

However, many elements of this transformation, particularly those related to privatization and other institutional changes, resulted to be inherently slow and prone to possible setbacks: as a consequence, the more rapid and successful stabilization and liberalization policies have emerged, till now, as the cornerstones of the transition process. In particular, the experiences of Hungary and Poland in 1990 and of Czechoslovakia in 1991 suggest that trade liberalization, combined with devaluation and tight expenditure-switching measures, can stimulate a rapid increase in exports to Western markets, a change which is in itself a critical component of their economic transformation.

While the first results of the stabilization-liberalization policies have been positive, the new strategy appears to be already losing some of the initial vigour: the main restraining factors derive from the high social and economic costs of the transition and from the relative weakness of the costituencies favouring trade liberalization efforts. Some countervailing movements toward an increased protection of domestic industry have already emerged in Poland, Hungary and Czechoslovakia, and seem to be rapidly acquiring strength.

The political economy of protection is increasingly becoming an important issue in these countries, where new or revived nationalistic and protectionist tendencies found some of their best interpreters in the left-wing parties (social-democratic and socialist) that took over part of the heritage of the ruling elites ousted from power after 1989. The strong commitment to liberalization policies of the governments, moreover, has been put severely under strain by their equally strong attraction towards the EEC. As stressed by Nuti (Nuti 1992, p. 13) the contradiction between the pursuit of free trade policies and the desire to join a trading bloc like the EEC was not immediately understood. This meant not only that the negotiation of the Association Agreements with the European Community 'required' the reimposition of higher trade tariffs as a bargaining chip, but also that during 1991 the internal constituencies in favour of protectionism acquired new strength and visibility [20].

From this point of view, in the transitional economies of Eastern Europe the major issue of the economic policy debate is now increasingly becoming the possible contradiction between the policies under the responsibility of functional bodies like the ministry of finance and the central bank, firmly backing the stabilization-liberalization strategy, and those falling within the sphere of the ministries for industry or for regional development, increasingly in favour of protectionist and safeguarding measures (Gawlikowska-Hueckel and Zielinska-Glebocka, 1992).

Notes

[1] Like a seminal study by two Hungarian economists (Liska-Máriás, 1954), in which Ricardo's theory of comparative ad-

vantage was 'rediscovered', as one of the authors said many years later.

[2] Because of the necessity of evaluating more correctly, in the calculus of foreign trade profitability, the level and structure of domestic costs, many different formulas were devised to replace the internal wholesale prices with more reliable indicators that take into account, for instance, the prices of imported goods used as inputs in the production of exportables, or the 'investment intensity' of the exported production. For a thorough account of the methodological debates on these issues in the Soviet Union, see Stouracová, J.- Roubalová (1977).

[3] These ratios can in fact be equated to effective exchange rates, but it should be stressed that they differ from those calculated for market economies because they are based on average rather than marginal costs of earning a unit of foreign exchange.

[4] In the literature it has become customary to distinguish between 'traditional centrally planned economies' (TCPEs), relying mostly on quantity-oriented central plans, with plan fulfillment rather than profit as the main evaluative criterion for enterprises, and 'modified centrally planned economies' (MCPEs), characterized by the elimination of detailed central planning and the increased role of enterprise profitability (see Bornstein 1980). Hungary after 1968 and Poland after 1982 are generally considered to be MCPEs.

[5] For thorough descriptions and comments on various aspects of recent reforms in the foreign trade field, see Tosi (1985), Lavigne (1988) and Wolf (1989).

[6] But the same applies, in fact, also to other CPEs. It is sufficient to cite the following comment of an economist from the People's Republic of China, reported in Johnson (1986): 'We write many articles about the Hungarian economy, but as you read them, you should understand that Hungary is an euphemism for the Republic of Korea. We are not really all that interested in Hungary.' (Johnson 1986, pp. 559-60).

[7] No doubt also because in recent years the Eastern European economies did meet a rapidly increasing competition, on western markets for manufactured goods, from countries like Argentina, Mexico and Brazil in Latin America, and Singapore, South Korea, Taiwan and Hong Kong in East Asia). See: Poznanski (1986).

[8] For an early criticism of the assumptions and consequences of IS policies, with reference to the Prebisch 1959 article, see Aubrey 1959.

[9] See Lavigne 1985, pp. 17-23.

[10] A thorough comparative study of industrialization policies in various developing countries shows that, among the sample chosen for the analysis, the first countries that started to change their strategy were, at the end of the 1950s, Pakistan and Spain, followed by Taiwan, South Korea and Israel in the early sixties. The change of strategy was delayed (beginning in the second half of the 1960s), and less radical, in Brazil, Colombia, Egypt, India, Yugoslavia, and Mexico. (Donges 1976, pp. 644-5)

[11] Refer, for instance, to the following statement by Donges: '... the more outward-looking economies, by their very nature, disposed of a business community capable of quickly discovering selling opportunities in world markets and then offensively exploiting them. On the other hand, these economies used to enjoy considerable creditworthiness, they thus had relatively easy access to international capital markets and so they were able to reduce growth-restricting financial stringencies. Moreover, outward-looking countries tended to have an import-to-GDP ratio high enough to allow some import curtailment without severely curbing long-term economic growth.' (Donges 1976, pp. 656-7)

[12] 'For Latin America, already industrialized and with higher income and wages, the export market was never conceived as the basis for growth of the manufacturing sector; its function was to supply needed foreign exchange, and the structure of exports continued top depend heavily on resource-based exports. For Asian NIC's, the foreign market oriented domestic investment in industry, first in labor intensive goods compatible with low wages, and later in others. Exports were the instrument of industrialization.' (Fishlow 1987, pp. 11-12).

[13] 'The most acceptable version is that which stresses the difficulty involved in an LDC (or any country) setting up an industry which from the start is heavily oriented toward foreign markets. There are examples of such industries, but the normal cycle seems to be for an activity to first start operating with sales to the domestic market, with or without competition from imports, and then, once its domestic base and overhead are assured, move on abroad in search of markets, most frequently using marginal

cost pricing ("dumping"), and often using protective schemes to monopolize the home market. A stronger version of the argument stresses the need to have an integrated and diversified industrial structure before one can develop substantial manufactured exports. While the former version points to a "normal" cycle in specific industrial activities, the latter emphasizes the whole industrial sector.' (Diaz Alejandro 1974, 221-2).

[14] 'Since it is the opinion of every analyst that — despite non-negligible difficulties — it is normally possible to change from a policy of turning inward to an outward turning one and to shift from an import substituting policy to export orientation (in other words, to open to the world market), there is no reason to question this possibility with regard to the economic policy of the CMEA countries.' (Köves 1989, p. 6).

[15] Among the 41 developing economies considered in the 1987 World Bank Report, the countries considered to be strongly or moderately outward-oriented were only 13 in the 1963-73 period and 11 in the 1973-85 period. Moreover, the outward policy stance has not been a stable one: from the first to second period, while four countries switched from strongly or moderately inward- to outward-orientation, six countries moved back from moderately outward- to moderately inward-orientation. (Rajapatirana 1987, p.4).

[16] On the problems faced by domestic producers under import-substitution regimes, refer for instance to the following considerations by Marer: 'efficient manufacturing entails the use of a wide variety of inputs. In countries pursuing import substitution policies, producers are often forced to obtain inputs from protected domestic suppliers, whose costs, quality control, design, engineering, product innovation and timeliness of delivery may leave much to be desired. Forced reliance on their products thus raises the costs and lowers the quality of output throughout the economy'. (Marer 1988, p. 209). On the necessity of relatively liberal import regimes in order for outward oriented policies to be successful, see: Krueger 1980, p.291; Krueger 1985, p. 22; Inotai 1988, p. 55.

[17] 'Close to 30 years ago, the economic reasoning on export subsidies suggested that they would result in greater export diversification and performance. In contrast, experience shows that, at the macro-level, this has generally not occurred. ... the reason

for this has been that, in a majority of cases, export subsidies were not supported by more open import policies. As a result, export subsidies reduced only marginally the anti-export bias of Latin-American countries. (Nogués 1990, p. 112).

[18] These aspects have been stressed by authors dealing with the problem of the appropriate sequencing and speed of liberalization programmes. See, among others: Little, Scitovsky and Scott 1970; Krueger 1981; Choski and Papageorgiou 1986; Edwards 1989).

[19] These problems have been analysed in the literature on the political economy of protection, particularly by the authors dealing with the so-called 'rent-seeking societies' (Baldwin 1982 and 1985; Krueger 1974 and 1989).

[20] It is only apparently paradoxical, from this point of view, that some of the strongest protectionist pressures on the governments of Poland and Czechoslovakia did come from some Western European enterprises, so well acquainted with the Community trade policies, that have invested heavily in these countries by acquiring majority stakes in their major manufacturing enterprises.

References

Aubrey, H.G. (1959), 'Discussion', *American Economic Review*, Papers and Proceedings, May, vol. 49, n. 2, pp. 284-8.

Baldwin, R.E. (1982), 'The Political Economy of Protection', in: Bhagwati, J., Srinivasan, T.N. (eds), *Import Competition and Response*, University of Chicago Press, Chicago, pp. 263-86.

Baldwin, R.E. (1985), *The Political Economy of Postwar U.S. Import Policy*, M.I.T. Press, Cambridge (Mass.).

Berend, I.T.- Ranki, G. (1977), *East Central Europe in the 19th and 20th Centuries*, Akademiai Kiadó, Budapest.

Bornstein, M. (1980), 'Systemic Aspects of the Responses of East European Economies to Disturbances in the International Economy', in: Tyson, L.-Neuberger, E., (eds), *The Impact of International Disturbances on the Soviet Union and Eastern Europe*, Pergamon Press, New York.

Brabant, J.M. van (1985a), 'Eastern European Exchange Rates and Exchange Policies', in *Jahrbuch der Wirtschaft Osteuropas*, Band 11, 1. Halbband, pp. 123-71.

Brabant, J.M. van (1985b), 'Exchange Rate Policies in Eastern Europe in the late 1980s. A Perspective', paper presented at the Colloquium "East-West Trade and Financial Relations", Florence, European University Institute, 4-6 June (mimeo).

Brown, A.A.- Marer, P. (1973), 'Foreign Trade and East European Reforms', in: Bornstein, M., *Plan and Market. Economic Reform in Eastern Europe*, Yale University Press, New Haven, pp.153-205.

Choski, A., Papageorgiou, D. (1986) (eds), *Economic Liberalization in Developing Countries*, Blackwell, Oxford.

Comisso, E. (1986), 'State structures and political processes outside the CMEA: a comparison', in *International Organization*, vol. 40, n. 2, Spring, pp. 577-98.

Corbo, V. (1991), 'World Bank-Supported Adjustment Programs: Lessons for Central and Eastern Europe', in: Corbo, V.- Coricelli, F. - Bossak, J. (eds), *Reforming Central and Eastern European Economies. Initial Results and Challenges*, The World Bank, Washington (D.C.).

Csikós-Nagy, B. (1968), *Altalános és szocialista árelmélet*, Budapest, Kossuth, p. 250, cited in: Brown-Marer 1973, p. 154, note 3.

Diaz-Alejandro, C.F. (1965), 'On the Import Intensity of Import Substitution', *Kyklos*, vol. XVIII, fasc. 3, pp.495-511.

Diaz-Alejandro, C.F. (1974), 'Some Characteristics of Recent Export Expansion in Latin America, in Giersch, H. (ed.), *The International Division of Labour. Problems and Perspectives*, Tübingen, J.C.B. Mohr (Paul Siebeck), pp.215-36.

Donges, J.B. (1974), 'Conditions for Successful Import Substitution and Export Diversification in LDCs: a Summary Appraisal', in: Giersch, H. (ed.), *The International Division of Labour. Problems and Perspectives*, Tübingen, J.C.B. Mohr (Paul Siebeck), pp. 336-56.

Donges, J.B. (1976), 'A Comparative Survey of Industrialization Policies in Fifteen Semi-Industrial Countries', *Weltwirtschaftliches Archiv*, Band 112, Heft 4, pp. 626-59.

Edwards, S. (1989a), 'Openness, Outward Orientation, Trade Liberalization and Economic Performance in Developing Countries', NBER Working Paper n. 2908, March 1989.

Edwards, S. (1989b), 'On the Sequencing of Structural Reforms', NBER Working Paper n. 3138, October 1989.

Fishlow, A. (1986), 'The East European debt crisis in the Latin American mirror', in *International Organization*, vol. 40, n. 2, Spring, pp. 567-75.

Fishlow, A. (1987), 'Some Reflections on Comparative Latin American Economic Performance and Policy', WIDER Working Paper n. 22, August.

Gawlikowska-Hueckel, K. - Zielinska-Glebocka, A. (1992), 'Motivation for protectionism in Poland in the light of transition to a market economy and association with the EC', paper presented at the Conference: *Impediments to the transition: the East European countries and the policies of the European Community*, Florence, European University Institute, 24-25 January.

Gács, J. (1986), 'The Conditions, Chances and Predictable Consequences of Implementing a Step-by-step Liberalization of Imports in the Hungarian Economy', in *Acta Oeconomica*, vol. 36(3-4), pp. 231-49.

Hanson, P. (1982), 'The End of Import-Led Growth? Some Observations on Soviet, Polish, and Hungarian Experience in the 1970s', *Journal of Comparative Economics*, (6), pp.130-47.

Havlik, P. (1985), 'The Scope and Structure of Czechoslovak Foreign Trade: Effects of Applying Realistic Exchange Rates', in *Comparative Economic Studies*, XXVII, Spring 1985, pp. 1-19.

Holzman, F. (1974), *Foreign Trade under Central Planning*, Harvard Univ. Press, Cambridge (Mass.).

Inotai, A. (1988), 'International Competitiveness and Imports', in *Acta Oeconomica*, vol. 39(1-2), pp. 44-59.

Johnson, Ch. (1986), 'The nonsocialist NICs: East Asia', in *International Organization*, vol. 40, n. 2, Spring, pp. 557-65.

Köves, A. (1989), 'Opening to the World Economy and Renewing Hungarian Relations with the CMEA', *Acta Oeconomica*, vol. 41 (1-2), pp. 1-26.

Krueger, A.O. (1974), 'The Political Economy of the Rent-Seeking Society', *American Economic Review*, June, vol. 64, n. 3, pp. 291-303.

Krueger, A.O. (1980), 'Trade Policy as an Input to Development', *American Economic Review*, Papers and Proceedings, May, vol. 70, n.2, pp. 288-92.

Krueger, A.O. (1981), 'Interactions between Inflation and Trade-Regime Objectives in Stabilization Programs', in Cline, W.R., Weintraub, S. (eds), *Economic Stabilization in Developing Countries*, Brookings Institution, Washington.

Krueger, A.O. (1983), 'The Effects of Trade Strategies on Growth', *Finance and Development*, June, pp. 6-8.

Krueger, A.O. (1985), 'Import Substitution versus Export Promotion', *Finance and Development*, June, pp. 20-23.

Krueger, A.O. (1989), 'Asymmetries in Policy between Exportables and Import-Competing Goods', NBER Working Paper n. 2904, March.

Lavigne, M. (1988), 'Comments on the devaluation of the rouble', Florence, European University Institute, Working group on comparative economic systems, December (mimeo).

Levine, H. (1968), 'The Effects of Foreign Trade on Soviet Planning Practices', in Brown.A.-Neuberger, E. (eds), *International Trade and Central Planning*, University of California Press, Berkeley.

Liska, T. - Máriás, A. (1954), A gazdaságosság és a nemzetközi munkamegosztás' (Optimum Returns and International Division of Labour), Közgazdasági Szemle, n.1, pp.75-94, reproduced as extracts in: U.N.-E.C.E. 1955, pp.131-5.

Little, I., Scitovsky, T. and Scott, M. (1970), *Industry and Trade in Some Developing Countries: a Comparative Study*, Oxford University Press, London.

Marer, P. (1988), 'Comparing the Foreign Economic Strategies of Market and Centrally Planned Economies', in Saunders, C.T. (ed.), *Macroeconomic Management and the Enterprise in East and West* Macmillan, London, pp. 183-216.

Mérey, I. (1983), 'Hungarian Export Problems and the Economic Environment', in *Acta Oeconomica*, vol. 30 (2), pp. 179-91.

Nogués, J. (1990), 'The Experience of Latin America with Export Subsidies', *Weltwirtschaftliches Archiv*, Band 126, Heft 1, pp. 97-115.

Nuti, D.M. (1992), 'Economic Inertia in the Transitional Economies of Eastern Europe', paper presented at the Conference: *Impediments to the transition: the East European countries and the policies of the European Community*, Florence, European University Institute, 24-25 January.

Okólski, - Winiecki, J. (1983), 'Structural change and adaptation. On reintegrating planned economies into the world economy', paper presented at the 7th World Congress of Economics, Session 8: Theoretical Aspects of Change in Productive Structures, Warsaw, June (mimeo).

Poznanski, K. (1986), 'Competition Between Eastern Europe and Developing Countries in the Western Market for Manufactured Goods', in *East European Economies: Slow Growth in the 1980s, Vol. 2: Foreign Trade and International Finance*, Congress of the United States, Joint Economic Committee, U.S. Government Printing Office, Washington.

Prebisch, R. (1950), 'The Economic Development of Latin American and its Principal Problems', Lake Success, New York.

Rajapatirana, S. (1987), 'Industrialization and Foreign Trade', *Finance and Development*, September, pp. 2-5.

Salgó, I. (1986), 'Economic Mechanism and Foreign Trade Organization in Hungary', in *Acta Oeconomica*, vol. 36(3-4), pp. 271-87.

Stouracová, J.- Roubalová (1977), L., 'The Contribution of Soviet Economists to Studying the Effectiveness of External Economic Relations', in *Soviet and Eastern European Foreign Trade*, Spring, vol. XIII, n.1, pp. 69-100.

Szymkiewicz, K. (1977), *La planification du commerce extérieur. L'exemple polonais*, Economica, Paris.

Tosi, D. (1984), 'Tendenze e fasi delle riforme del commercio estero nei paesi dell'Est europeo nei decenni 1950-1970', in *Est-Ovest*, n. 4, pp. 7-58.

Tosi, D. (1985), 'Le riforme di commercio estero nei paesi dell'Est europeo durante i quinquennati 1976-80 e 1981-85', in *Est-Ovest*, n. 4, pp. 7-68.

Tyson, L. (1984), *Economic Adjustment in Eastern Europe*, Rand Publication Series, September.

Tyson, L. (1986), 'The debt crisis and adjustment responses in Eastern Europe: a comparative perspective', in *International Organization*, vol. 40, n. 2, Spring, pp. 239-85.

U.N.-E.C.E. (1955), *Economic Survey of Europe in 1954*, Geneva.

U.N.-E.C.E. (1969), *Economic Survey of Europe in 1968*, New York.

U.N.-E.C.E. (1973), 'Recent Changes in the Organization of Foreign Trade in the Centrally Planned Economies', in Economic Bulletin for Europe, vol. 24, n.1, pp. 36-49.

Vanous, J. (1986), 'Commercial Exchange Rates of East European Countries and Realistic Dollar/Ruble Exchange Rates for Soviet

Trade with Eastern Europe', in *Soviet and Eastern European Foreign Trade*, Spring, vol. XXII, n.1, pp. 83-99.
Winiecki, J. (1985), 'Central Planning and Export Orientation in Manufactures. Theoretical considerations on the Impact of System-Specific Features on Specialisation', in Economic Notes, n.2, pp. 132-53.
Winiecki, J. (1988), 'East European Economies: Forced Adjustment Forever?', Seminar Paper n. 413, August, Institute for International Economic Studies, Stockholm.
Winiecki, J. (1989), 'STE-LDC Comparisons: a Neglected Field of Comparative Systems Analysis', *Communist Economies*, vol. 1, n. 1, pp. 61-77.
Wolf, T.A. (1989), 'Market-Oriented Reform of Foreign Trade in Planned Economies', paper presented at the conference on "Market Forces in Planned Economies", organized by the International Economic Association and the U.S.S.R. Academy of Sciences, Moscow, 28-30, March (mimeo).